Praise for *The Triple Bottom Line*

"Informative, persuasive, and practical, containing valuable advice for anyone seeking a more responsible and profitable approach to business."

—**Steve Reinemund**, former chairman and chief executive officer, PepsiCo

"An engaging mix of powerful ideas and practical advice. Values matter, and Savitz shows how profitability and responsibility can and must go hand in hand."

—**Michael Morris**, former president and chief executive officer, American Electric Power

"'Some circumstantial evidence is very strong,' Savitz and Weber recall Thoreau saying, 'as when you find a trout in the milk.' The flood tide of corporations they profile provides powerful evidence that the triple bottom line is going mainstream."

—**John Elkington**, founder and chief entrepreneur, SustainAbility

"A timely contribution to why big corporations engage in sustainable development and how managers can implement it in their companies."

—**Bjorn Stigson**, former president, World Business Council for Sustainable Development

"Must-reading for any corporate manager or investor seeking the 'sweet spot' where financial and stakeholder interests meet. It provides powerful arguments, cogent analysis, great stories, and dozens of real-world insights into how companies are enhancing profits through sustainability strategies."

—**Mindy Lubber**, president, CERES; former regional administrator, U.S. Environmental Protection Agency

"Savitz and Weber's *The Triple Bottom Line* offers a perspective that is already influencing the wisest and most socially responsive corporations in the world. This well-written, insightful, and practical book will guide executives for decades to come."

—**Max Bazerman**, Jesse Isador Straus Professor of Business Administration, Harvard Business School

"Amidst the proliferating number of books on corporate sustainability topics, Savitz's *The Triple Bottom Line* is a refreshing relief. Its accessible style, jargon-free language, and thematic organization avoid the tendency toward cheerleading and case study overdose characteristic of the field. Savitz speaks with clarity, authority, and good humor."

—**Allen White**, senior fellow, Tellus Institute; cofounder, Global Reporting Initiative

"*The Triple Bottom Line* is full of practical advice based on Savitz's hands-on experience working with corporate managers. This book is a very readable guide for those who want to build a successful and sustainable business for the twenty-first century."

—**Arnold S. Hiatt**, former chairman and CEO, the Stride Rite Corporation

"Most executives have a superficial or misguided understanding of sustainability. *The Triple Bottom Line* should be required reading for business leaders who seek to enrich their shareholders, society, and themselves."

—**Scott Cohen**, former editor and publisher, Compliance Week

"Responsible leadership ensures that what we have today will be around for future generations. This book shows us both what it takes to lead responsibly and what happens when people fail to do so. An insightful book for those who seek how they can personally make a difference."

—**Samuel DiPiazza**, former global chief executive officer, PricewaterhouseCoopers LLP

"Andy Savitz puts sustainability in a clear, practical framework supported with real business examples."

—**Travis Engen**, former president and chief executive officer, Alcan, Inc.; chair, Prince of Wales' International Business Leaders Forum; chairman, World Business Council for Sustainable Development

the TRIPLE BOTTOM LINE

*How Today's Best-Run Companies Are Achieving
Economic, Social, and Environmental
Success—and How You Can Too*

REVISED AND UPDATED

Andrew W. Savitz

with Karl Weber

JB JOSSEY-BASS™

A Wiley Brand

Jacket design by Faceout Studio

Published by Jossey-Bass
A Wiley Brand
One Montgomery Street, Suite 1200, San Francisco, CA 94104-4594—www.josseybass.com

Jossey-Bass books and products are available through most bookstores. To contact Jossey-Bass directly call our Customer Care Department within the U.S. at 800-956-7739, outside the U.S. at 317-572-3986, or fax 317-572-4002.

Wiley publishes in a variety of print and electronic formats and by print-on-demand. Some material included with standard print versions of this book may not be included in e-books or in print-on-demand. If this book refers to media such as a CD or DVD that is not included in the version you purchased, you may download this material at http://booksupport.wiley.com. For more information about Wiley products, visit www.wiley.com.

Library of Congress Cataloging-in-Publication Data
Savitz, Andrew W.
  The triple bottom line : how today's best-run companies are achieving economic, social, and environmental success—and how you can too / Andrew W. Savitz, with Karl Weber.— Revised and updated.
     pages cm
  Includes bibliographical references and index.
  ISBN 978-1-118-22622-3 (cloth); ISBN 978-1-118-33317-4 (ePDF); ISBN 978-1-118-33037-1 (ePub)
  1. Success in business. 2. Social responsibility of business. 3. Industrial management—Environmental aspects. I. Weber, Karl, 1953-II. Title.
  HF5386.S346 2014
  658.4′08—dc23

                                                                                    2013030805

SECOND EDITION
HB Printing 10 9 8 7 6 5 4 3 2 1

To Penelope
and to our children, Noah, Zuzzie, and Harry;
their cousins, Louis, Sarah, Daniel, Olivia, Julianna, Elliot, Sophia,
Jacob, and Jonah;
and their offspring, who will hold us accountable.

Contents

the TRIPLE BOTTOM LINE

Introduction

The whaling industry personified American prosperity for more than one hundred years. It employed seventy thousand sturdy seafarers and fueled hundreds of thousands of homes and businesses here and abroad, earning fortunes for boat owners and more than a few enterprising crewmates. The intrepid whaler was celebrated in song, story, and even high art, including what is arguably the greatest American novel, Melville's *Moby-Dick*. Whaling was a tale of courage and initiative—a tale of America.

Today nearly all the whales are gone, and so is the industry built around them. The decline began in the mid-1840s, when hunters ignored decreasing stocks and continued harpooning grays, rights, humpbacks, and other species of this enormous, elegant mammal. Within a few years, the industry that had thrived for a full century collapsed entirely. The era of American whaling still stands as a symbol—but now it represents the shortsightedness of businessmen whose thirst for profit made their enterprise unsustainable.[1]

Sadly, the lessons of the past have still not been fully absorbed by today's fishing industry or by the governmental agencies that regulate it. Fishing grounds the world over are being depleted as the industry exploits valuable species to the point of extinction. Predator species like tuna, swordfish, and salmon have been especially hard hit, with the prized Pacific bluefin tuna having suffered a population decline of more than 96 percent. In the Gulf of Mexico, species like red snapper, grouper, and amberjack have fallen to just a fraction of the population deemed capable of supporting itself.[2] Another once-great industry, it seems, may be on the verge of becoming unsustainable.

This is a book not about the whaling or fishing industries but about how to avoid their fate. It is a look at how businesses can prosper financially while protecting and renewing the social, environmental, and economic resources they need—and how they can fail if they do not tend to those resources.

The centerpiece of this book is the concept of *sustainability*. The term originated around a growing awareness, in the 1980s, that nations had to find ways to grow their economies without destroying the environment or sacrificing the well-being of future generations. Sustainability has since become a buzzword for an array of social and environmental causes, and in the business world it denotes a powerful and defining idea: *a sustainable corporation is one that creates profit for its shareholders while protecting the environment and improving the lives of those with whom it interacts.* It operates so that its business interests and the interests of the environment and society intersect. And as we will show, a sustainable business stands an excellent chance of being more successful tomorrow than it is today, and of remaining successful, not just for months or even years, but for decades or generations.

Sustainable organizations and societies generate and live off interest rather than depleting their capital. Capital, in this context, includes natural resources, such as water, air, sources of energy, and foodstuffs. It also includes human and social assets—from worker commitment to community support—as well as economic resources, such as a license to operate, a receptive marketplace, and legal and economic infrastructure. A company can spend down its capital for a while, but generally not for long. A firm that honors the principles of sustainability, by contrast, is built to last.

• • •

Sustainability in practice can be seen as *the art of doing business in an interdependent world.* Sustainability in the broadest sense is all about interdependence, which takes several forms.

Sustainability respects the interdependence of living beings on one another and on their natural environment. Sustainability means operating a business in a way that causes minimal harm to living creatures and that does not deplete but rather restores and enriches the environment. The whalers of the nineteenth century failed to respect this form of interdependence and destroyed their industry as a result.

Although most people think first of the environment when they hear the term, sustainability also respects the interdependence of various elements in society on one another and on the social fabric. Sustainability means operating a business in a way that acknowledges the needs and interests of other parties (community groups, educational and religious institutions, the workforce, the public) and that does not fray but rather reinforces the network of relationships that ties them all together.

Sustainability also respects the interdependence of differing aspects of human existence. Economic growth and financial success are important and provide significant benefits to individuals and society as a whole. But other human values are also important, including family life, intellectual growth, artistic expression, and moral and spiritual development. Sustainability means operating a business so as to grow and earn profit while recognizing and supporting the economic and noneconomic aspirations of people both inside and outside the organization on whom the corporation depends.

The only way to succeed in today's interdependent world is to embrace sustainability. Doing so requires companies to identify a wide range of stakeholders to whom they may be accountable, develop open relationships with them, and find ways to work with them for mutual benefit. In the long run, this will create more profit for the company and more social, economic, and environmental prosperity for society.

The concept of sustainability is sometimes confused with other terms that are widely used in business today. Many businesspeople, authors, and experts use the expression *corporate social responsibility* (CSR), for example, to refer to a company's obligations to society at large. It's a useful term, and we will occasionally use the expressions "responsible business" or "corporate responsibility" as shorthand for the kinds of managerial practices we recommend. We prefer the term sustainability, however, because responsibility emphasizes the benefits to social groups outside the business, whereas sustainability gives equal importance to the benefits enjoyed by the corporation itself.

Similarly, the term *business ethics*, which is commonly used to describe the social and moral responsibilities of businesspeople, is too narrow in its focus for our purposes. Business ethics emphasizes specific choices made by individual managers: What should I do when I'm asked or tempted to pay a bribe, cut corners on safety, or fudge the corporate accounts? It doesn't address broader operational questions, such as the following: Who should be consulted when decisions are being made that affect large numbers of people outside the company? To whom are business managers responsible? How should companies systematically measure the impact of their activities on society?

Sustainability has developed as a unified way of addressing a wide array of business concerns about the natural environment, workers' rights, consumer protection, and corporate governance, as well as the impact of business behavior on broader social issues, such as hunger, poverty, education, health care, and human rights—and the relationship of all these to profit.

•••

Many books about sustainability focus on how society can benefit if companies take a more responsible approach. This book turns that lens around, examining how companies can become more profitable by doing the right thing. One powerful way to grasp this connection is the concept of the *Triple Bottom Line (TBL)*, originally proposed by sustainability guru John Elkington. Elkington suggested that businesses need to measure their success not only by the traditional bottom line of financial performance (most often expressed in terms of profits, return on investment [ROI], or shareholder value) but also by their impact on the broader economy, the environment, and the society in which they operate.[3]

In conducting their businesses, companies use not only financial resources (such as investment dollars and sales revenues) but also environmental resources (such as water, energy, and raw materials) and social resources (such as community employees' time and talents, and infrastructure provided by governmental agencies). A sustainable business ought to be able to measure, document, and report a positive ROI on all three bottom lines—economic, environmental, and social—as well as the benefits that stakeholders receive along the same three dimensions.

The TBL captures the essence of sustainability by measuring the impact of an organization's activities on the world. A positive TBL reflects an increase in the company's value, including both its profitability and shareholder value and its economic, environmental, and social capital (see Figure I.1).

The table shown in Figure I.1 is an oversimplification, of course. Just as meaningful financial reporting cannot be reduced to one number, so sustainability does not sum precisely. There is yet no way to accurately or completely describe environmental benefits or social benefits using a number, and some of the numbers themselves require a great deal of explanation, which is precisely why most financial reports include pages of management discussion and analysis.

The TBL exists currently as a kind of balanced scorecard that captures in numbers and words the degree to which any company is or is not creating value for its shareholders and for society.

	Economic	Environmental	Social
Typical Measures	Sales, profits, ROI	Pollutants emitted	Health and safety record
	Taxes paid	Carbon footprint	Community impacts
	Monetary flows	Recycling and reuse	Human rights; privacy
	Jobs created	Water and energy use	Product responsibility
	Supplier relations	Product impacts	Employee relations
	Total	Total	Total

Figure I.1   The Triple Bottom Line

Elkington's formulation is central to understanding sustainability. Whereas the practice of sustainability is still an art, the measurement of sustainability is becoming a science, including specific goals and parameters by which businesses can measure and judge their own progress. As we'll explain in detail later, thousands of companies around the world have been measuring and reporting their performance in the environmental, economic, and social spheres. And growing numbers of institutional and individual investors, consumers, and workers are beginning to evaluate companies according to the TBL.

Sustainability, then, is not simply a matter of good corporate citizenship—earning brownie points for reducing noxious emissions from your factory or providing health care benefits to your employees. Nor is it merely a matter of business ethics—of doing the right thing when confronted with a particular moral dilemma that arises in the course of doing business. Sustainability is now a fundamental principle of smart management, one that's all too easy to overlook or take for granted in a world where the financial bottom line is often treated as the only measure of success. And as we will show, even well-run companies with good intentions and with years of success behind them can now fall hard if they ignore the principles of sustainability.

• • •

If sustainability is more important today than ever before, it's probably because corporations have, over the past few decades, entered what we call the Age of Sustainability. They are increasingly being held responsible for a wider range of activities and impacts, not just for their financial ones. They are accountable not only for their own activities, but for those of their suppliers, the communities where they are located, and the people who use their products. They are being called to account not only by investors and shareholders but by politicians, whistleblowers, the media, employees, community groups, prosecutors, class-action lawyers, environmentalists, human rights advocates, public health organizations, and customers. These stakeholders come from every corner of the world, armed both with the traditional media and with global megaphones called the Internet and social media.

As a result, businesses are being forced to respond to social, economic, and environmental changes in the world around them. Just as the issue of climate change is fundamentally altering the commercial and regulatory landscape for energy and auto companies, so the aging of the population in the developed world and the availability and cost of health care are changing the basic business model for hospitals, pharmaceutical companies, and makers of medical devices. Just as Nike was transformed by the discovery of children working in its overseas factories, so Wal-Mart has had to come to grips with "the high cost of low wages," and McDonald's with the growing public concern over childhood obesity. No sooner had Google and Facebook invented new ways to connect people and ideas around the world than they had to grapple with social issues ranging from online hate speech and government censorship to data privacy and copyright protection.

The best-run companies, large and small, are responding to these challenges. Toyota develops the gas-electric hybrid engine, and the Prius catalyzes an entirely new category of vehicles that every other carmaker seeks to emulate. DuPont moves away from chemicals to become the world's largest producer of soy protein. Procter & Gamble goes head-to-head with Unilever to figure out how to develop and sell products to the desperately poor in ways that will help lift them out of poverty. And most of these moves are generating enormous financial benefits. Toyota became the number-one car company in the world, largely on the basis of the hybrid; Wal-Mart and its suppliers are saving billions on the basis of its environmental programs to reduce waste; and PepsiCo claims annual revenue increases of $250 million from new purchasing programs that seek out companies owned by women and members of minority groups.

Perhaps most significant, corporations are reaching out to their harshest critics, demanding to know how they can improve, and seeking new forms of collaboration, innovation, and partnership to improve their results—many with startling success. They are publishing TBL reports and revealing their successes and even their failures using Facebook, Twitter, and other forms of online media, driven not by governmental mandates or journalistic sleuthing but by the new transparency that is a natural outgrowth of the Age of Sustainability.

This book will show you how and why companies are making such previously unheard-of changes in their behavior, and it will provide you with a road map you can follow as you start or speed your own journey toward the goal of sustainability.

•••

We come at these issues not as though they were abstractions, but through more than two decades of working on them with some of America's biggest, most robust corporations. Andy Savitz led the sustainability practice at PricewaterhouseCoopers, one of the world's foremost financial advisory services companies, and has helped senior executives and midlevel managers apply the Triple Bottom Line at their firms and in their departments, in the process making them more sustainable. He has since begun to work more closely with employees and human resources professionals to embed sustainability within the cultures and employee life-cycle processes of their organizations. Karl Weber gained similar insights through his research and writing on a series of books exploring business strategy, corporate decision making, and the innovative practices of many of the world's most successful companies, as well as his collaborations with such innovative social entrepreneurs as Nobel Peace laureate Muhammad Yunus, pioneer of microcredit and founder of Grameen Bank.

In these pages, we'll provide you with a set of tools—must-dos, don't-dos, and simple charts and lists—and stories to carry you down the road to sustainability for your business. In the end, you should emerge with an understanding of why and how this transformation is occurring and what you can do to become part of it.

Correctly understood and applied, sustainability is about strategy, management, and profits. But in today's interconnected world, thinking about profits as if they were unrelated to the environmental and social impacts of what you do to earn them is shortsighted and counterproductive. Social and environmental issues are creating risks and opportunities that fundamentally change the playing field for individual firms, industries, and business itself. The best-run companies see this and are turning these trends to their advantage. *The Triple Bottom Line* will help you apply the same advanced thinking to your own business.

• • •

The *Triple Bottom Line* was first published in 2006. We've been gratified by its success. Thousands of business leaders, consultants, students, researchers, and others concerned about the future of free enterprise and human society have examined our ideas, and many have generously shared their feedback and experiences with us. Guided by reader comments and questions, we've prepared this second edition, bringing the ideas, stories, examples, and recommendations up-to-date. We've also expanded the contents to incorporate fresh insights that we've developed in the course of our continuing research and Andy's ongoing work with a variety of corporate and nonprofit clients.

We hope this revised and updated version of *The Triple Bottom Line* will prove valuable both to those who appreciated the first edition as well as to a new generation of readers.

PART ONE

THE SUSTAINABILITY IMPERATIVE

1

A Bitter Aftertaste

Hershey Struggles to Master the Sustainability Challenge

Utopia of Chocolate

Hershey is an iconic American brand. Founded as the Hershey Chocolate Company in 1894 by entrepreneur and philanthropist Milton S. Hershey, the Hershey Company (as it's now known) has come to be synonymous with chocolate in the minds of millions of consumers. Its classic brown-wrapped bar is almost as recognizable as the curvaceous Coke bottle. Today the company boasts annual revenues of over $6 billion, employs some fourteen thousand workers, and sells candies and confections under names that include not only Hershey itself but also Kit Kat, Twizzlers, Jolly Ranchers, and a growing array of "premium and artisan" chocolate brands.

Perhaps even more intriguing, Hershey has managed to expand into a global giant with operations in countries around the world and a growing presence in markets from China to Mexico, while steadfastly clinging to its image as a classic American company. At the heart of this image is Hershey's home base, the bucolic Pennsylvania town once called Derry Church but long since renamed in honor of the man and the company whose history dominates the community.

Indeed, Hershey, Pennsylvania, is much more than the home of a chocolate factory. It's a popular tourist attraction whose mission is to combine chocolate with family fun. On a typical summer day in Hershey, you'll find tourists strolling Chocolate Avenue, gawking at streetlights shaped like Hershey Kisses and shopping for candy-themed souvenirs at the dozens of gift shops. Bedazzled children and obliging parents can be seen lining up for tours of Hershey's Chocolate World and squealing with delight on the ten roller coasters at nearby Hersheypark, while those with more sedentary tastes relish a whipped cocoa bath or chocolate hydrotherapy at the Hotel Hershey's pricey spa, or simply savor the sweet aromas wafting from the factory.

All these pleasures have one thing that unites them even more than their chocolate flavor: the steady stream of income they produce for Hershey's twelve thousand residents, nearly all of whom have some connection to the company. It's a heartwarming image—a charming American city built on the heritage of a classic company and a product loved by almost every child—and plenty of adults.

Making the story even more charming is the history of the connection between the Hershey Company and the town it dominates. Their fates are closely entwined, and that's the way Milton S. Hershey wanted it.

The deeply religious Hershey, a member of the socially conservative Mennonite sect, wanted his wealth to be used "for a purpose of enduring good," and he viewed his little Pennsylvania town as a utopian community, designed and managed for the good of all its inhabitants.[1]

Hershey himself largely built the town in the early years of the twentieth century. Through his Hershey Improvement Company, he founded most of its leading institutions, including the local bank, department store, zoo, and public gardens modeled on those at the French royal court in Versailles. He laid out the bucolic street design, built a trolley company, and designed houses for factory workers and bigger houses for corporate executives. He even founded a community college that local residents and company employees could attend free of charge. During the Great Depression, despite a 50 percent drop in chocolate sales, he kept the workers from his factory busy building a hotel, a community center, a sports arena, and public schools—all, of course, bearing the Hershey name.

Milton also founded the Hershey Industrial School—now known as the Milton Hershey School—which today provides free room and board, clothing, medical care, and schooling for some eighteen hundred disadvantaged children. The charitable trust that Hershey created in 1909, which owns and operates the school, also owns or controls about 70 percent of the voting shares of the Hershey Company. As the company's website declares with justified pride, "Students of Milton Hershey School are direct beneficiaries of The Hershey Company's success."[2]

Yet despite the noble intentions of Milton Hershey and the undoubted good the company has done, Hershey's once sugar-sweet reputation has turned increasingly bitter in recent years. Headlines about Hershey no longer focus solely on happy customers, enthralled tourists, or charitably sponsored schoolkids. Instead, the news about Hershey has centered on a series of embarrassing controversies that have put the company in a startlingly negative light.

The Dark Side of an Icon

Consider, for example, the rash of disturbing stories that hit the presses in August 2011—the height of the tourist season in Hershey—when some four hundred young foreign workers at a Hershey plant in Palmyra, Pennsylvania, staged a noisy walkout over their mistreatment by the company. The students had been brought to the United States from such countries as Costa Rica, China, Poland, Turkey, and Romania through the State Department's J-1 guest worker visa program. They'd been told, in the words of a recruiting brochure, "You will gain valuable work and life experience, expand your resume, improve your English, have opportunity to travel in the U.S., make great memories and form lasting relationships. No matter where you end up in the U.S., your Work and Travel Program is sure to be a summer you will never forget!"[3]

Sure enough, it was an unforgettable summer—but not in the way the students expected. Rather than experiencing American culture and making lifelong friendships, the students found themselves laboring in candy warehouses, packing and lifting fifty-pound boxes of Reese's Pieces, often on the 11 PM overnight shift. They earned so little that they couldn't even cover their grossly inflated living expenses—one group of six students was reportedly charged $2,400 per month to share a three-bedroom apartment normally rented for $970.

"There is no cultural exchange, none, none," said one twenty-year-old Chinese student. "It is just work, work faster, work." A Ukrainian student added, "All we can do is work and sleep."

With the help of organizations including the National Guest-worker Alliance and the Service Employees International Union, the students brought their plight to the attention of authorities—and the world. Officials at the Labor and State Departments promised to launch investigations. Making matters worse for Hershey, critics in the media were quick to link the apparent abuse of student workers to a broader picture of questionable labor practices by the company. In a scathing op-ed titled "America's Sweatshop Diplomacy," Fordham University law professor Jennifer Gordon pointed out that the work done by the students had previously been handled by unionized Hershey workers earning between two and four times as much. Their jobs had been eliminated, their productivity replaced by that of unorganized workers who were easier to exploit. She called Hershey's use of low-wage foreign students "a microcosm of the downsizing and subcontracting that so many American companies have pursued during the past few decades in search of ever cheaper labor."[4]

It's arguable that the negative spotlight on Hershey was somewhat unfair. As company spokespeople were quick to point out, Hershey had not hired the student workers directly. Hershey owns the Palmyra plant where they labored, but the facility was managed for Hershey by a logistics company called Exel. Exel, in turn, had outsourced its staffing to a vendor called SHS OnSite Solutions, which in turn recruited the student workers through a nonprofit organization known as Council for Educational Travel, USA (CETUSA). The glowing promises of "opportunity to travel" and "great memories" had come from CETUSA, not Hershey itself.

These mitigating factors are undeniable. But there's also no doubt in the public's mind that a company like Hershey is ultimately responsible for conditions in a factory it owns and profits from. Yet Hershey's only response to the revelations was a belated effort to pressure its labor suppliers to offer the student workers a week's vacation.

Subsequent investigations made it clear that the members of Hershey's shadowy chain of labor suppliers had behaved very badly. In February 2012, the Occupational Health and Safety Administration fined Exel for failing to report forty-two serious injuries between 2008 and 2011. And in November 2012, the federal government fined all three contractors $143,000 and ordered them to pay more than $213,000 in back pay to the foreign students.[5]

The Hershey Company wasn't named in the case. Nonetheless, the company's reputation had been seriously damaged by the ongoing publicity. Understandably, every news story focused on the Hershey connection and the harsh light it shed on a classic American institution. Which makes it strange that, when news of the government findings appeared, spokespeople for Hershey refused to respond to questions from the media. Hershey's own website—which carefully tracks most news about the company—contained no references at all to the ongoing controversy. And Hershey's corporate social responsibility (CSR) report for 2011—which devoted eight pages to the company's labor policies and practices, all avowedly designed to keep Hershey "a great place to work"—failed even to mention the guest worker case.[6]

It was a troubling story that left many people wondering about the reality behind the glowing Hershey image.

A Habit of Secrecy

Hershey's odd refusal to publicly address the mistreatment of young guest workers—for which many people held the company liable, regardless of its legal responsibility—is unfortunately totally consistent with a company tradition of operating behind closed doors that, over the years, has done much to tarnish the proud legacy of Milton Hershey.

For example, although Hershey has always boasted of its philanthropy, details of how the company operated and its impact on the communities that hosted it have traditionally been hard to come by. Media analysts and social activists seeking such information were routinely turned away. It wasn't until 2010 that Hershey finally joined competing firms in the confectionary industry by issuing its first CSR report. This long-overdue report finally addressed some of the more controversial aspects of the company's business, including its environmental practices, its labor policies, and the impact of chocolate candies in a world where childhood obesity is a growing public health problem.

Hershey's report claimed that the company had made an exemplary commitment to responsible behavior in all these areas. In his "Letter to Stakeholders," John P. Bilbrey, Hershey's CEO since May 2011, declared, "I am confident that Hershey's CSR strategy will help support and advance our growing global business. It is based on our values, aligned with our culture, focused on partnerships, open to change and evaluated through continuous improvement measures."[7]

But many of Hershey's critics were less impressed. Consider, for example, the company's record on ethical sourcing of cocoa, which is of course a major component of Hershey's most popular products.

Around 70 percent of the world's cocoa crop is harvested in West Africa, where abusive human rights practices such as forced labor, child labor, and human trafficking are rampant. In countries like Ghana and Côte d'Ivoire, children are pulled from school, forced to work in the cocoa fields and factories, and frequently injured on the job. Human rights activists have been protesting these conditions for years, and a number of food companies have responded with substantive changes. They've instituted programs to trace the sources of their raw materials, moved to enforce decent labor standards, and sought certification for their products by Fair Trade, which provides the strictest system of external monitoring in this arena.

On these issues, Hershey trails others in its industry. Its CSR report lists a number of initiatives aimed at ensuring more responsible sourcing, including a five-year, $10 million investment in "cocoa sustainability efforts" and a project called CocoaLink that uses mobile technology to deliver training on topics including child and forced labor to farmers in Ghana.[8] At first glance, this sounds impressive. But back in 2009, a rival chocolate firm—the Swiss-based Nestlé—had announced plans to invest $110 million in sustainability initiatives over a ten-year period, just one of several industry programs than dwarf Hershey's comparatively tiny effort.[9]

Business magazine *Fast Company* summed up the company's track record by saying, "Hershey, despite having a market share in the U.S. of over 40%, is doing the least in the area of fair trade."[10] In October 2012, Whole Foods announced that it was halting orders of Hershey's "artisan" Scharffen Berger chocolates due to concerns over child labor among Hershey's West African suppliers.[11] And a consortium of environmental and labor groups was so underwhelmed by Hershey's claims of social responsibility that it issued its own analysis rebutting the company's official CSR report: *Time to Raise the Bar: The Real Corporate Social Responsibility Report for the Hershey Company*. The report concluded,

> Hershey, one of the largest and oldest chocolate manufacturers in the United States, prides itself on its commitment to supporting its community and underserved children in the United States, yet it lags behind its competitors when it comes to taking responsibility for the communities from which it sources cocoa. Hershey has no policies in place to purchase cocoa that has been produced without the use of labor exploitation, and the company has consistently refused to provide public information about its cocoa sources.[12]

Look closely at that last sentence. The issues of stakeholder engagement, trust, and transparency leap to the surface. The more one studies the Hershey track record, the less the 2011 student worker fiasco looks like an outlier. Instead, history suggests that Hershey's continuing sustainability problems are linked to a consistent corporate culture whose negative features—especially a penchant for secrecy—repeatedly undermine the company's attempts to live up to its self-image as a model of responsible business.

The Hershey Heritage Goes Up for Sale

One of the most dramatic episodes highlighting Hershey's failure to practice the principles of transparency and stakeholder engagement burst into the news on July 25, 2002.[13] On that date, which the townspeople of Hershey came to call Black Thursday, a story in the *Wall Street Journal* revealed that the board of the Hershey Trust, the charitable organization that owned a controlling stake in the Hershey Foods Company and thereby in the future of everyone in town, had suddenly decided to sell the company to the highest bidder.[14]

The news flashed through town. The questions followed in an instant. Why sell Hershey? Who might the new owners be? What would they do with the Hershey plant, the theme park, the spa and hotel and gardens, and all the other attractions that had made their town a center of tourism? What would happen to the chocolate-related jobs that drove the local economy? Would Hershey, Pennsylvania, become a ghost town?

No one could say.

Of course, the idea of putting a company up for sale is far from unprecedented. It's a story that has been told in one company town after another all across America: corporate interests decide to sacrifice the local economy, culture, and tradition in pursuit of profit. And in most towns, after a period of dismay and anger, the citizens quietly accept their fate.

Not in Hershey.

A coalition of angry citizens formed within hours. It included former CEOs of Hershey who hated the idea of selling the company they'd nurtured; leaders and members of Chocolate Workers Local 464 of the Bakery, Confectionery, Tobacco Workers and Grain Millers International, the union that represented twenty-eight hundred employees at the Hershey plant; alumni of the Milton Hershey School; and thousands of business owners and residents of central Pennsylvania who feared the death of a town they cherished.

A week later, five hundred townspeople converged on Chocolatetown Square for the first protest rally in the history of bucolic, conservative Hershey. The emergence of a broad coalition of activists vowing to fight the sale was the last thing Hershey's leaders had expected. And on August 12, an ambitious state politician—Pennsylvania attorney general Mike Fisher—got involved. That day, Fisher filed a petition with the seemingly named-for-TV Orphans' Court Division of the Court of Common Pleas of Dauphin County, Pennsylvania, calling for prior court approval of any deal to sell Hershey. This was an ironic turn of events, considering that the impetus for selling Hershey seemed to have originated with a suggestion by a member of Fisher's own staff. In December 2001, the staff member had urged the board of the Hershey Trust to diversify its stock holdings, 52 percent of which were in Hershey Foods. Fisher would later say that his office simply had in mind a sale of a portion of the Hershey stock—not a complete divestiture. But by then the damage from the misunderstanding—if that's what it was—had already occurred.

The remarkable battle for control of Hershey that followed illustrates many of the complexities of running a responsible business in an age when stakeholders of every stripe are increasingly assertive, outspoken—and powerful. And it raises a host of questions that business leaders everywhere need to consider—questions like these:

- Do the responsibilities of a business manager go beyond earning the highest possible profits? If so, what are those responsibilities, and how should they be balanced with the pursuit of profits?
- What responsibilities does a company have to its workers, their families, the community where they live, and society at large? Is it enough to pay fair wages, provide competitive benefits, and supply needed goods and services—or should a company do more?
- What information should be disclosed about corporate decisions and activities to those who have a stake in them? How should the leaders of a company take into account the viewpoints and concerns of those stakeholders? And who should have a say about the fate of the company?

- How should the answers to these questions impact the daily decisions made by leaders of a company? If a company does have responsibilities to society that demand the involvement of a wide range of stakeholders, how do these responsibilities affect the management methods and strategic approaches of leaders in every department of the business?

The leaders of the Hershey Company and the Hershey Trust were upstanding citizens of the corporate world and the local community. Yet when challenged to chart a course for future decades in a rapidly changing world, they stumbled, hurting the company financially and leaving Wall Street and the American public with a badly damaged image—one that subsequent events have failed to repair. The reason, we believe, is that they failed to adequately address the questions we've just raised. It's a mistake that other business leaders must avoid.

The Chocolate Hits the Fan

The news that Hershey Foods was in play was big news on Wall Street. Hershey's stock rose from $63 a share into the seventies, and a list of potential buyers quickly emerged, including such international food industry powerhouses as Kraft Foods, Nestlé, and Cadbury Schweppes. Sale prices of up to $12 billion were mentioned in the press, and lawyers, bankers, and fund managers began licking their chops at the prospect of enormous fees and profits.

But in Hershey, Pennsylvania, the news produced shock and dismay. Bruce Hummel, business agent for the union, recalls being stunned when he heard that Hershey was for sale. "The National Labor Relations Board rules stipulate that the company is supposed to inform the union when a major change like a sale is in the works. They never said a word to us."[15]

Local folks also wondered: Why had Hershey kept them completely in the dark? That isn't how people in small-town America treat their friends and neighbors . . . unless they are ashamed or embarrassed about what they are doing.

In retrospect, some Hershey residents felt that the decision to sell the company must have been in the works for months. CEO Rick Lenny had been the first outsider named to direct the fortunes of Hershey Foods. Shortly after his arrival at the company in March 2001, a number of long-term company executives had been quietly pushed toward early retirement in what some employees called "the purge." Now that the sale plan had been announced, many concluded that Lenny had been hired specifically to clean house and make the company more attractive to a would-be buyer. Hershey confirmed no such thing. But under the circumstances, the locals were now unwilling to accept the company's word.

Stunned and angry townspeople felt they had no choice but to launch a grassroots campaign to oppose the sale, including the formation of a watchdog group they called Friends of Hershey.

The international fame of Milton Hershey's charming town had always drawn positive attention to Hershey Foods. Now it fueled controversy. People from around the world took an interest in the fate of the much-loved company and the town that millions had visited as tourists. Columnists and commentators who had recently gorged on the greed and duplicity of companies like Enron, WorldCom, and Adelphia found the Hershey story a tempting treat, writing feature stories on the saga with zinger headlines like "A Bittersweet Deal," "Putting the Bite on Hershey," and the seemingly irresistible "Kiss of Death."

Everyone had something to say about the proposed sale, most of it negative. *BusinessWeek*'s feature story "How Hershey Made a Big Chocolate Mess" excoriated the trust's handling of the sale, citing its failure to anticipate public protests, failure to win advance support from key constituencies, and failure to study the impact of any sale on the Milton Hershey School and its students.[16]

Outside groups connected the Hershey controversy to their own causes. A closely linked trio of nonprofit organizations—the Campaign for Tobacco-Free Kids, Essential Action, and Global Partnerships for Tobacco Control—weighed in with a strong protest against the sale. One of the potential buyers was Kraft Foods, whose parent company was the tobacco firm Philip Morris. "It would be terribly ironic if the School Trust were to effectively force the sale of Hershey Foods to a company associated with the orphaning of thousands upon thousands of children worldwide," wrote Matthew Myers, president of the Campaign for Tobacco-Free Kids, in a September 12, 2002, letter to Robert C. Vowler, CEO of the trust. "Hershey and Philip Morris go together like chocolate and poison."

Executives at the company and the trust hunkered down. Apparently stunned by the reaction of the town and bewildered by the avalanche of bad press—a new phenomenon for Hershey at the time—they refused comment when besieged by newspaper and TV reporters, and failed to provide spokespeople to air their side of the controversy at public forums. The investment world, initially delighted, began to voice displeasure and doubts. In early August, two Wall Street analysts downgraded Hershey shares as a result of the mishandling of the company sale. Others, certain that the sale would go through despite the controversy, began bidding up the stock price—typical behavior, of course, when a company is in play. Hershey stock reached a high of $79.49 on July 29, then stayed in the upper seventies as the company management began weighing potential offers, while all around them protests and legal maneuverings swirled.

About-Face

Community outrage grew steadily. A petition demanding the ouster of the trust's board grew to 3,000 signatures, then to 6,500, then to 8,000—in a town whose total population was only 12,000. The protests attracted all sorts of unlikely allies, from staunchly Republican small-business owners who contributed truckloads of pizzas and bottled water to sustain picketing union workers, to prosperous local realtors who showed up wearing fur coats to take lessons in carrying protest signs from union leader Bruce Hummel.

Determined to press on with its plans despite the outcry, the trust set a deadline of September 14 for prospective buyers to submit bids. By September 17, 2002, a deal was all but finalized to sell Hershey to the Wrigley Company for $12.5 billion. The sale price represented a 42 percent premium over the price of the stock prior to the sale announcement. It was also a full billion dollars richer than the only other offer on the table, a joint bid from Nestlé and Cadbury Schweppes. All in all, it was an excellent financial package, reflecting confidence that the Pennsylvania courts would ultimately approve the deal.

But as in any good small-town drama, there was a surprise ending. Just before midnight, Hershey Foods issued a terse statement: "Hershey Foods Corporation announced today . . . that the Trust's Board of Directors has voted to instruct the company to terminate the sale process that the company initiated at the direction of the trust."[17]

The board had decided to kill its own deal—despite the $12.5 billion on the table and the $17 million in banking and other fees it had already invested in the scheme.

Board members refused to explain their reasons for quashing the sale, just as they had for putting it on the auction block. But media leaks from sources close to the board indicated that the overwhelming and continuing protests from the community had eventually split the board in two. Feeling like pariahs among the angry employees and people of Hershey, first one, then several board members had backed away from the plan. Finally, support for the sale utterly collapsed.

Hershey Foods CEO Rick Lenny, who had negotiated the deal with Wrigley, was deeply embarrassed and furious at the sudden turnaround, reportedly screaming at board members, "We had a deal! You told me if I brought you a deal that was acceptable we would all go ahead."[18] The investment bankers involved in arranging the deal were equally angry. One banker barked, "This has nothing to do with anything other than the politics."[19]

Media around the world reported the startling outcome of the business battle in David-slays-Goliath tones. Thousands of Hershey employees, residents of Hershey, and Hershey School alumni celebrated, feeling that they had saved their company and their community through the power of protest.

The mood at Hershey headquarters was somber. Hershey stock fell nearly 12 percent to $65 the day after the sale was cancelled.

By contrast, Wrigley stock fell just eight cents; conservative investors who favored Wrigley may have been relieved to be taken off the hook by Hershey's reluctance to consummate the deal. The *Wall Street Journal* observed, "Hershey now is left to chart a course as a stand-alone player that effectively can't be sold—but whose controlling shareholder [the trust] has shown it is ambivalent about its long-term commitment to the company."[20]

Two months later, under pressure from the community, the employees, and the Pennsylvania attorney general's office, ten members of the board of the Hershey Trust were ousted. A new eleven-member board was created that included four members not on the earlier board, all inhabitants of Hershey or nearby communities. Two months after that, as the dust was finally settling, *BusinessWeek* magazine enshrined the Hershey Trust Company among its "Ten Worst Managers of 2002."[21]

In the years since then, some things have changed while others have remained the same. Attorney general Fisher ended up being named by President George W. Bush to the United States Court of Appeals for the Third Circuit. Hershey has remained an independent business, majority control still firmly in the hands of the Hershey Trust. Richard Lenny served several more contentious years as Hershey CEO, battling his way through more labor disputes, plant closings, and intensified global competition until his retirement in 2007. And Hershey stock plummeted from its high price in the upper seventies, spending almost the entire next decade in the thirties and the forties. It failed to reach the $70.00 level again until June 2012.

Lessons from the Chocolate Mess

The story of Hershey in the twenty-first century, from the failed sale attempt in 2002 through the student worker fiasco of 2011 and the child labor controversies of 2012, is the saga of a company that is continuing to grope for answers in a complicated and contentious business and social environment. But of course Hershey isn't the only company to face these sorts of challenges. Business managers of all kinds, in all industries, can learn some crucial lessons of sustainability from the experiences of Hershey.

Focusing on profit alone can backfire. The managers who made the decision to sell Hershey Foods back in 2002 and those who, almost a decade later, hired student workers and paid them rock-bottom wages were doing the right thing by purely financial yardsticks. They were trying to maximize returns to the company. But in today's business world, the financial bottom line is not the only or even the most important measure of success. Executives also must consider the social, economic, and environmental impacts on anyone with a stake in the outcome.

The protests that derailed the Hershey sale were based on non-financial concerns: the economic impacts of the sale on company employees and their families; the social disruption it would cause to the community; and long-term effects on students, teachers, and alumni of the Milton Hershey School. Those nonfinancial concerns ultimately trumped the financial ones, causing what looked like a good deal to crater.

Businesses are accountable to more people than they may realize. In the abortive company sale, Hershey management acted as if their fiduciary duty was the only interest that mattered. They forgot about other crucial stakeholders with a vested interest in their actions. Some stakeholders had obvious connections to the company—the employees of Hershey Foods, residents of Hershey, alumni of the Milton Hershey School. Others proved to be equally important: the citizens of Pennsylvania; the media; and millions of Americans who knew, loved, and patronized the company and town. Board members even managed to overlook the legacy of Milton S. Hershey himself, whose vision for his company and town was repeatedly invoked against the sale.

The Hershey deal had aspects that may appear unique, but almost every company these days faces special circumstances that can disrupt its plans. Some are subject to activist investors who push hard in the opposite direction from where they want to go. Others rely on government contracts or public permits that can be held hostage by politicians or threatened by environmentalists or the media. Some executives wake up to a demonstration by animal rights activists, an unexpected visit by a cameraman and correspondent from 60 *Minutes*, the news that their headquarters is being occupied by Greenpeace, or a call saying, "The state attorney general's office holding for you on line two." Many rely on sensitive natural resources or suppliers in distant places who can upset the apple cart in dozens of ways.

So don't lull yourself by thinking, "Nothing like this can happen to me, because my stock isn't owned by a trust." Chances are good that the world is still watching what you do and will react—strongly—if you make a Hershey-style blunder.

You are responsible for those who act on your behalf. Many businesses today sit at the center of a network of companies—suppliers, manufacturers, warehousing and shipping companies, wholesalers, retailers, and customer service specialists—that together form a complex value chain. As a result, most of the operations involved in bringing your product or service to customers may be performed by companies you don't own or directly control. But this doesn't reduce your sphere of responsibility—just the opposite. Stakeholders including consumers, the media, activist organizations, government agencies, and the general public will hold you accountable for actions taken by organizations in your network—such as a cocoa grower that employs child labor or a logistics company that exploits foreign students. In the Age of Sustainability, the excuse "We didn't do it, our business partner did" simply doesn't fly.

Bad things can happen to good companies that fail to take a broad view of accountability. Well-intentioned, well-managed organizations like the Hershey Trust and Hershey Foods that focus exclusively on shareholders as if they were the only stakeholders that matter are headed for trouble just as certainly as those that knowingly violate societal norms in pursuit of profit.

The outcome of the failed company sale could have been different. John Dunn, a former marketing executive at Hershey, emphasizes that the board could have succeeded if they had understood and managed their accountability: "In the end, it's really not that important for Hershey Foods to stay in the hands of the trust. They could have sold the company if they'd handled it properly. But by blundering ahead without communicating with the community, they sent the message that they were willing to endanger the sense of continuity and tradition that the people and businesses of central Pennsylvania had been counting on. That was just plain dumb."[22]

Among the most important stakeholder groups to whom businesses are accountable is the one that Dunn himself represents—employees. Most companies at least pay lip service to the importance of employees; slogans like "Our most valuable assets walk out the front door every evening" are featured in plenty of CEO speeches and annual reports. But many organizations fail to fully inform, involve, and engage their employees; many fail to provide them with the opportunity to express their deepest values on the job. By contrast, companies that take employee engagement seriously reap huge rewards: they enjoy better morale, productivity, and profitability (as well as avoiding needless destructive controversies like the one that Hershey suffered).

Transparency is crucial to success in an era of empowered employees and demanding stakeholders. Hershey has a long history of keeping to itself. In researching the story of the botched Hershey sale for this book, we spoke to numerous sources in and around the town of Hershey, including former employees and officers of the company—yet no company spokesperson or current executive would speak with us in any detail about the firm. Even such basic information as the identity of the products made in Hershey's various chocolate plants is treated as a closely guarded company secret.

Companies often have legitimate reasons for keeping secrets and for confining decisions to internal leaders and Wall Street bankers, as did Hershey and the trust. But bringing your stakeholders inside the tent on matters that might affect them is increasingly a matter of responsible corporate citizenship and sophisticated risk management.

When Hershey suddenly sprang its proposed sale on the general public, it was taking an unnecessary business risk, especially in light of recent warning signs (including a rare strike settled just weeks before the announcement). The furious reaction that derailed the sale was driven, in large part, by the fact that everyone except the bankers had been kept in the dark. According to John Dunn, "The way the company handled the controversy compounded the problem. Instead of reaching out, they went into a bunker. They refused to make any public statements, failed to show up at community meetings, ignored calls for an open forum or debate."

It's hard not to agree with Dunn's conclusion that this "was a textbook example of what not to do in a corporate controversy."

Corporate culture has a powerful yet often invisible impact on a company's sustainability. A year after the 2002 showdown, Hershey Foods CEO Rick Lenny was asked to name the most important qualities of a good chief executive. He emphasized "openness and transparency with the multiple constituents."[23] It's excellent advice, even if Lenny and his leadership team ignored it during their crisis and there is reason to believe their successors still don't adequately practice it today.

Was Lenny being dishonest or hypocritical? Perhaps. But it's also possible that he was quite sincere in his praise of transparency, yet equally unaware of the powerful undertow that Hershey's traditional, deeply ingrained corporate culture exerted, making true transparency almost impossible. In the twenty-first century, companies can no longer get by with an attitude of father-knows-best paternalism. If your company culture isn't evolving to meet the new expectations, even the best-intentioned sustainability program is likely to founder.

It's instructive to compare Hershey's corporate culture with the more savvy and responsible approach of one of Hershey's biggest competitors and former suitors, Cadbury Schweppes. Part of the Kraft Foods family since 2010 (and now known simply as Cadbury), the British-based firm has long been considered one of the world's most socially responsible companies. Among other enlightened practices highlighted in the company's two-hundred-page sustainability report for the year 2004 (titled *Working Better Together*) is this description of how Cadbury Schweppes managed the closing of a plant that manufactured cough drops and chewing gum in Avenida, Brazil:

> To increase production, logistics and distribution efficiencies and support our plans for growth and innovation, we decided to consolidate the Avenida production site into the modern facility at Bauru [also in Brazil]. We began the transition in October

2003 and aim to complete it by July 2004. While the closure of Avenida do Estado involves the loss of 300 jobs, 212 new jobs will be created in Bauru.

We have managed the impact of the changes by being open and transparent about what has to be done and by working with employees to do it in the right way. We informed all employees in advance of the closure and hired a firm that specializes in supporting large scale restructuring. The firm devised a programme, New Professional Project, to coordinate the redeployment of employees in the most supportive way. The programme included researching job vacancies with local companies and matching employees' capabilities, wishes and ambitions within the current job market and business environment.[24]

Comparable openness and responsiveness by Hershey Foods in regard to the possible loss of jobs in Hershey, Pennsylvania—a community that is far more tied to the history and reputation of Hershey Foods than Avenida, Brazil, was to those of Cadbury Schweppes—might have defused resentments stirred up by the proposed sale and paved the way for its completion.

Politics is an inescapable part of business. The anonymous investment banker who complained bitterly that the cancellation of the sale "has nothing to do with anything other than the politics" was not wrong. The board's decision to pull back was a political one, in the sense that it was motivated by the belated recognition that most concerned stakeholders opposed the deal and would, in various ways, have withdrawn their support from the company if the sale had gone through. To a doctrinaire advocate of the free market, the fact that business leaders must consider the political impact of their decisions may be abhorrent. But it's a reality. Hershey's lack of political judgment and skills was a direct cause of the company's misfortune.

•••

The Hershey story shows that even a well-run company with a proud history of business and philanthropic achievement can stumble and fall when the principles of sustainability are ignored. Why has sustainability become such a crucial issue for today's businesses? And what must they do to address it successfully and avoid the kinds of mistakes that Hershey has made? The rest of this book will answer those questions.

The Sustainability Sweet Spot
How to Achieve Long-Term Business Success

It's up to us to use our platform to be a good citizen. Because not only is it a nice thing to do, it's a business imperative... If this wasn't good for business, we probably wouldn't do it.

—Jeffrey Immelt, CEO, General Electric[1]

Where Profit Meets the Common Good

Business leaders with a superficial understanding of sustainability think of it as a distraction from their main purpose, a chore they hope can be discharged quickly and easily. "We're responsible corporate citizens, so let's write a check to the United Way or allow employees to volunteer for the local cleanup drive or food kitchen and get back to work."

This approach reveals a fundamental misunderstanding. Sustainability is not about philanthropy. There's nothing wrong with corporate charity—in fact, in times of natural disaster or other crisis, emergency assistance from businesses can be essential. But sustainability goes deeper. The sustainable company conducts its business so that benefits flow naturally to all stakeholders, including employees, customers, business partners, the communities in which it operates, and, of course, shareholders.

It could be said that the truly sustainable company would have no need to write checks to charity or "give back" to the local community, because the company's daily operations wouldn't harm the environment or deprive the community, but would improve the world. Sustainable companies find areas of mutual interest and ways to make "doing good" and "doing well" synonymous, thus avoiding the implied conflict between society and shareholders.

The vision of a company that renews society as it enriches its shareholders may seem remote, and for most companies it is. But we propose a way to think about your company's current operations that might suggest an avenue for moving in that direction.

Think about sustainability as finding the common ground shared by your business interests (those of your financial stakeholders) and the interests of the public (your nonfinancial stakeholders). This common ground is what we call the Sustainability Sweet Spot: the place where the pursuit of profit blends seamlessly with the pursuit of the common good, including the creation of both environmental and social benefits for all of the company's stakeholders (see Figure 2.1). The best-run companies around the world are trying to identify and move into their sweet spots, where benefits to their financial

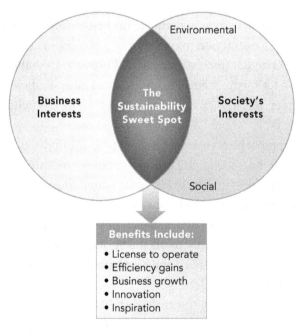

Figure 2.1   The Sustainability Sweet Spot.

performance are naturally generated. And they are developing new ways of doing business in order to get there and stay there.

General Electric (GE) was long considered an environmental scofflaw. It fought the U.S. Environmental Protection Agency for years, trying in vain to avoid responsibility for polluting the Hudson and Housatonic Rivers with over one million pounds of toxic waste.[2] Jack Welch, GE's CEO and chairman, personally led the attack, which included arguing over settled science and challenging parts of the federal hazardous waste cleanup program as unconstitutional, tactics widely considered irresponsible.

When Welch retired in 2001, many of the flattering reviews referred to GE's environmental record as Welch's one black eye. In the years since then, his successor Jeffrey Immelt has plotted a new course—not because he and the company are born-again environmentalists, but because being pro-environment is smart business for GE. In Immelt's words, tackling environmental challenges on behalf of GE's client companies is a way of repositioning the corporation as "a company that solves big problems for customers and the world."[3]

As its first major push in this direction, in 2005 GE announced an initiative called ecomagination. (Following GE's corporate practice, we will spell the words *ecomagination* and [later] *healthymagination* with a lowercase initial E and H.) It is a powerful example of finding and working toward the sweet spot, representing "action that goes beyond compliance to benefit both society and the long term health of the enterprise," in the words of Ben Heineman, then GE's senior vice president of law and public affairs.[4] Ecomagination's main thrust is to create clean technologies to help GE's customers reduce their environmental impacts, including carbon emissions and excessive consumption of valuable resources.

Addressing environmental problems has provided GE with huge business opportunities. For example, despite the economic slowdown following the Great Recession of 2008–2009, GE's wind energy business has already generated over $30 billion in revenues since it was acquired in 2002 from Enron, and its fuel-efficient jet and locomotive engines and natural gas turbines are proving to be essential to customers needing additional ways to reduce their emissions.[5] By November 2012, GE had installed twenty thousand wind turbines in markets from Latin America to India and China—enough to provide all the energy needed to power Hong Kong and London for an entire year—including over five thousand turbines in 2012 alone.[6]

By mid-2012, the entire ecomagination portfolio of clean-tech products and solutions had generated more than $105 billion in revenue, exceeding the ambitious growth targets originally set for the program and growing at a faster rate than the rest of GE.[7] Ecomagination also includes internal initiatives that are reducing GE's own footprint on the planet—for example, by using less energy and water.

GE has found a significant overlap between its business interests and protecting the environment. And if climate change regulations ultimately impose carbon restrictions on businesses in the United States, placing an even greater premium on the use of clean energy, GE will be ready to take advantage of the increasing area of overlap. The bigger the overlap, the better for an environmentally friendly GE (see Figure 2.2).

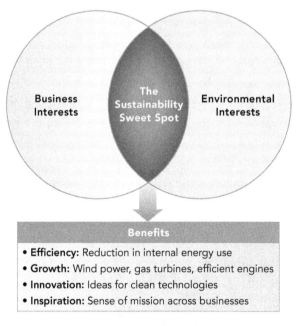

Figure 2.2   GE's Ecomagination Sweet Spot.

Buoyed by the success of ecomagination, GE has followed it with another sweet spot initiative called healthymagination. Its goals are to reshape the health care business by improving access to quality care, use innovative technology to make better care more widely available and affordable, and give individual consumers greater control over their own care.

Some healthymagination products are natural outgrowths of GE's existing health technology business—for example, newly designed neonatal incubation units for at-risk infants and portable electrocardiogram machines, each costing just a fraction of the traditional price for such devices. These innovations will enjoy a huge market in the developing world, where hundreds of millions of people lack access to medical equipment many in North America take for granted. In time, versions of the same devices customized to the U.S. market may also help slow the out-of-control growth of health care costs that has been plaguing policymakers and providers alike.

Other healthymagination services are being created to serve GE's own employees. For example, Health Coach provides an 800 number and a smartphone app that makes the advice of a trained nurse available, 24/7, whenever a family member needs help. GE believes that the service will help employees make better decisions about choosing doctors or obtaining emergency care while also eventually reducing the cost of health care coverage for the company—a social and economic sweet spot that benefits everyone (see Figure 2.3).

Products like wind turbines occupy a sweet spot where GE's business interests overlap with environmental concerns; low-cost medical devices serve both GE's interests and society's interest in making high-quality health care available to families in the developing world. In still other cases, GE's interests overlap with both environmental and social interests. For example, GE has been building a business around advanced water filtration systems capable of providing pure, potable water for communities in the developing world at minimal cost. These systems produce benefits across the entire spectrum of the Triple Bottom Line (TBL): they help protect the environment (consuming minimal amounts of energy and other resources) while also meeting social and economic needs (saving lives and freeing poor

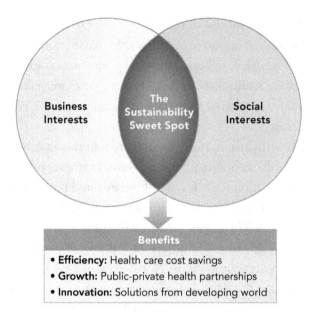

Figure 2.3   GE's Healthymagination Sweet Spot.

people from the unproductive drudgery of daily treks for drinking water) (see Figure 2.4).

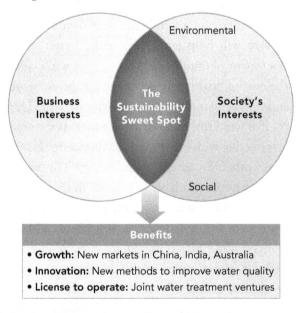

Figure 2.4   GE's Water Filtration Business Sweet Spot.

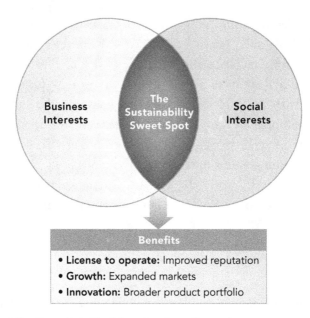

Figure 2.5   PepsiCo's Healthier Products Sweet Spot.

GE's ecomagination and healthymagination initiatives embody the observation by Ian Davis, former chairman and worldwide managing director of the management consulting firm of McKinsey & Company, that "large companies need to build social issues into strategy in a way that reflects their actual business importance."[8]

• • •

The overlap between winning increased market share and supporting healthier lifestyle habits is a sweet spot for PepsiCo (see Figure 2.5). If the idea of healthy products sounds like a stretch for a company famous for its sugary sodas and salty snacks, think again. With the purchase of brands like Tropicana and Quaker Oats, as well as the launch of a global nutrition group focused on dairy products, juices, and other healthful snacks, PepsiCo's healthy-product sweet spot now represents 20 percent of the company's annual revenues.[9] What's more, CEO Indra Nooyi expects to more than double the revenues derived from "good for you" products to over $30 billion by 2020.[10] PepsiCo is using its expertise to develop other projects that will both enhance the company's bottom line and improve the nutritional status of people around the world—for example, by working with the UN World Food Program and the U.S. Agency for International Development to help farmers in Ethiopia improve the yield and quality of their chickpea crop. PepsiCo will use some of the resulting harvest in its popular hummus products (sold under the Sabra brand), while the rest goes to make new ready-to-eat foods designed to help address rampant hunger in countries like Pakistan.[11]

● ● ●

The world's largest retailer, Wal-Mart, has long had a troubled relationship with organizations that advocate sustainable business policies. The company has come under fire for the low wages and scanty benefits some of their workers receive, for labor infractions allegedly committed by some of its many global suppliers, and for violations of environmental regulations, such as local pollution laws. As a gigantic, almost ubiquitous symbol of American capitalism, Wal-Mart makes a tempting, highly visible target for those who seek publicity for social and environmental causes.

At one time, the company's response to such criticism was combative and defensive. Then, in 2005, CEO H. Lee Scott had an epiphany. He decided it was time to transform the company from an environmental offender into a corporate leader. Scott's change of heart was driven by several factors: a growing personal conviction that global climate change is real, and that one of the world's largest corporations has a special responsibility to help address the issue; Scott's becoming a grandfather, which led him to ponder the legacy he would be leaving to future generations; and the gradual realization that more responsible environmental stewardship could save Wal-Mart money and contribute to its quest to remain the world's leading low-price retailer.[12]

The environmental results have been impressive. Wal-Mart Stores now reuses or recycles more than 80 percent of the waste produced in its U.S. operations—an improvement on the 64 percent figure from 2009, but short of its ultimate zero-waste goal. It has reduced greenhouse gas emissions from existing stores by 12.74 percent compared with 2005, short of its 20 percent target.[13] Wal-Mart's efforts to reduce packaging used by its suppliers is on track to save between $12 and $13 billion by 2015. Many environmental activists give Wal-Mart credit for its efforts. Some have converted from adversaries to advisers; for example, the Environmental Defense Fund has opened an office in Bentonville, Arkansas, making it easy for its experts to confer with company executives at Wal-Mart headquarters.

On the social front, however, Wal-Mart's record has been far less impressive. The issue of the company's health care benefits for workers has been a sticking point with advocates for years. And recently Wal-Mart's reputation for economic and social justice has suffered major blows: an international scandal centered on bribery of local officials to obtain preferential regulatory treatment for Wal-Mart expansion plans, and a tragic garment-factory fire in Bangladesh that killed more than one hundred workers employed by a Wal-Mart supplier.[14] (Wal-Mart subsequently severed its business ties to the supplier company, but the damage to its reputation had already been done.)

Wal-Mart itself has suffered as a result of its social responsibility failures. For years, the corporation has been unable to win regulatory approval for a store location in Boston, with critics citing its poor record on labor issues as a prime reason to reject its applications. It's probably no coincidence that Wal-Mart gave up its long-standing efforts to win approval for a New York City store in the aftermath of the Bangladesh factory fire. For Wal-Mart, therefore, the Sustainability Sweet Spot—still not truly attained by the company—is clearly an area where Wal-Mart's business interests (including its desire to increase its market presence by opening stores in two of America's prime retail locations) overlaps with improved performance on environmental and social issues (see Figure 2.6).

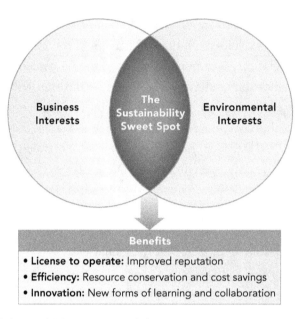

Figure 2.6   Wal-Mart's Sustainability Sweet Spot.

Sweet spots like the ones we've looked at embody the literal meaning of sustainability: making your company viable for the long term by managing according to principles that will strengthen rather than undermine the company's performance in environmental, social, and economic areas. A business that occupies the Sustainability Sweet Spot (or that strives to fit as much of its activities into that favored zone as possible) should have real long-term advantages over its rivals. We'll explain why that is the case when we discuss in Chapter Three the increasing pressures that companies are under, and we'll provide an in-depth discussion in Chapter Nine on how to find your own organization's Sustainability Sweet Spot.

"Prove It!"

Many businesspeople find the simple logic behind the sweet spot compelling, but others require proof that sustainability creates financial benefits. They seek an assurance that's as good as gold— incontrovertible evidence that they can and will make more money practicing sustainable management than they will with good old-fashioned, short-term, profit-only thinking.

Let's consider some of that evidence. It includes the share prices of companies listed in the Dow Jones Sustainability Index and the FTSE4 Good Indexes. These prestigious indexes of companies on sustainable pathways have outperformed various market indexes. Similarly, companies that belong to the World Business Council for Sustainable Development outperformed their respective national stock exchanges by 15 to 25 percent over the past three years. From 1999 through 2003, the Winslow Green Index of one hundred "green-screened" companies increased in value by over 73 percent, whereas the members of the comparable benchmark Russell 2000 Index increased by less than 17 percent.[15] The outperformance by socially responsible funds continued later in the decade. The FTSE KLD 400, an index of socially responsible stocks, produced annualized returns of 9.51 percent between 1990 and 2009, whereas the S&P 500 earned just 8.66 percent during the same period. Even during the economic meltdown late in the 2000s, the pattern persisted: large-cap mutual funds dedicated to socially responsible investments outperformed the S&P 500 by 6 percent during 2009.[16]

A recent study by researchers from Harvard Business School reflected similar results. Robert G. Eccles, Ioannis Ioannou, and George Serafeim created two matched sets of companies, one defined as "high sustainability" based on their governance systems, business policies, and cultural characteristics, and the other defined as "low sustainability." They then tracked the stock market results achieved by each of these sets of ninety otherwise comparable companies. They found that $1.00 invested in 1993 in a portfolio made up of the high-sustainability companies would have grown, by 2010, to $22.60, whereas $1.00 invested in the low-sustainability companies would have grown to just $15.40. They conclude, "This finding suggests that companies can adopt environmentally and socially responsible policies without sacrificing shareholder wealth creation. In fact, the opposite appears to be true: sustainable firms generate significantly higher profits and stock returns, suggesting that developing a corporate culture of sustainability may be a source of competitive advantage for a company in the long-run."[17]

It cannot be proved that sustainability is the reason for the strong market performance of the companies that have embraced it, but when similar results continue year after year, the correlation implies causation. (As Henry D. Thoreau, the American essayist and philosopher, famously remarked, "Some circumstantial evidence is very strong, as when you find a trout in the milk.")

Those seeking the gold standard should recall that the cases for such strategic initiatives as Total Quality Management, Six Sigma, and reengineering—or, more recently, business model reinvention, crowdsourcing, and big data—were not proved before thousands of businesses invested billions of dollars in them. These concepts won widespread support because of case studies that illustrated their effectiveness, endorsements from well-known business leaders, their resonance with the zeitgeist of their times, and eventually (in some cases) because of financial results. The initial evidence supporting those programs was largely anecdotal, but, as Travis Engen, former CEO of Alcan, likes to say, "the plural of anecdote is data"—and many companies, perhaps including yours, have benefited from one or more of these ideas.

Like most business strategies, sustainability is not a guarantee of financial success. It requires commitment, resources, and a change of direction, which entail costs and risks. The real question to ask yourself, as with all important business decisions, is this: Is sustainability a good bet for me and my company?

More and more companies are answering yes. Sustainability is quickly becoming mainstream. Socially responsible initiatives, from the Prius to natural foods, from green buildings to ecofriendly clothes and cosmetics, from responsible outsourcing to diversity in hiring, have migrated from being considered heretical, to impractical, to visionary, and finally to common sense—usually as soon as they begin to turn a profit. Eventually they become part of business as usual, their controversial origins all but forgotten.

When Ralph Nader first began to argue that cars in the 1960s could be made much safer, he was dismissed by Detroit and most of the public as an agitator and a nutcase. Now all car companies strive for increased safety, and some, such as Volvo, have made it the centerpiece of their marketing.

Can a sustainable business strategy enhance profitability? Of course, but when it does, it usually travels on our mental maps from the space now labeled "sustainability" into the one more simply known as "good business."

Three Ways Sustainability Enhances Your Business

Whether you find or even look for the sweet spot, the principles of sustainability can improve the management of your business in three fundamental ways—by helping you protect it, run it, and grow it.[18]

Protecting the Business

Protecting the business includes reducing risk of harm to customers, employees, and communities; identifying emerging risks and management failures early; limiting regulatory interventions; and retaining the explicit or implicit license to operate granted by government or by the community at large.

When low rainfall in Kerala, India, caused a water shortage in 2002, political activists staged protests against both the Coca-Cola and Pepsi plants in the state, blaming the beverage companies for withdrawing too much water from the local aquifers.[19] Pepsi's hydrogeologists proved that their plant drew water from a *separate* deep-well aquifer with no connection to the public water source. But this failed to stop the protests, and Pepsi's managers quickly recognized that thirsty people couldn't care less about the science—that bottling water and soft drinks in the plant while people nearby lacked water for their homes and their families was unacceptable to the community and presented a significant business risk.

Using technical information that had been gathered when Pepsi built its plant, the company improved the community well, thereby restoring water to Kerala, and began a program to build community wells in other areas. At the same time, aggressive water management procedures were established at the Pepsi plant, including the creation of ponds on the plant premises to increase the recharge of the aquifer. These steps mollified the protesters, protecting Pepsi's business interests and gaining permission for the company to continue operating in Kerala.

Meanwhile, protests continued against Coca-Cola, and the Coke plant was shut down in early 2004 by the local government. With the Coke plant shut, political activists driven by anti-U.S. sentiments turned their attention to Pepsi. Bowing to political pressure, the Kerala government ordered the Pepsi plant closed, but with little local support, the protests failed, and the plant reopened almost immediately. In fact, when political activists tried to shut the Pepsi plant down again in late 2005, they were stopped by the local villagers.

As of 2012, lingering anti-American sentiment in Kerala is continuing to make the production of soft drinks by U.S.-based companies controversial. But Pepsi is still operating its Kerala plant, while Coke remains shut out.

By contrast, the story of how biotechnology giant Monsanto botched its entrance into the field of bioengineering crops in the mid- to late 1990s illustrates the downside of failing to protect your business through sustainable practices. Monsanto's genetically modified (GM) seeds—corn containing natural insecticides, and soybeans able to withstand potent weed killers—were supposed to offer farmers enormous competitive benefits. Monsanto had a powerful sweet spot proposition: that its pioneering efforts would give the company a leading position in a major new marketplace and provide a powerful new weapon in the battle against world hunger. "Monsanto is in a unique position to contribute to the global future," declared biodiversity advocate Peter Raven.[20]

But Monsanto executives, like those at Hershey, failed to work with stakeholders in their development of the new initiative—a core principle of sustainable business. Monsanto dismissed early critics of GM products as antitechnology fanatics and failed to mount a concerted effort to educate consumers about the science behind genetic engineering.

Monsanto consequently found itself beset by a variety of attacks. Several European supermarket chains as well as American natural food retailers announced that they would remove GM foods from their shelves, and major food companies, such as baby-food maker Gerber, vowed to keep their products free of GM ingredients. Embarrassingly, even the staff canteen at Monsanto's own UK headquarters announced that it would ban GM food from its menu "in response to concern raised by our customers."[21]

In the years since then, Monsanto has had to fight a prolonged "ground war" against opponents of GM foods, winning victories in some parts of the world (such as Asia and Latin America) while facing fierce resistance in others (Western Europe and Africa).[22] Lawsuits and legislative initiatives seeking to limit the use of GM products or force their labeling on consumer products—both staunchly opposed by Monsanto—continue to surface. And organizations ranging from Greenpeace and Friends of the Earth US to Physicians for Social Responsibility and the Sierra Club continue to speak out against Monsanto's efforts to win government support for its GM research programs.[23]

More than fifteen years after the controversy first erupted, the entire biotech industry is still struggling to win general public acceptance for bioengineered products—largely because of Monsanto's early failure to consider the demands of sustainability before launching this major business initiative.

Running the Business

Running the business includes reducing costs, improving productivity, eliminating needless waste, and obtaining access to capital at lower cost.

Eco-efficiency is a basic component of sustainability that applies to running your business. It means reducing the amount of resources used to produce goods and services, which increases a company's profitability while decreasing its environmental impact. The underlying theme is simple: pollution is waste, and waste is anathema because it means that your company is paying for something it didn't use. Given the clarity of this logic, it's amazing how few companies have diligently pursued eco-efficiency.

Consider the financial benefits from eco-efficiency enjoyed by Unilever, which has been pursuing a multiyear program designed to reduce carbon emissions, water and energy use, and production of hazardous wastes in its manufacturing facilities. The company has now developed technical tools that enable it to measure the financial benefits from these improvements in eco-efficiency with fair precision. Unilever reports, "During 2011, the financial benefits of reductions in energy and water alone reached approximately €36 million [$47 million]. Raw material and packaging material waste delivered another €11 million, giving a total of approximately €47 million [$61 million]. The cumulative savings of our eco-efficiency programme achieved since 2006 are approximately €250 million [$328 million]."[24] As the Unilever website goes on to observe, "This clear financial benefit reinforces our belief that sustainability is good for business."

Growing the Business

Growing the business includes opening new markets, launching new products and services, increasing the pace of innovation, improving customer satisfaction and loyalty, growing market share by attracting customers for whom sustainability is a personal or business value, forming new alliances with business partners and other stakeholders, and improving reputation and brand value.

Sustainability is a powerful engine of economic and business growth, driving innovation and new technologies. In 2004, $5.8 billion was spent on "green building" initiatives—the design and construction of ecofriendly, healthy, and efficient buildings; by 2011, the sum had mushroomed to $87.1 billion.[25] Entire new businesses have been developed in support, including energy-saving home appliances, low-flow toilets, improved technologies for heating, solar heating, lighting, and electricity, and superefficient cooling and insulation systems.

The sustainability mind-set is also helping companies think creatively about how to gain access to vast new markets that were once dismissed as unprofitable or even impossible. Significant businesses are being built at the "base of the pyramid," among the four billion people living on less than $2 per day, who collectively represent enormous untapped buying power. Companies that figure out how to sell goods and services to the poor will reap huge rewards in the decades to come and create new opportunity for those in need.

The late C. K. Prahalad, the business consultant who, along with Professor Stuart Hart, studied opportunities at the base of the pyramid, explained how companies that respect the rights, needs, and interests of the poor can create new business models that in turn create economic opportunity for business and society.[26]

Prahalad cited Casa Bahia, a Brazilian retailer (now part of the Viavarejo chain), which operates exclusively in the favelas, or shantytowns, where the poorest people of Brazil are found; Annapurna Salt, a Unilever brand that has captured a significant share of the market in India, Ghana, Kenya, Nigeria, and other African nations with small, low-priced packages of iodized salt specifically designed to help combat rampant iodine deficiency disorder among the poor; and Hindustan Unilever Ltd., the largest soap producer in India, which has achieved that status through innovative production, packaging, and marketing techniques that reach into many of the smallest and poorest villages in the subcontinent. Businesses like these represent large sweet spots, creating profit while providing access to needed and affordable consumer goods, thereby stimulating economic growth and improving the quality of life.

It takes ingenuity and creativity to find ways to reach customers at the base of the pyramid. But the effort is worthwhile, not just because of the sizeable profits to be earned in the short run but because of even greater long-term benefits to companies that win the patronage and loyalty of this huge group of consumers at the start of their march toward middle-class status—a transition that base-of-the-pyramid programs will help accelerate.

Additional Business Benefits of Sustainability

So far, we've focused on the quantitative side of the case for sustainability—the direct and measurable costs of ignoring your stakeholders and their concerns, and the financial benefits that companies are enjoying by managing themselves or producing goods and services to assist others in the pursuit of the principles of sustainability.

There's also another side, one that turns on opportunities and risks that may be harder to quantify: company reputation, employee engagement, customer goodwill, and the value of being considered a leader in your industry.

Wegman's, a privately held grocery chain with sales of $6.2 billion in 2011, has been named one of the best companies to work for in America by *Fortune* magazine every year from 1998 through 2012. The reasons aren't difficult to fathom. The company offers higher-than-average wages, high-end training programs, college tuition assistance, and, perhaps most important, jobs designed to empower workers to make decisions to help customers. Wegman's commitment to these practices is expensive: the company spends 15 to 17 percent of sales on labor costs as opposed to the industry average of 12 percent. Wegman's has also spent more than $85 million in tuition assistance over the past twenty-nine years.

But employee satisfaction creates sizeable financial rewards for Wegman's. The company's costs related to turnover (for example, unemployment insurance, severance, training, lost productivity) are 6 percent of revenues compared to the industry average of 19 percent, which translates to a savings of approximately $300 million per year, far more than needed to cover the costs of the programs.

Moreover, the family-owned company is thriving in the face of competitive pressure from companies like Wal-Mart and Costco, and sees its employee retention programs as fundamental to its success. Wegman's margins are double those of America's four biggest grocery firms, and its sales per square foot are twice the industry average.[27]

Hard Cases

Unfortunately, sustainability isn't always an easy win-win. Many situations arise, especially in the short term, where being sustainable imposes additional costs or redirects money away from shareholders and toward other stakeholders. Some of these situations are resolved as being in the long-term interest of shareholders, but others represent genuine, perhaps permanent conflicts of interest between shareholders and other stakeholders. These are the hard cases.

Many companies try to avoid those situations by seeking new sweet spot opportunities where the needs of the business and the needs of society overlap. But avoidance isn't always possible. The realities of the U.S. automobile industry, for example, include both consumer demand for gas-guzzlers and a cost structure that currently makes big cars more profitable than small ones. It's impossible, not to mention highly unsustainable, for a company to act against its own financial interest. Simply demanding that the car companies or their executives do so is, to put it mildly, counterproductive.

There's a useful distinction between being sustainable and being responsible. The responsible action is for the automakers to meet the current demand for traditional gasoline-powered vehicles, including SUVs and other relatively inefficient models, while working to alter consumer preferences and expanding the availability, attractiveness, and profitability of high-tech, high-efficiency alternatives. Thus, when Bill Ford Jr., executive chairman of the automaker that bears his family name, talks about Ford's transition to "global platform" vehicles that include a growing number of hybrids, plug-in hybrids, and pure battery electric cars, his behavior can be considered highly responsible even though his industry, his company, and his main products are not yet sustainable.[28]

Similarly, we can't expect, nor do we want, the energy companies to give up on oil and gas production today because extracting and burning fossil fuels is unsustainable in the long term. But we can and should expect them to work hard to help society make the transition to renewable energy sources—as companies like Royal Dutch Shell and even the once-recalcitrant ExxonMobil are now beginning to do, even while they maintain a high percentage of their current operations in oil and gas extraction.

Hardest of all is when there is no sustainable or responsible action to be taken. If, for example, genetically modified food is conclusively proved to be dangerous for consumers and bad for the planet (like leaded gasoline or asbestos-based insulation), the only responsible approach for companies in that business will be to close down their operations as fast as possible while trying to mitigate the adverse impacts of doing so. Any other choice would be socially irresponsible, making such companies the legitimate target of activists, responsible businesses, and society, while at the same time exposing their shareholders to ever-growing liability risks.

Why Now?

We believe that sustainability enhances profitability for the vast majority of companies. It serves as a road map for doing business in an interdependent world where environmental and social challenges are creating growing problems both for businesses and for humankind as a whole. It offers new ways to protect your company from environmental, financial, and social risks; to run your company with greater efficiency and productivity; and to grow your company through the development of new products and services and the opening of new markets. It provides intangible benefits that include an improved corporate reputation, higher employee morale, and increased customer goodwill. Sustainability will set you and your organization on the path to long-term success.

So far, so good. But if these assertions are correct, why has sustainability only recently made its way onto the agenda? What is different about today's business environment that is making sustainability a crucial factor in twenty-first-century business success? To answer this question, we need to make a brief detour into business history and examine the emergence of some of the most potent trends now at work on the global stage.

3

The Age of Sustainability

Sorry, I can't talk right now—I'm uploading a live
satellite feed onto the Web. We're watching Greenland
break apart.
—Kert Davies, research director, Greenpeace,
during a telephone conversation with
Andrew W. Savitz

Sustainable Business—an Old Idea
Made New Again

Business practices that promote specific aspects of sustainability have
been around for a long time. Some great companies have always tried
to behave responsibly in terms of their resources and impacts. But the
areas that make up today's sustainability movement—the environment, community relations, labor practices, responsible investment,
and others—were historically seen in isolation from one another;
companies addressed specific issues based on their special circumstances or business requirements, or because of the personalities
or interests of their leaders. So when we try to trace the history
of sustainable business, we find scattered, disconnected anecdotes
that describe the pioneering efforts of a few organizations in a few
areas. In retrospect, these efforts foreshadow the much more powerful, widespread, and integrated sustainability movement that is
transforming business today.

None of the companies that deserve a place in the early history of
sustainability have scored consistently high marks over the years in
all three areas of social, environmental, and economic responsibility.

Take the chemical company DuPont, for example. Only in the 1990s did DuPont begin transforming itself from a company notorious for polluting the environment in the 1960s into a more environmentally responsible business and ultimately sustainable enterprise. By then, DuPont had helped create close to 350 hazardous waste sites, which it has spent billions to clean up. Today the company faces environmental concerns related to the possible impacts of the chemicals used to manufacture Teflon and a range of potentially dangerous pesticides.[1] The company's own reports (through 2010) show that DuPont continues to produce over nine hundred million pounds of hazardous waste every year—a 62 percent drop from the 1990 figure, but essentially unchanged since 2005.[2]

But in terms of safety and community involvement, the leaders of the new DuPont can draw historical connections to the earliest days of the company, when the firm was an explosives manufacturer.[3] The first DuPont plant was housed in a three-sided building designed to funnel unplanned explosions toward the neighboring Brandywine River. The underlying social principle was simple and suited to the times: "Don't blow up the workers—and mind the town as well." Thus company founder E. I. DuPont and the other early leaders of the firm embraced two basic aspects of sustainability—worker and community safety—from the company's earliest days. (Undoubtedly they also recognized the financial price they'd pay if a disastrous accident occurred, as it did in 1818, when an explosion attributed to a foreman's drinking killed forty workers, which forever ended any drinking on DuPont sites.[4]) To this day, safety is DuPont's number-one priority. The company is now drawing on this one aspect of its socially conscious policies—its commitment to safety—to lay a foundation for becoming a more broadly sustainable organization.

Ford Motor Company pioneered the element of today's sustainability movement that centers on economic benefits to workers and the community.[5] In 1913, when hourly wages for skilled workers ran as low as $.15, the company's founder, Henry Ford, startled the world by announcing that he would pay a guaranteed daily wage of $5 to every worker, because "everyone who works at Ford should be able to afford the product he produces." It was a shrewd business move as well as a humane one. Labor turnover at Ford virtually disappeared, with the result that the company's total personnel costs fell, enabling Ford to lower the price of a Model T while increasing profits.

Ford can't claim an unblemished record on labor relations. During the Great Depression, the company engaged union-busting thugs to beat up striking workers, and it has used enormous, disruptive layoffs to control payroll costs during business downturns. Yet Ford is now working to find the Sustainability Sweet Spot, not just in regard to its treatment of workers but also on the environmental front, generally facing its challenges straightforwardly and often in collaboration with other affected parties.

DuPont and Ford were sustainability pioneers, each developing a specific aspect of corporate responsibility based on their specific circumstances. Both are now striving to achieve true economic, social, and environmental sustainability by building on their historic strengths and working to overcome their historic weaknesses, experiencing both successes and setbacks along the way. They represent the way hundreds of companies of historic stature are mounting serious efforts to combine a commitment to all three elements of the TBL with profitable growth over the long haul.

New Pressures on Business

In philosophical terms, one of the earliest appearances of the notion that corporations might have some ethical responsibilities to the larger society may have been the business philanthropy of the 1920s, as exemplified by the charitable foundations created by the great capitalists John D. Rockefeller, Henry Ford, and Andrew Carnegie. Having created huge business empires—often using competitive methods that many considered ethically questionable—these moguls moved, in their later years, toward returning some of their wealth to the communities that created it, building universities, hospitals, museums, libraries, schools, and churches that enhance the quality of life to this day.

Even earlier, many businesses had begun building entire communities around their factories, creating housing, stores, recreational facilities, and churches for their workers. In some cases, the business owners were motivated by an idealistic desire to create a better world. That was the case with Milton S. Hershey and his beloved Hershey, Pennsylvania, which he built around both his eponymous chocolate factory and the Milton Hershey School, supported by company profits and dedicated to educating underprivileged children. In other cases, greed and the desire to control the lives of workers were more powerful motivations. In some mining, steel, and factory towns, living conditions were squalid or dangerous. The legacy of company towns whose environment was despoiled by irresponsible businesses lives on today in such communities as Anniston, Alabama, and Bethlehem, Pennsylvania, which are still working to restore the damage done by decades of toxic dumping.

In the 1930s and 1940s, the concept of corporate responsibility expanded beyond philanthropy to include workers' rights. Labor unions battled to organize workers, achieve recognition by management, and win concessions, such as increased wages, shorter hours, and improved working conditions. Roosevelt's New Deal pushed through a series of laws protecting the rights of labor, including the National Labor Relations Act (1935), which guaranteed the right to collective bargaining, and the Fair Labor Standards Act (1938), which established the minimum wage and the forty-hour workweek. However, unions and the federal government were the primary forces behind these efforts; many businesses fought against the expansion of workers' rights.

During this period, most business thinkers were not focused on the social implications of how businesses operated. Business's social responsibility was considered a matter of making charitable donations to organizations like the local Community Chest. As Peter Drucker put it in his classic *Management*, "Where an earlier generation had looked to the 'rich businessman' to endow a hospital, post–World War II big business was expected to support worthy causes. Emphasis was still on [supporting] outside 'causes' rather than on the behavior and actions of business itself."[6]

The focus on the impact of business on society intensified in the 1960s as part of a general social awakening. Rachel Carson's book *Silent Spring* (1962) galvanized a generation of political activists, spearheaded the campaign to ban the pesticide DDT, and is widely credited with launching the modern environmental movement. The two decades that followed saw a series of landmark events that exemplified the growing power of environmentalism, including (in the United States) the creation of the Environmental Protection Agency and passage of a host of laws—the Clean Air Act, the Clean Water Act, Superfund, the Resource Conservation and Recovery Act, the Safe Drinking Water Act, and others—that focused on how businesses operated.

Consumer rights and product safety also emerged as major corporate issues, driven in part by the groundbreaking work of Ralph Nader. His dramatic congressional testimony about auto safety and the revelations in his book *Unsafe at Any Speed: The Designed-In Dangers of the American Automobile* (1965) led to a series of auto safety laws and helped launch the consumer movement. In 1972, Congress established the U.S. Consumer Product Safety Commission, and subsequent years saw a series of trends that continued to put the spotlight on business, including the rise of product safety litigation focused on consumer goods ranging from the Dalkon Shield contraceptive device to asbestos to tobacco. Attention had shifted to the responsibility of companies for the impacts of their products and how they were made.

As the 1970s, 1980s, and 1990s unfolded, more social movements emerged, each creating new pressures on businesses to fulfill newfound social responsibilities: the civil rights movement (focused initially on equal rights for blacks, and later broadened to include Latinos or Hispanics, Native Americans, and other ethnic groups); the women's rights movement; the anti-apartheid movement focused on South Africa; the gay rights movement; and other similar efforts.

Today the business environment continues to evolve in ways that make the increasing demand for corporate responsibility dangerous to ignore and profitable to embrace. In the rest of this chapter, we'll look at some of the most important trends contributing to this evolution.

A Freer World

When World War II ended in 1945, only about twenty-two nations had democratic forms of government. The rest were either totalitarian or authoritarian. And even these few democratic governments operated in a style of benign paternalism, exemplified by the Eisenhower administration, in which major decisions were made by a handful of political leaders who took advice almost exclusively from the heads of large, established institutions—major corporations, leading universities, the military. Western governments weren't under pressure to be responsive to the people, who were just glad to have survived a brutal world war and mainly wanted government to jump-start their economies and protect them from the new threat of Communist domination.

Today, between 78 and 115 nations are democratic (depending on the precise definition one uses).[7] And with the spreading worldwide acceptance of free enterprise and democracy as the way of the future, people everywhere are taking it for granted that they deserve more say about their own futures.

The government paternalism of the 1950s has long since been replaced by activism and citizen involvement. Groups that were once effectively disenfranchised—women, racial and religious minorities, gays, students, consumers, and the elderly—have forced their way into the political dialogue, claiming rights and influence once enjoyed only by powerful elites. This spreading democratic spirit underlies the explosion of rights movements touched on earlier in this chapter, and the trend feeds on itself: the more freedom and power people have, the more they expect and are in a position to demand.

For businesses, this change offers fabulous opportunity. The demise of communism has opened up new markets all around the world. The widespread acceptance of free enterprise has liberated vast industries from nationalization and created broad new horizons for business in the former Soviet Union and its erstwhile satellites. Vast new markets are being created in once-destitute nations, such as India and

China. And in the United States, working women, blacks, Latinos, Asians, and gays have become far more significant in the consumer marketplace.

Procter & Gamble (P&G), the world's largest packaged goods company, is one of many business that recognize the enormous growth opportunities available in the developing world and in countries newly opened to Western-style consumer markets. P&G has launched a host of sustainability initiatives designed to nurture those new markets and create strong connections between its brands and millions of potential customers. These programs include Live, Learn and Thrive, which provides such essentials as vaccinations, hygiene education, and nutritional help to children in 120 countries around the world; the Safe Drinking Water Program, active in sixty-five countries; the Hope Schools project, which supports educational programs in poor districts of rural China; and many more.[8] Thanks in part to the "good neighbor" aura created by these social efforts, P&G has been enjoying rapid business growth in the developing nations, including the all-important BRIC countries (Brazil, Russia, India, and China), where sales have grown at an average rate of 20 percent annually over the past decade.[9]

Of course, the new market opportunities create new responsibilities for businesses that choose to pursue them. The newly empowered people who are your customers, your workers, your investors, and your neighbors will demand a voice in how your business is run and its impact on their lives. Consider, as just one example, the rise of civil society in China, with newly formed citizens' groups demanding a voice in such issues as local pollution control. As members of China's emerging middle class demand an ever-greater degree of democratic participation, it will be harder and harder for businesses—whether based in China or anywhere else in the world—to ignore their legitimate concerns.

It will be challenging to reshape your business practices to address the needs and aspirations of millions of new stakeholders—but that's exactly what many of today's smartest businesses are doing.

A More Interdependent World

The world in which we live and do business is also becoming more closely interdependent, a profound change created by several related trends.

Products and services, distribution, and marketing are all becoming more complex, demanding that companies and individuals work more closely together both within and between enterprises and also across regional and national borders. Many of the world's most successful companies today operate not as centrally controlled monoliths but as networks of loosely connected units, each with a high degree of autonomy. And as these relationships multiply, they are becoming more complicated. The relationship between vendors and purchasers, once a simple zero-sum game in which each fought for a larger piece of the pie, has become far more complex. P&G and Wal-Mart, for example, recognizing their financial and operational interdependence, now work closely together to develop information and logistics technologies that will benefit both.

What does all this have to do with sustainability? As companies become increasingly dependent on one another, their interests become more closely entwined. The traditional doctrines of "buyer beware" and "arm's-length transactions" work less well in a world where your company's long-term health requires stable business relationships and economically healthy and ethically responsible partners, joint venturers, suppliers, distributors, and marketers with whom to do business. And when those parties may be located anywhere in the world, you and your company suddenly have good reason to care about the practices of companies and nations far from corporate headquarters.

Mutual dependence isn't merely financial. It is also reputational and legal. Apple, for example, publishes a list of over 150 companies it relies on to provide materials, parts, and manufacturing services for its products.[10] Any one of those suppliers that uses prison labor, employs a ten-year-old worker in one of its factories, or dumps toxic waste into a river can create embarrassment as well as political and legal problems for Apple—as the widely publicized problems (including worker suicides) at the giant Foxconn plants in China, which make iPads, iPhones, and other Apple gadgets, have made abundantly clear. And advocacy groups are prepared to exploit the new interdependence to put pressure on companies. "We attack the weakest link in the company's value chain," Kert Davies, director of research at Greenpeace, told us.

Most managers don't yet realize that they may be held responsible for the illegal or irresponsible actions of their suppliers and vendors, or that their customers may be held responsible for those actions. Management of social issues all the way up and down the supply chain is one of the new challenges posed by the sustainability imperative in an interconnected world.

A Networked World

The spread of freedom, the growth of a worldwide economy, and the business interdependence we have just described are all being driven by an astounding explosion of global communications advances.

Social critics were surprised by the impact of television on American culture and politics in the early 1960s. Electronic media had begun to turn the planet into a global fishbowl. Today, as the quotation from Kert Davies at the head of this chapter suggests, anyone concerned about the impact of global warming on the polar ice cap can literally watch it happening via live satellite feed on the Internet. The proliferation of twenty-four-hour news sources, from the cable networks to individual tweeters, means that information about your company, whether true or false, can circle the globe in an instant, with potentially devastating effects. And the journalistic filters that once served to control and limit the kinds of stories being disseminated have largely vanished. Today, any individual concerned about, or aggrieved by, the activities of any corporation can easily find, speak to, and join forces with like-minded people via mobile communications and social networking media—Facebook, Twitter, YouTube, and other tools that allow anyone to become a writer, filmmaker, reporter, broadcaster, and publisher.

Of course, companies can also use social networking and other new media technologies to their advantage. But these communications channels are so decentralized that it's impossible for any company, no matter how large, rich, and powerful, to control the messages being disseminated about it. And fragmented communications tools reaching niche audiences (such as the customers of a particular company) are easily leveraged by advocacy groups—at a cost close to zero.

You are now doing business in a world where what you say can easily be drowned out by a multiplicity of voices over which you have no control. And this new vulnerability is increasing just as corporate reputation, brands, and other intangible assets are becoming dominant value drivers. A corporation like Nike, which outsources virtually all of its global manufacturing to almost nine hundred companies in forty-seven countries, owns almost no tangible assets.[11] What the company does own is intangible: ideas and patents, financial and management resources, business relationships, brands, knowledge, and goodwill—most of which, in turn, depend on its reputation.

If 75 percent of your assets are intangible, as is now the case on average for the Fortune 500, it's obvious that an attack on your reputation can be financially devastating—especially with hundreds of millions of people now following the markets, glued around the clock to business channels, finance websites, and social media sources like Twitter and Facebook. Bad news, true or false, is apt to prompt investors to flee first and ask questions later—fairly or not.

Well-managed businesses recognize these new realities and have adjusted their business strategies accordingly. Thus, when Greenpeace launched a campaign against the use of toxic chemicals in the manufacture of sportswear in 2011, it quickly garnered massive attention on websites and social media as well as in print media and on radio and television. Nike responded within weeks, announcing an ambitious program to make its factories toxin free by 2020. Competitors Adidas and Puma followed suit shortly thereafter.[12]

An Imperiled World

The sense of living in a world of physical limits was profoundly underscored for billions of people by the first pictures of Earth taken from *Apollo 8* as it circled the moon in December 1968. The image of our home planet rising above the empty lunar landscape against the infinitely deep background of space proved beyond any doubt that we were stewards of a small and precious vessel.

A host of events and trends have since reinforced that sense of a shared and fragile world:

- The growing damage to the global ecosystem caused by carbon dioxide and other greenhouse gases, with impacts thousands of miles from their source
- The felling of rain forests in the Amazon Basin and around the world, driven by economic forces that originate in North America and Europe and producing climatic effects around the world
- Repeated oil shocks in which political, military, or financial troubles in a handful of Middle Eastern countries create economic dislocations in Japan, the United States, Europe, and dozens of other nations
- Ecological disasters, such as the *Exxon Valdez* and Deepwater Horizon oil spills, the Bhopal chemical disaster, and the Chernobyl nuclear accident in Ukraine
- The HIV/AIDS catastrophe, along with other, lesser global pandemics, such as SARS and Avian flu, spread via expanded international travel, trade, and migration
- The 2004 tsunami in which 230,000 people perished, and the increasing number and severity of weather-related disasters, including the enormously destructive Hurricane Katrina (2005) and Superstorm Sandy (2012)
- The growing threat of water shortages in a world where an estimated 3.4 billion people live in regions where the freshwater supply is deemed insecure[13]

- The persistence of poverty, disease, hunger, and lack of drinking water and sanitation in large regions of the world, affecting more than two billion people—one-third of the world's population
- Conversely—and paradoxically—the rise of a rapidly urbanizing and enriched middle class in countries like India and China, where more than ten thousand new cars are flooding the highways *every day*, putting enormous stress on natural resources (fossil fuels, metals, glass, rubber) and contributing to pollution
- Underlying and exacerbating these trends, the continuing growth of world population, which mushroomed from around four billion in 1975 to more than seven billion in 2012 and is projected to surpass nine billion by 2050[14]

In what seems a much smaller and highly imperiled world, it is difficult for any business, much less the business community, to say that social, economic, or environmental problems across the state, nation, or globe are irrelevant or "not our concern." People assume that anything that happens anywhere on Earth may affect them, directly or indirectly, sooner or later—and that therefore they must take it all seriously, looking closely at how their actions may affect others (and even, potentially, the fate of the world). And many are extending the same assumptions to the businesses they patronize or for which they work.

A Socially Conscious World

It's natural that today's young people, who were born and raised in a world whose sustainability has been questioned for as long as they can recall, should be especially conscious of these issues. It seems obvious that younger people are more in touch with the smallness of our planet, having grown up with the Internet and the globalization of communications and culture, as well as with constant reminders of its fragility; today's twenty-five-year-olds grew up watching reports of social and environmental disasters, from the Indian Ocean tsunami

(2004) to the Deepwater Horizon oil spill (2010) and the Fukushima Daiichi nuclear emergency (2011).

Popular culture reinforces these concerns. Movies from *Erin Brockovich* (2000) and *Syriana* (2005) to *Milk* (2008) and *The Hurt Locker* (2008) have turned environmental and social problems into the stuff of heart-stopping drama; *An Inconvenient Truth* (2006) won an Academy Award and helped its star, Al Gore, earn the Nobel Peace Prize; and even fantasies like *Avatar* (2009), *Wall-E* (2009), and *The Lorax* (2012) reinforce environmental and social themes. Every young adult knows that Academy Award–winning actor Leonardo DiCaprio drives a hybrid Toyota Prius, that director and actor Matt Damon has posted a video in which he vows not to go to the bathroom until the world water crisis is solved, and that Grammy-winning singer Alicia Keys has toured Africa to help children afflicted with AIDS and raised money for the relief of Haiti after that island nation's 2010 earthquake. The outpouring of funds in response to Hurricane Sandy followed naturally on the heels of similar outreach efforts—Live Aid, Band Aid, Farm Aid, and tsunami relief. Tens of millions of today's young people know what's happening around the world, and they care.

In response to this burgeoning of interest, courses on environmentalism, corporate social responsibility, and sustainability have taken root in colleges. The Triple Bottom Line is now being taught at business schools all over the world, and over half of U.S. business schools mandate courses in corporate responsibility. As a result of this expanded consciousness, we're seeing the birth of organizations like Net Impact, a thirty-thousand-member network of business students and young professionals, whose mantra is that "it is possible to use business to effect positive social, environmental and ethical change."[15]

Social activism is also on the rise among the young. For example, a study conducted by the nonprofit organization Take Part found that 70 percent of young Americans consider themselves "social activists," with 50 percent saying they donate time to causes they care about, one third saying they've either boycotted or patronized businesses to express social concerns, and one fifth having participated in rallies, meetings, or legislative lobbying.[16] Under the circumstances, the emergence of the Occupy movement in response to the financial meltdown and Great Recession of 2008–2009 was not so much anomalous as inevitable.

Younger generations to come are likely to be even more sensitive to these issues. Today's youngsters—who are, of course, tomorrow's consumers, activists, government officials, and corporate leaders—are learning about environmental and social issues in the classroom, from the news media, through their favorite social networking sites, and, increasingly, through personal experience.

A Corporate World

Even as our world increases in complexity and interconnectedness, governments in many regions have been in retreat—practically, philosophically, and politically—from some of their traditional social responsibilities. (Although this trend has ebbed and flowed from time to time—as seen, for example, in the partial return to government activism in the United States under the Obama administration—the long-term pattern remains basically intact.) This is a natural outgrowth of the triumph of laissez-faire capitalism and the collapse of socialism that occurred throughout Europe, Asia, and much of the developing world during the past twenty-five years.

In much of the developed world, many countries have deregulated industries, privatized businesses that were once government controlled, reduced trade restrictions, opened their borders, adopted regional or global rather than local or national standards, and shifted from the traditional command-and-control model of regulation to free-market mechanisms or jointly negotiated settlements between the private and public sectors.

As these trends unfold, businesses—especially large corporations—are becoming richer and more powerful than ever. When the world's 175 largest economic entities are ranked in terms of gross domestic product (that is, the value of goods and services produced), just 64 are countries—the other 111 are multinational corporations. The individual businesses Royal Dutch Shell, ExxonMobil, and

Wal-Mart are each larger than 110 countries, including such notable powers as Argentina, South Africa, and the United Arab Emirates.[17] This is an enormous concentration of wealth and power—not in the hands of presidents or parliaments, but in the hands of CEOs and corporate boards.

A graphic example of the shift in power and efficacy from the public to the private sector came in the immediate aftermath of the Hurricane Katrina catastrophe on the U.S. Gulf Coast in 2005. While the entire U.S. government, notably the Federal Emergency Management Agency, fumbled the disaster relief effort, giant companies with powerful logistical capabilities, such as Wal-Mart, Home Depot, PepsiCo, and Federal Express, not only got their own operations up and running but also provided more effective relief than the government, getting emergency supplies of water, food, and building materials to law enforcement officials and the stranded masses days before federal, state, or local could respond.

Many advocacy organizations devoted to social and political causes have thus shifted their efforts away from lobbying government to lobbying the free market and the businesses that operate in it. Pressure on companies to develop and adhere to high standards of behavior when it comes to the environment, labor practices, human rights, and other social issues is consequently at an all-time high.

As if to mark this role reversal, businesses are even being pressured to change or resist the behavior of governments, as when advocacy groups demand that companies use their influence to promote change in countries whose policies they deem unacceptable. Human rights groups attacked Yahoo's Beijing division for assisting the Chinese government in identifying an email user—a journalist who was ultimately sentenced to ten years in jail for emailing documents related to the Tiananmen Square protest. And Microsoft and Google have come under attack for cooperating with the Chinese government in making it harder for activists to use their search engines to research political issues.

The shift in power from the public to the private sector means that societies at large will be looking to business to help solve social, environmental, and economic problems that were once considered solely the province of government. These new pressures will be felt in every sector of the business world. And if you run or work for a small or medium-size company, don't assume you will escape. As we'll explain later, many large companies have transferred these new requirements to suppliers, distributors, marketers, and others throughout their value chains. Although your small company may be less visible to the public than McDonald's, Apple, or IBM, the chances are good that you will ultimately be subject to exactly the same demands for corporate accountability now faced by the global giants, especially if you do business with them.

A World of Empowered Employees

Many of the trends we've already outlined—the spread of freedom and democracy, the introduction of powerful tools for instantaneous communication, and the growth of social consciousness, particularly among the young—have combined to give today's rank-and-file employees greater impact on the future of businesses than ever before. Today's workers aren't content to simply follow orders from on high. They are aware of and concerned about worldwide economic, social, and business trends; they're likely to be continually in touch with friends and colleagues around the corner or around the world; and they are more inclined than their counterparts from past generations to question the dictates of authority.

Add to these traits the central importance of employee talent in a world where a company's competitive edge is based mainly on the knowledge, skills, attitudes, and energy of its workforce. One result is today's "global war for talent," which pits corporations against one another in a battle for the world's best minds, whether those minds emerge in New York, Frankfurt, and Rio or in Beijing, Mumbai, and Jeddah. The outcome of the war for talent will help shape tomorrow's business landscape—and companies with a reputation for sustainability will have a big edge in winning that war.

It all adds up to a world in which attracting and retaining the best employees is more crucial to business success than ever.

And sustainability is proving to be a vital tool in these efforts. As Beth Comstock, a leader of GE's sustainability programs, has said, "Ecomagination has helped make GE an unmatched magnet for talent. And healthymagination is beginning to develop some of the same appeal. So the positive impact of sustainability on GE's corporate and employer brands is huge."[18] Leaders at other companies echo her observation.

From a different perspective, the whistleblower phenomenon is another striking example of growing employee power—an illustration of what can happen when companies ignore the impact that their workers' attitudes can have. In a networked world, it's increasingly easy for employees outraged at their companies' perceived social or environmental misdeeds to leak documents or information to the media or the general public. And insiders who expose corporate malfeasance of many kinds are now protected against firing or other punishment by numerous laws, with additional protections and incentives conferred by the Sarbanes-Oxley Act. When their accusations lead to fines or money recovered, whistleblowers can even collect a piece of the settlement—up to 30 percent of sums recovered—under the Federal False Claims Act.

Popular culture has even glorified the role of the whistleblower. *The Informer*, *Silkwood*, and other films have idealized whistleblowers, and individuals like Julian Assange of WikiLeaks, convicted leaker Bradley Manning, and NSA leaker Edward Snowden have been treated as folk heroes in some quarters. (Witness, for example, the statements in support of Assange by media personalities on the left ranging from author Naomi Wolf and Pentagon Papers leaker Daniel Ellsberg to filmmakers Michael Moore and Oliver Stone. As a business leader, you may not consider such voices credible—but millions of others do.)

So employee power is an important force that is making the demands of sustainability increasingly dangerous to ignore. The people who work for you know whether or not you're living up to your social and environmental obligations. If you're not, they have the power to make you pay a heavy price.

A World of Investor Activists

Corporate shareholders are becoming more engaged with social issues. From mainstream investors to endowment managers for religious and educational organizations, investors have begun to push corporations to pay more attention to nonfinancial risks. The Interfaith Center on Corporate Responsibility, which represents religious pension funds, maintains a database of shareholder resolutions related to TBL issues as a source of information for individuals and organizations that want to use shareholder activism as a way of pressuring public companies to behave in more socially and environmentally responsible ways.[19] Recent resolutions cover a mind-boggling range of topics, including "sexual orientation discrimination," "weaponization of space," "parabens in beauty products," "glass ceiling," "smokefree facilities," "HIV reporting," "report global warming impact on operations," "China business principles," "drilling in the Arctic Wildlife Refuge," "amusement park safety," "foreign military sales," "limit CEO pay," "diversity on the board of directors," and many more.

Both the number of resolutions and their success at drawing votes from shareholders have been steadily increasing. A study by Ernst & Young found that fully 40 percent of shareholder resolutions in 2011 focused on environmental and social causes (up from 30 percent just a year earlier). And each year, dozens of resolutions are withdrawn by corporate dissidents after negotiated settlements are reached with companies that have found it's more expedient to work with their critics than to battle them publicly.[20]

In addition, more and more investors are choosing investment opportunities on the basis of companies' environmental and social records, a practice commonly referred to as socially responsible investing (SRI). SRI started to take off in the United States during the Vietnam War, when investors who opposed U.S. participation moved their money out of companies that profited from war-related contracts. During the 1970s, the list of issues gradually expanded to include labor rights and the environment.

But it was the struggle against apartheid in South Africa that first demonstrated the growing social and political clout of SRI. Opponents around the world exerted significant economic pressure on the apartheid regime, helping accelerate its collapse in 1993 and its replacement by the current majority-rule government. The dramatic impact of the South Africa divestment campaign drew increased interest in SRI. So did the gradual accumulation of research demonstrating that corporations with good social records tended to outperform corporations with bad social records, as did investment portfolios created using SRI selection systems (often called screens). Managers of the portfolios of many churches, universities and colleges, and state and city pension funds began to follow SRI principles; and the number of bond, equity, mutual, and money market funds that used some type of social screening increased from just a handful in the early 1980s to well over one hundred by 1997. SRI mutual funds, such as the Dreyfus Third Century Fund, the Neuberger & Berman Socially Responsible Fund, the Parnassus Fund, and the Pax World Fund, began to attract large numbers of investors, and their positive investment results drew increasing respect from investment analysts and the press.

By the late 1980s, interest in SRI had spread from North America to Australia, Japan, Austria, France, Germany, Switzerland, and many other countries. Today over three hundred SRI mutual funds screen using Triple Bottom Line criteria, and SRI portfolios account for an estimated $3.74 trillion in investment capital—more than 11 percent of the total sum invested in the United States.[21]

SRI has become an important presence in the world of investing. Any public company that wants access to the widest possible pool of investment capital must look for opportunities to participate in this burgeoning market. That involves, of course, making one's company an attractive investment according to all the traditional financial benchmarks. But it also entails solid performance according to the social, environmental, and economic indicators that complete the Triple Bottom Line.

A World of Stakeholders

The term *stakeholder* was introduced in 1984 by Professor R. Edward Freeman, who defined a stakeholder as anyone who is affected by, or can affect, an organization.[22] It includes internal stakeholders (such as your employees), stakeholders in your value chain (from your suppliers to your customers), and external stakeholders (communities, investors, nongovernmental organizations [NGOs], government agencies, regulators, the media—even future generations who may be affected by your company's actions today).

Today the network of stakeholders that affect every business has become more vocal, skillful, influential, tenacious, and effective than ever before. Hence stakeholder concerns—the environment, labor and human rights, community relations, consumer protection, and social responsibility—are becoming more important to corporations.

Many nonfinancial stakeholders are gaining credibility, influence, and power thanks to their access to the mass media and their roots among the general population. For example, the Edelman Trust Barometer, a widely known and respected survey of global opinion concerning public attitudes toward government, business, the news media, and other institutions, has found that NGOs are the single most trusted category of organizations in the world and have been so for the past five years (2008–2012).[23] Thus when a well-known NGO like Greenpeace, Amnesty International, Oxfam, or the World Wildlife Fund criticizes the behavior of a particular company, it's likely that most of the public will immediately assume that the charges are correct and that the company's attempts to defend itself are self-serving and probably dishonest.

That's only the beginning of the public relations challenges for many corporations. Certain stakeholder organizations believe they have a vested interest in fomenting crises for businesses. A dramatic confrontation with a major corporation—a multibillion-dollar lawsuit, a demonstration or strike that threatens to shut down a factory, a journalistic exposé of alleged corruption or abuse of power—draws enormous publicity to the stakeholders' cause, supports fundraising and membership drives, and puts business on the defensive. A world of empowered stakeholders is thus inevitably a world of ticking time bombs for business.

Stakeholders embody the new expectations of corporations to be more responsible, and the near universal use of the term indicates that companies are more accountable, not just to shareholders, but to others who have a stake in their activities.

Perhaps the simplest and most visceral way to sum up these new challenges is this: for every issue your company has to deal with, imagine someone—perhaps many someones—in your face, pulling at you, demanding action, and refusing to go away or let go until they are satisfied.

Welcome to the new world of stakeholders.

When Global Trends Arrive on Your Doorstep

The trends we've just enumerated describe in broad terms the challenging business environment in which companies must operate today, as well as changes that will only intensify the challenges in the years to come. Many industries and businesses are grappling with these issues already, but even the most forward looking can't possibly see what the future holds for them. What is clear is that these trends will eventually affect your industry and your company in a powerfully focused fashion at a time and in a way that no one can accurately predict. The resulting risks and opportunities are enormous, and you need to be prepared.

For example, the growing power of stakeholders, the increased power of modern communications media, and the emergence of new tactics and strategies in the legal community have led to massive suits involving thousands, even millions of plaintiffs, arrayed against collections of large corporations in a particular industry. One by one, major business sectors have been targeted by such enormous lawsuits: chemicals (Agent Orange, the gasoline additive MTBE), pharmaceuticals and health care (the Dalkon Shield, DES, and Vioxx), construction (asbestos, mold, "sick building syndrome"), tobacco, and the oil and gas industries (in connection with oil spills and fracking).

Plaintiffs are successfully reaching further and further back in time. Holocaust victims are demanding and receiving compensation from German companies for their illicit profiteering and expropriation of property seventy years ago; descendants of American slaves are suing companies for the enslavement of their ancestors 160 years ago; and Indian tribes have received redress for claims going back even further.

The dramatic expansion of legal liability, the explosion of lawsuits, the remuneration of whistleblowers, and the piling on by public prosecutors are important wake-up calls for corporations everywhere, not just in the United States; a similar transformation is under way in Europe. These changes in law reflect a far broader transformation of societal expectations related to corporate behavior.

What does the future hold? How will corporate responsibilities expand in the years to come? Will hospitals and insurance companies be sued over shortages of affordable health care or care for the elderly (as pharmaceutical companies have already been forced to make HIV/AIDS medication accessible to the poor)? Will coal-burning utility companies be held liable for the deaths of coal miners or for harm to entire neighborhoods if their emergency response plans fail to protect surrounding communities in the event of foreseeable emergencies or natural disasters? How will the changing expectations of society translate into new risks and liabilities for your industry or company?

The expansion of corporate responsibility is like the buildup of carbon dioxide in the atmosphere—gradual, almost imperceptible (see Figure 3.1). But just as global warming is expected to ultimately produce sudden, local effects that are shockingly destructive—droughts, tornadoes, tsunamis, and hurricanes—so these growing expectations are already causing major disruptions in specific industries and specific companies. That is why you can't afford to ignore these mounting expectations, even if your own business has (so far) remained unaffected by them.

Doing business in this emerging world—freer, more interdependent, wired, and filled with powerful, vocal stakeholders—demands

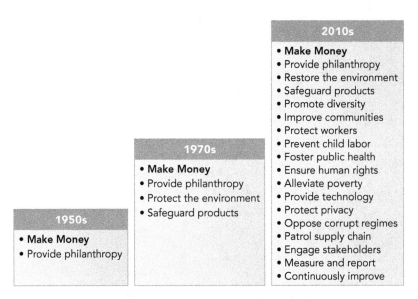

Figure 3.1   The Rise of Corporate Accountability and the Age of Sustainability.

a high degree of accountability. You can't pretend that you are operating in a vacuum. Instead you're in a crowded neighborhood where everyone knows your business, has an opinion about it, and feels that he or she has the right to express that opinion and try hard to change your behavior. Call this period the Age of Sustainability, a new era for business in which responding to the demands of stakeholders is a necessity, not an option.

4

Business Responds

*We thought we could sit in Bentonville, take care of
customers, take care of associates—and the world would
leave us alone. It doesn't work that way anymore.*
—H. Lee Scott, CEO, Wal-Mart[1]

Sustainability Reaches the C-Suite

The current generation of leaders would appear to be well positioned
to respond to today's sustainability crises. They are highly educated,
globally conscious, technology savvy, and the most diverse generation
of corporate chieftains in history. As they enter their forties and fifties
and assume leadership in business, politics, social causes, academia,
religion, the arts, and every other sphere, they bring along their
generational sensibility, forged in the political, social, and economic
crises of the 1960s and 1970s as well as in the epoch-making traumas
of the early years of the twenty-first century, from the terrorist attacks
of September 11, 2001, to Superstorm Sandy in 2012.

With this background, many of today's business leaders and managers are looking for social, philosophical, even spiritual meaning and
satisfaction in their lives and their work. They recognize the superfi-
ciality and fragility of past booms (the financial boom of the "Greed
is good" 1980s, the dot-com boom of the 1990s, the real estate boom
of the 2000s) and accept the need to create organizations that will
survive and thrive not just for a quarter or two but for years, decades,
and generations.

Furthermore, as this cohort of leaders ages, many are becoming
more sensitive to legacy issues, such as environmentalism, poverty,

business ethics, and social progress—the very currents that are pushing sustainability into the mainstream. The wave of religious and personal searching reflected in a spate of philosophically centered best sellers, from Rick Warren's *The Purpose-Driven Life* and Mitch Albom's *Tuesdays with Morrie* to Rhonda Byrne's *The Secret* and Randy Pausch's *The Last Lecture*, mirrors the same trend.

A generation of people in search of deeper meaning in their lives is now making its mark in the corporate suites. Their personal quests are intersecting with the drive toward sustainability, making it part of the daily mission of companies around the world.

Motivations vary among CEOs who have endorsed sustainability. Some, like Howard Schultz of Starbucks, John Mackey of Whole Foods, and Indra Nooyi of PepsiCo, have made sustainability a personal mantra. They have strong personal concerns about the environment and society, driven in some cases by direct involvement or something they heard from their spouse or their children.

Other CEOs recognize the image benefits, for their companies and themselves, of being in the forefront of the sustainability move-ment. Some have been persuaded by colleagues or highly motivated employee groups. Many see the business risks involved in ignoring the TBL; others are excited by the economic opportunities sustainability offers. And in many cases, the personal satisfaction of trying to put their enterprise on the side of the angels plays a role.

In the end, the reasons are unimportant. What is crucial is that more and more CEOs are driving sustainability harder and harder, making it a key focus of their management style and corporate strategies.

We've noted the generational shift at GE from the feisty Jack Welch who battled the EPA to Jeffrey Immelt—twenty-one years younger—whose signature initiatives include ecomagination and healthymagination. When Immelt set off in this direction in 2005, the step was widely viewed as revolutionary. Today most regard it as mainstream.

As of this writing, over seven thousand CEOs leading companies in 145 nations have signed the UN Global Compact. Launched by UN Secretary General Kofi Annan in January 1999, this initiative aims "to unite the power of markets with the authority of universal ideals ... to reconcile the creative forces of private entrepreneurship with the needs of the disadvantaged and the requirements of future generations" (in other words, to encourage businesses to seek their sweet spots).[2] The compact captures these universal ideals under four headings: human rights, labor standards, environment, and anticorruption. Together they describe a TBL agenda that a growing number of companies have adopted as their own.

At the same time, numerous leaders within specific industries are working together to develop sustainability definitions, guidelines, and practices for their industries. This group includes some of the world's most controversial industries, often viewed as inherently unsustainable, such as forestry, cement, oil, and mining. Even the nuclear energy industry, once uniformly reviled by environmentalists, is working to redefine itself as offering a sustainable, carbon-free alternative to today's environmentally dangerous reliance on fossil fuels.

The TBL is now a regular focus at the annual World Economic Forum at Davos, where many of the world's most powerful business and political leaders gather annually to reflect on the key challenges of the year ahead. In 2012, its influential annual risk survey rated water supply crises, food shortage crises, greenhouse gas emissions, failure to adapt to climate change, and land and waterway mismanagement as five of the top ten global risks in terms of likelihood and severity.[3] Therefore, it isn't altogether surprising that surveys of corporate leaders by PricewaterhouseCoopers and others consistently show that a high percentage of CEOs are willing to sacrifice short-term profits in the interests of long-term sustainability.

The growth of executive leadership associations and programs focused on sustainability is both a sign and a driver of change. The World Business Council for Sustainable Development is the leading CEO organization dedicated to sustainable development. Founded after the 1992 Earth Summit in Rio de Janeiro, it includes over two hundred international CEOs, leading many of the world's best-known and most-respected companies from every business sector. The U.S. Conference Board now hosts four conferences a year on corporate citizenship. Business for Social Responsibility, created in the 1980s, was a relatively small organization until about five years ago. Now its membership is growing rapidly, and its annual conference draws standing-room-only crowds.

Organizational Support for the Sustainability Movement

Just as individual business leaders are responding to sustainability, so are many institutions that support business—a sign of the staying power and growing long-term impact of the movement. In turn, this burgeoning institutional base offers powerful support to companies and managers who want to pursue TBL goals but aren't sure how to get started.

Colleges and business schools have dramatically expanded coverage of sustainability issues in their curricula. Many universities have launched academic centers focused on corporate social responsibility (CSR) that work with and develop case studies about companies tackling social and environmental challenges. Leading MBA programs now require students to take courses on corporate responsibility, and many of the world's highest-ranked business schools (including Harvard, Stanford, Wharton, Yale, MIT, Chicago, Columbia, INSEAD, and Ashridge) emphasize their CSR offerings when promoting themselves to students and corporate sponsors. More than 250 business schools have chosen to support the MBA Oath, a voluntary pledge taken by graduating students to follow ethical business principles.[4]

The investment world has also begun to recognize the significance of the TBL as a measure of corporate performance. The Dow Jones Sustainability Index (DJSI), created in 1999, tracks the financial performance of the leading sustainability-driven companies worldwide, helping investors examine sustainability as a defining measure of corporate performance. Currently the DJSI World (the dominant brand in the DJSI portfolio) includes 342 firms drawn from fifty-nine business sectors in twenty-three countries, including such industry giants as GE, Toyota, Hewlett-Packard, Citigroup, Pfizer, Unilever,

3M, and P&G. Other indexes that are part of the same family are the DJSI Europe, DJSI North America, and DJSI United States. DJSI North America is drawn from the largest North American companies and includes firms rated in the top fifth of each industry sector in terms of the DJSI's economic, environmental, and social criteria—currently a total of 143 companies.

Companies listed in the DJSI World enjoy benefits including improved access to investment capital (because shares of DJSI members are recommended for sustainability investing), prestige, and brand enhancement (because recognition as a global sustainability leader can enhance a company's reputation in the eyes of stakeholders, financial analysts, and the public at large).[5] Most important, DJSI-listed companies are a good investment, having outperformed the market since the launch of the index in 1999.

Governmental and quasi-governmental agencies have also come to recognize the importance of the sustainability movement. For example, the U.S. Environmental Protection Agency has made sustainability (rather than simple pollution prevention) an explicit element in its regulatory and scientific work, and the U.S. State Department has launched a Greening Diplomacy Initiative to reduce its environmental footprint and costs. Meanwhile, the European Union has mainstreamed sustainable development and the shift to a low-carbon economy into a host of its policies.

Sustainability, then, is not simply a cause that has captured the imagination of thousands of CEOs and other individual business leaders. It is also at the heart of an impressive array of organizations that are developing systems, practices, and bodies of knowledge around which sustainability initiatives can be built—a kind of "sustainability infrastructure" that is growing every year.

Sustainability—a Story of Success and Failure

We've seen that top business leaders the world over have publicly embraced the value of sustainability, thousands of leading corporations have committed themselves to studying and reporting their own environmental and social performance, and hundreds of prestigious educational institutions are placing CSR at the center of their curricula. Does this mean that a utopia of sustainable business has been achieved—or is it at least within striking distance?

Far from it. The transformation from business as usual to true sustainability is a long and difficult one. Many organizations that take the need for sustainability very seriously are still in the early stages of that journey. Others that have publicly espoused sustainability have failed to engage in the deep process of self-examination, strategic rethinking, and culture change that sustainability demands; their efforts, though well intentioned, are often superficial and ineffective. And still others (though a dwindling number) have failed to take even the first steps on the journey, perhaps assuming (or hoping) that sustainability is a mere fad that will disappear if they ignore it.

One obvious sign that business, in general, has not yet achieved sustainability is the persistence and, in some cases, the worsening of many of the environmental and social problems we listed in Chapter Three—disturbing climate trends, ecological disasters, global epidemics, widespread poverty, water and energy shortages, population stresses, and so on. Not all of these problems are caused by business activities, but many have been exacerbated by them—and surely no one would claim that businesses have done all they could to address them as part of their day-to-day activities.

Another, perhaps even more troubling indicator of the degree to which we've fallen short in the quest for sustainability is the fact that a number of organizations that have launched major efforts to achieve specific environmental and social goals have suffered significant setbacks, damaging their reputations and sometimes calling into question the genuineness of their commitment to sustainability.

For example, BP, once known as British Petroleum, rebranded itself as "Beyond Petroleum" to publicize its commitment to developing renewable energy sources and helping reduce the world's dependence on shrinking supplies of environmentally damaging fossil fuels. CEOs Sir John Browne (1998–2007) and Tony Hayward (2007–2010) were widely praised for their progressive leadership, illustrated by such bold actions as the 2004 firing of 252 employees in a crackdown on bribery and corruption, as well as by their public pronouncements describing environmental and worker safety as BP's number-one priority. But BP's reputation as a sustainability leader collapsed in the wake of a series of devastating accidents, culminating in the Deepwater Horizon disaster of April 2010, which killed eleven workers and poured over two hundred million gallons of oil into the Gulf of Mexico, causing untold environmental and economic damage. The company's stock price collapsed as well, falling from $60.98 to $26.75 in just two-and-a-half months, and BP has had to set aside $42 billion to pay for the damage and the resulting lawsuits and government penalties.

Similarly, as we saw in Chapter Two, giant retailer Wal-Mart, a frequent target of critics for its environmental, labor, and community relations policies, launched a significant effort to earn a reputation as a responsible corporate citizen through environmental and social initiatives, only to lose some of the trust it had earned through major missteps, such as the massive international bribery scandal that came to light during 2012.

Reasons for Failure

We think that most executives and employees at companies like BP and Wal-Mart are sincere about their commitment to manage their businesses in ways that are environmentally and socially responsible. Why, then, have these and other companies experienced such significant failures in their efforts to pursue sustainability? We believe there are several reasons.

Perhaps the most basic reason is the simple fact that, like any significant business challenge, *sustainability is hard*. Like superlative customer service, innovative product design, and consistent manufacturing quality, sustainability is a complex challenge that can't be met overnight. Companies that commit to sustainability should bring patience to the task and plan for a long campaign with both successes and failures, rather than expecting instant success.

Another reason is that companies are under enormous countervailing pressures—in particular, the pressure to maintain and increase profits in both the short term and the long term, even when doing so may harm the environment, local communities, workers, and other stakeholders. The Great Recession of 2008–2009 and the period of sluggish growth that followed has tempted many companies to jettison or de-emphasize their sustainability programs with the explanation (or excuse), "In hard times like these, we need to focus on short-term survival, not sustainability." We consider such thinking shortsighted and, in the long run, self-defeating. But it's true that finding ways to create environmental and social benefits while pursuing growth in revenues and profits—in other words, identifying and occupying sweet spots—is a complex challenge that many managers find unfamiliar and daunting. It's no wonder they sometimes backslide on their TBL goals.

Still another reason is the inconsistency of customer attitudes concerning sustainability. Although most measures suggest that public awareness of and concern about environmental and social problems are higher than ever, research and experience suggest that most customers will not pay extra for products or services from companies that promise environmental or social benefits. Just as companies tend to focus on short-term profits, customers are generally focused on the price and quality of the goods they buy. Wal-Mart continues to lure customers with its wide product array and enticingly low prices; and although McDonald's has found that a growing number of consumers are demanding healthier menu options like salads, it's obvious that high-fat, salt- and sugar-laden items remain very popular.

Under the circumstances, it's not surprising that not all businesses are flocking to the sustainability banner. As one CEO told us, "I'll go green when my customers demand it."

We believe that responsible companies will identify their sweet spots and then work hard to change customer and consumer preferences to fill those spots. This is what P&G did when it developed and promoted Tide Coldwater detergent, what Toyota did when it introduced the hybrid Prius, and what PepsiCo and other companies are doing to foster greater demand for healthier foods. When customers move from accepting sustainable products and services to demanding them, the journey toward sustainability will accelerate dramatically.

Sometimes sustainability stumbles or fails in the face of opposi-tional cultures, both inside and outside companies. In our consulting work, we frequently encounter managers—particularly business vet-erans who rose through the ranks years before sustainability was on anyone's radar—who take a jaundiced view of the subject and even turn a blind eye to the convincing business case in its favor. These antisustainability "dead enders" are supported by a significant body of opinion shapers in the news media, think tanks, business schools, and government who consider the concept of the TBL a misguided doc-trine that threatens to undermine traditional notions of free enterprise, individual liberty, and other benefits generated by the "invisible hand" of unfettered capitalism. Although, over time, these antisustainability voices have become less numerous (particularly in executive suites and corporate boardrooms), they remain influential, and we'll address their major arguments in Chapter Five of this book.

From Superficial to Systemic Change

Within companies, perhaps the biggest obstacle to sustainable per-formance is that it requires cultural, strategic, and organizational changes that many organizations are not yet prepared to make. The transformation to sustainability requires complex, time-consuming, and long-term change, and change is always a risky proposition. It's one thing to love the sound of a slogan like "people, planet, and profits"; it's quite another to launch the serious intellectual, strategic, managerial, and even moral efforts required to change your company and its behavior, root and branch, and thereby make sustainability truly a part of its DNA.

Thus we see companies pursuing the TBL in many varied ways, some making changes at the margins, others trying to make more fundamental change, albeit incrementally.

Some companies take the path of least resistance, selecting aspects of sustainability with which they feel comfortable or in which they already excel, such as volunteering, philanthropy, or Earth Day events. These activities are worthwhile, but are often emphasized to the exclusion of other aspects of sustainability that are more fundamental to the business or have more material impacts on their stakeholders.

Some companies issue annual sustainability reports in which only good news appears—awards received, community projects supported, waste reduction goals met. Other issues or initiatives that obtained disappointing results are simply swept under the rug. Some organizations present misleading or incomplete data. We may be told that the volume of pollutants emitted by a particular plant has fallen by 10 percent—without being told that the main reason for the reduction is that production fell by 30 percent.

Other companies pursue sustainability projects in an incomplete fashion, excluding significant portions of their sphere of influence—for instance, companies that apply strict environmental and labor standards to their own operations while failing to oversee the activities of outside suppliers that provide them with products, services, or raw materials.

In a later chapter, we'll delve deeply into the cultural aspects of corporate change, especially in regard to the shift toward sustainability. Our point here is a simple but important one. Sustainability doesn't just happen. It takes more than a commitment from leadership and more than just piecemeal initiatives. Sustainability is about rethinking your organization from top to bottom—from competitive strategy to business design to policies and procedures. It may even, as we'll explore, demand a reexamination of some of our most fundamental assumptions about the nature of business itself—for example, the single-minded pursuit of profit and the supreme status of shareholders in the hierarchy of the corporation.

A Challenge for Every Manager and Every Department

So sustainability is hard, in part, because it demands systemic rather than superficial change. You can't make your company sustainable by publishing a set of environmental and social guidelines, by launching an isolated initiative or two, or even by appointing a vice president of sustainability with a staff and budget of his own. Sustainability means rethinking every aspect of how you do business, and making corresponding changes in all of your strategies, practices, and daily decision-making processes.

And because sustainability requires such far-reaching, deeply rooted changes, an understanding of how the new demands of sustainability affect one's job is increasingly important for *any* aspiring business leader. If your company hasn't yet incorporated sustainability into your job description, just wait. That change is on its way. And the sooner it happens, the better for you. In the years to come, leaders aware of and committed to sustainable management will have a distinct advantage over their less enlightened colleagues in the race to the top of the corporate pyramid.

So it's a serious mistake for managers below the executive level—business unit or division heads, plant or departmental managers, and vice presidents or directors in charge of particular functions—to assume that sustainability is irrelevant to them or is someone else's job. As sustainability grows in importance, the skills, knowledge, experience, and mind-set associated with it will be an increasingly necessary part of every manager's portfolio.

Structural shifts in business are also increasing the burdens carried by middle managers. The sustainability challenges of the coming decades will be addressed by corporations that have already downsized, reengineered, and reorganized themselves to be flatter, more open, more flexible, and more responsive than traditional businesses. Most middle managers now have more accountability, responsibility, and power than their counterparts of a generation or two ago. They need to use these tools to help drive the sustainability movement from the middle of the organization—in some cases abetted by enlightened CEOs working supportively from the top down, in other cases driven by rank-and-file employees using the power of social media to make their voices heard.

Virtually every business function is being linked into the sustainability movement:

- *Production, manufacturing, and operations.* Environmental protection, worker safety, and product liability have long been at the forefront for operations managers. Today, eco-efficient manufacturing processes, the beneficial reuse of waste, pollution prevention, and cradle-to cradle manufacturing (whereby products and materials are designed with reuse, remanufacture, or recycling in mind) are driving new waves of design, engineering, and management change. Correctly anticipating emerging environmental and social risks is an increasingly important ability in terms of the future success or failure of a product, which is why today's engineers are being trained to think about downstream issues at the beginning of the design process.

- *Supply-chain management.* Contractual issues related to the TBL, such as human rights, child labor, and worker safety, are hitting the desks of supply-chain managers. So are the economic concerns of workers and demands from community members to buy locally. Thus purchasing agents are being challenged to develop new business criteria for selecting and managing partners, and new monitoring mechanisms to ensure compliance.

- *Marketing.* Marketing managers for all kinds of products and services now have to deal with social and political questions around the promotion of their products. This involves increasing regulatory complexity around positive marketing (for example, "organic" or "all natural") as well as the more traditional concerns around marketing products like tobacco, alcohol, guns, and adult entertainment. Marketing professionals will continue to be challenged regarding appeals to children and such dilemmas as marketing goods to customers in the developing world for whom costly developed-world products may be inappropriate or even harmful.

- *Sales.* Sales professionals at all levels and in both business-to-business and business-to-consumer markets are being confronted with a wide range of customer concerns regarding the sustainability of their offerings.
- *Research and development.* Companies are analyzing environmental issues from the conception and design phase of a new product, using sophisticated tools such as life-cycle analysis, which evaluates the environmental impact of a product throughout its history. Some companies are expanding the use of these tools to forecast social and economic impacts as well.
- *Customer relations.* In some industries, customers are demanding more environmentally or socially responsible products. Now companies and managers are figuring out how to partner with their customers in the pursuit of the TBL, as well as struggling to tackle such thorny emerging issues as data privacy.
- *Human resources (HR).* HR is directly responsible for many issues that fall under the rubric of sustainability. Companies must have policies and practices in such areas as diversity, labor rights, privacy, and, most recently, child labor and human rights. Sustainability requires a high degree of employee development and engagement, continual communication with employees, and organizational capacity development. Finally, sustainability involves change for most companies, and the HR function is the lead organization when it comes to change management. For all these reasons, HR is increasingly at the forefront of the sustainability movement.[6]
- *Risk management.* Companies with specialists in insurance risk (to guard against disasters) and financial risk (to guard against interest and currency fluctuations) now need an ever-expanding expertise in evaluating today's complex, changing array of TBL risks.
- *Information technology (IT).* As stakeholders' demands for information related to management and the TBL grow, IT specialists will be called on to integrate and customize information systems that meet these needs. So-called big data may help us

understand the challenges and offer options for dealing with them. Such challenges as balancing the ever-growing demands for corporate transparency with the need to respect individual customers' right to privacy and control over their own intellectual property will only grow more complex as the era of big data continues to unfold.

- *Investor relations (IR)*. Although socially responsible investing (SRI) has been around for forty years, many IR specialists have previously been able to avoid this niche marketplace. Now, as SRI grows in popularity and importance, entirely new areas of knowledge and skill are required.

- *Finance and accounting*. Over one-third of the social and environmental indicators typically included in TBL reports involve information that is either created by or rolls up to the office of the CFO. Financial professionals face enormous challenges related to sustainability, including finding ways to track, verify, and present TBL information that is meaningful and credible to stakeholders.

- *Public relations (PR)*. PR professionals are in a pickle. They need to play a key role in stakeholder engagement regarding sustainability and make sure the company gets appropriate credit for its efforts—but they must do so without making those efforts appear to be "just a bunch of PR." It's a difficult balance to strike.

- *Communications*. The networking era has created a multiplicity of ways to communicate with key constituencies and a cadre of communications specialists to help. Too many companies tell us, "We don't do a very good job of telling our story when it comes to sustainability or corporate responsibility." This represents a huge opportunity cost. Companies must pay closer attention to the needs and expectations of their key constituencies and offer access to key information in support of their communications efforts.

- *Environment, health, and safety (EHS)*. EHS plays an important role in managing sustainability, and many EHS professionals have built careers trying to integrate environmental concerns into general management practices. Yet many EHS departments and managers, stuck in a command-and-control mind-set, have trouble making the transition to today's broader, market-based sustainability platform.

- *Legal and governmental affairs.* Given our highly litigious world, it's inevitable that lawyers, lobbyists, and governmental experts will play a critical role in companies' journey toward sustainability; in fact, some sustainability officers report to their company's general counsel. Furthermore, many corporate sustainability strategies depend on the ability to move regulations or laws in a certain direction. Corporate lawyers and outside counsel tend to have difficulty getting comfortable with increased outreach, reporting, accountability, and transparency.

- *The C-suite and the board of directors.* It's essential for any sustainability effort to have concrete support from the company's top leadership. Only the CEO and his or her team of advisers can set forth a company-wide sustainability vision, bring high-level cross-functional teams together to tackle TBL challenges, and encourage the kind of long-term, outward-focused thinking that sustainability requires.

It's hard to imagine any corporate office, department, or business unit that won't somehow be involved in your company's sustainability efforts. No manager can afford to ignore sustainability issues. In fact, these issues are already landing in your lap every day, whether you realize it or not.

Further, in today's extended enterprise, where businesses rely on multiple partnerships and networks with outsiders, managers at every level are expected to partner with others up and down their own value chains and outside the business world altogether, from government, social and community organizations, and academia. Sustainability thus poses challenges for you, not just as a business leader manipulating the usual levers of corporate control (pay, budgets, performance objectives, management systems, and so on) but also as an ambassador, politician, and negotiator seeking ways to reach out to and communicate with stakeholders of all kinds, some of whom will be friendly and supportive, others anything but.

For every manager, then, sustainability presents both opportunities and risks. From the risk perspective, a manager might well ask, "Given the environmental, social, and economic impacts of my operation, who is in a position to ruin my day—or maybe my career?" For most managers, the answer is "many people." For a director of EHS or a plant manager, it might be the maintenance shift worker who mistakenly empties a waste tank into the sewage system; for a purchasing agent or a head of investor relations, it might be the overseas supplier who has twelve-year-old children working in the factory; for a store manager or a manager in HR, it might be the cashier who uses racial slurs while addressing customers.

The opportunities may be less obvious than the risks, but they are more important. They include, for example, the opportunity to reduce costs by trimming waste or to create revenue by turning your waste into someone else's source material; the opportunity to expand into new markets by redesigning, repackaging, or repurposing products; or the opportunity to hire talented and committed employees who are attracted to an organization devoted to TBL goals.

Many managers are already helping their companies achieve these benefits. Some are doing so as part of formal company-wide programs; others have taken the initiative within their own domains. Either way, it's time for you to get on board.

As a business leader, you need to understand the enormous transformations that the Age of Sustainability is driving and be prepared to turn them to your advantage. If you don't, you may lose out—and so will your company.

5

The Backlash Against Sustainability

Sustainability is a pernicious fad.
—One manager's reply to PricewaterhouseCoopers'
first employee sustainability survey

In Newtonian physics, the Third Law of Motion states, "For every action, there is an equal and opposite reaction." Any major cultural, social, and economic shift in today's interdependent, wired, and politically polarized world also seems to invite a contrarian response. The enormous movement toward sustainability by businesses around the world has produced an inevitable backlash, most of it from one of two camps.

First, there are cynics, often associated with the politics of the left, who deride the sustainability movement as mere hype. They call for significant corporate reform in dealing with environmental and social issues, but regard current efforts by business to achieve such reform as inadequate at best, dishonest ploys to obscure continued corporate malfeasance at worst. The cynics usually want government to mandate more responsible behavior rather than relying on corporations to change themselves.

In the other camp are the skeptics, often associated with the politics of the right, who attack the concept of sustainable business on the grounds that business leaders have no business getting involved with the environment or social responsibility. The sole job of business managers is to maximize profits, and if they focus single-mindedly on that, the world will be better off in the long run.

In this chapter, we'll examine the arguments being made against sustainability by both sides. Some of these may reflect your own concerns; others may be arguments you've heard from colleagues inside or outside your organization. We believe that the principles of sustainability are supported by facts, experience, and logic, and in this short chapter we hope to convince you that sustainability stands up well to the best arguments against it.

The Cynics: "Sustainability Is Corporate Hype"

First, let's consider the criticisms raised by the cynics, who consider it unlikely or impossible that businesses in a capitalist society will ever voluntarily manage themselves in a socially and environmentally responsible fashion.

The cynics say that as long as investors reign supreme and Wall Street is the chief arbiter of a company's value, corporate leaders and managers will direct their every waking moment to increasing shareholder value, often at the expense of all other stakeholders. Until companies are valued in a different way, on the basis of their social and environmental impacts as well as their financial performance, nothing will change unless mandated by law.

As we'll discuss in Chapter Fifteen, we agree with the cynics that fundamental changes in the nature of business may ultimately be necessary if future generations hope to live in a prosperous, equitable, and sustainable society. But we disagree with the cynics' assertion that contemporary capitalism is incapable of positive change. As we've seen, sweet spots exist. They reflect the reality that environmental and social benefits can often coexist quite comfortably with financial rewards for shareholders—and may even help produce them. As a result, countless corporations, from GE and 3M to Wal-Mart and Toyota, have voluntarily improved their environmental and social performance for financial reasons. And many others have found ways to produce benefits for workers, consumers, and the community while generating excellent financial returns for shareholders. So even in a world of short-term profit maximizers, companies may behave responsibly, and they often do.

The cynics say that these changes have come at the margins, that they have not gone nearly far enough to save the world. We agree, but we see reason to be hopeful in the fact that business leaders are now realizing that many more forms of corporate responsibility can help maximize profits and minimize risk in the long run. And as that idea takes hold, more dramatic, positive changes are in store.

It will be a long time before Wall Street adopts the TBL as its dominant measuring stick of corporate value. But as potential risks and rewards inherent in the TBL are seen as increasingly material to a company's financial bottom line, Wall Street must and will take notice. And with more and more companies recognizing that they have been undervaluing the risks and rewards associated with environmental and social responsibility, corporate behavior is already beginning to shift.

The cynics also argue that most of today's supposed investments in sustainability efforts are really spent on advertising and public relations. They deride the environmental claims of many companies as mere "greenwashing" (a term we'll explain more fully in Chapter Seven) and denounce the social initiatives of others as being skin deep, sure to be jettisoned during the next business slowdown.

It's true that many companies have specific PR objectives under-lying their responsibility programs. But we think that relatively few responsibility programs are *solely* about PR—thanks, in part, to the spotlight focused on them by the cynics themselves. Traditional news media, the Internet, and social networking platforms like Facebook and YouTube have done a reasonably good job of subjecting the TBL claims of corporations to skeptical public evaluation. As the scrutiny, research, ratings, and comparisons intensify, companies whose sustainability programs are phony will either get real or get exposed. Corporations are already coming under legal pressure to demonstrate that their sustainability claims are valid, as when Nike was sued because of allegedly false claims about its human rights record. (More about the Kasky case, which Nike was forced to settle after a long stretch of negative publicity, in Chapter Eight.) Such pressures are likely to increase over time.

The cynics also claim that many widely publicized sustainability programs are designed primarily to fend off calls for additional government regulation. By putting a happy face on self-regulatory efforts, industries can convince government leaders and the general public that tougher mandates are unnecessary. Accordingly, the cynics see many responsibility initiatives as minimal, jerry-rigged efforts to avoid aggressive new regulations.

Again, there's some truth in this charge—maybe more than even the cynics realize. Most business executives would prefer to retain control over their own sustainability practices rather than be dictated to by a government agency. But many TBL initiatives go far beyond the minimal efforts that would be needed to satisfy government regulators—particularly today, with most government agencies strapped for cash and advocates of "big government" constantly on the defensive against assaults from corporate lobbyists and the conservative media. Governments may have to become far more aggressive to keep environmental and social challenges from overwhelming society. Unless businesses and other free-market entities find ways to address these problems, more stringent regulation may ultimately be unavoidable.

In any case, the motivations of business leaders are probably less important than the fruit of their efforts. After the 1984 disaster in Bhopal, India (in which a pesticide plant owned by a subsidiary of Union Carbide leaked deadly gases, killing nearly twenty thousand people and harming hundreds of thousands more), the entire chemical industry was understandably fearful of the likelihood of draconian government regulations being imposed on their factories and other facilities. So they created Responsible Care, a self-regulatory program that has assisted the industry in achieving a 70 percent reduction in emissions and an employee safety record that is four times better than the average for the U.S. manufacturing sector. Responsible Care may have originated as a way of fending off government regulation, but it has proved to be a meaningful step toward TBL objectives by an industry that was once among the world's most dirty and dangerous.[1]

The cynics' most fundamental line of criticism, represented by such proponents of sustainability as Paul Hawken, author of *The Ecology of Commerce*, faults today's businesses—even those that are energetic and committed—on the grounds that their sustainability efforts are woefully inadequate to address the scope of tomorrow's environmental and social crises. Ray Anderson, founder and CEO of Interface, Inc., and author of the book *Mid-Course Correction*, has eloquently expressed this point of view, beginning with his fire-breathing 1998 speech "A Spear in the Chest" in which he called for "another, better industrial revolution" and declared, "Pedaling harder will not prevent disaster if the aircraft can't fly. We need to discover the principles of sustainability that will allow us to build a civilization that can stay aloft, a civilization that flies."[2]

We agree that the seriousness of the challenges facing humankind today demands economic and social reforms more far-reaching than any yet attempted. But even if today's efforts toward sustainability are inadequate, that does not invalidate them or suggest that they should be abandoned until far more dramatic, radical steps are possible. Neither businesses nor the public are likely to support extreme shifts in business practices until they've tested and become accustomed to the changes produced by more modest initiatives.

Someday we may look back on today's TBL programs and regard them as mere baby steps. But baby steps are necessary when you're learning to walk.

The Skeptics: "The Business of Business Is Business"

In contrast to the cynics, the skeptics argue against the very idea of sustainable business on grounds of economic principle. Most often, the skeptics claim to be defenders of laissez-faire capitalism, the economic theory described originally by Adam Smith and elaborated and defended by such modern economists as F. A. Hayek and Milton Friedman. Some skeptics are simply promoting the (perceived) short-term interests of businesses. Others are driven by fears that government overregulation invariably weakens the economic structure that has created such great wealth throughout the developed world. Some are hostile to the very notion of "society" as an entity that can make legitimate demands on individuals. As British prime minister Margaret Thatcher famously declared—in words that many still delight to quote—"There is no such thing as society."[3]

It would take an entire book to address the arguments of the skeptics in detail. But the challenges they raise are critical. In the next few pages, we'll address those that are most commonly heard.

Isn't profitability, not social responsibility, the primary objective of business? Yes, it is, and our view is that sustainability is consistent with and supportive of long-term profit maximization. But laissez-faire economists, including most notably Milton Friedman, go further, claiming that every other goal that a business might pursue is illegitimate or a distraction from the main event of creating profits. Friedman even takes the position that corporate philanthropy is suspect because it deprives shareholders of the right to determine what to do with their money. In this view, social responsibility is a needless, even counterproductive, concern for managers.

This is a quintessential economist's argument: bulletproof in theory, useless in reality. The fact is that even the most hard-nosed free marketer accepts the fact that there are social responsibilities that all businesspeople implicitly acknowledge.

Andy once had a conversation with a purchasing manager for a large telecommunications company who insisted that social responsibility had nothing to do with his job.

"All right, then," Andy asked him, "how would you describe your job?"

"My job is to buy products for our company at the lowest price," he replied.

"And would you buy from a foreign supplier that you knew was employing ten-year-old girls and paying them sixty cents a day for their labor?"

"Oh, well, of course I wouldn't do that," he replied.

"Not even if they offered you the lowest prices, by far?"

"No way."

"What if child labor was legal in the supplier's home country? And what if you could somehow guarantee that no one would ever find out?"

"No, I still wouldn't buy from them. It just isn't right."

"And do you think your company would support your decision to sacrifice profit in this case?" Andy asked.

"Absolutely. I'm certain of it," said the purchasing agent.

Case closed. Despite his strongly held *theoretical* opposition to the concept of social responsibility, this purchasing manager implicitly accepted the reality that social responsibility was part of his job. In fact, he and his company were already practicing socially responsible management, even when, in the short run, it conflicted with their responsibility to maximize profits. If Andy had posed a similar question about buying goods from a U.S. supplier with a horrible worker safety record, or one embroiled at every turn in bitter disputes with the local community, the answer probably would have been the same. And most businesspeople behave in much the same way.

Once we accept that managers and businesses in fact behave as if they have responsibilities other than maximizing profit, the only questions are, How exactly do we define the other proper responsibilities of businesses? and How can businesses most effectively discharge those responsibilities? Not that these are simple questions—in effect, this entire book is devoted to trying to answer them! But they are the *real* questions on which we need to focus, rather than the red-herring question as to whether businesses have any social responsibilities at all.

We aren't advocating imposing one's personal moral choices in business. The purchasing manager shouldn't quiz potential suppliers about their religious beliefs or political preferences. Such personal matters would be irrelevant in almost any business context. A distinction between private morality and the demands of sustainability needs to be drawn, and can be. But the need for such distinctions doesn't invalidate the notion of sustainable business; this objection, too, is more theoretical than real.

Don't business leaders and managers have a legal obligation to maximize profits (and therefore to disregard all other claims on company resources)? In fact, no. Harvard Law School professor Einer Elhauge notes that although all companies need to make profits to stay in business, "no corporate statute has ever stated that the sole purpose of corporations is maximizing profits for shareholders" or even making them the top priority. As Elhauge goes on to explain, most lawyers and legal scholars agree that managers are free to pursue other objectives; and in the United States at least, almost thirty states have adopted laws that explicitly authorize managers to "consider non-shareholder interests, specifically including the interests not only of employees, but also of customers, suppliers, creditors, and the community or society at large."[4]

If a company's shareholders are dissatisfied with management's orientation toward profits, they can exercise their rights to change the board, oust management, or sell their stock. But in the absence of criminal conduct, fraud, or negligence, they can't sue managers for considering "non-shareholder interests" like those involved in sustainability. And in practical fact, many corporations spend considerable money on a wide range of causes that shareholders may or may not approve and whose relationship to profit maximizing is questionable at best, from philanthropic donations to the local art museum or opera house to political lobbying in support of legislation the company management happens to favor. Spending on "non-shareholder interests" like these rarely draws a protest from those who say they're offended by investments in sustainability.

In truth, there is nothing illegal about managers' pursuing goals beyond profit, and those who assert otherwise are either repeating a widespread urban legend or stretching the concept of fiduciary duty to make a point they find ideologically attractive. In any case, we believe that this issue should rarely arise, considering that strong sustainability initiatives should serve to increase profits in the long term.

Shouldn't social, economic, and environmental issues be the government's concern (rather than a matter for business to address)? Of course the government has a major responsibility to address problems that threaten the safety and well-being of citizens. But as we have seen repeatedly—for example, in the inadequate government responses to disasters like Hurricanes Katrina (2005), Irene (2011), and Sandy (2012); the Indian Ocean tsunami (2004); and the Haiti earthquake

(2010)—business is now often better equipped to deal with certain social and environmental issues than are governments. And business is the only sector that can create meaningful, long-term economic growth, which is the *sine qua non* of sustainable development. Surveys show that a growing percentage of citizens share these perceptions and agree that business has a crucial role to play in addressing TBL issues such as climate change.[5]

For the past fifty years, social and political trends have served to increase our reliance on business. While the strength and reach of the free market and the private sector have grown, the role of the public sector has shrunk in most countries, partly due to pressure for less regulation, lower taxes, and decreased social activism by government. Many community organizations, social activists, and environmentalists have practically given up on government and are now focusing their efforts on trying to get businesses to address issues for the long-term benefit of society. Some activist organizations that once dedicated themselves to limiting corporate power now seek to harness or even unleash that power to serve the public interest. As a result, the line separating the responsibilities of government and those of business has blurred considerably in recent years, and business is increasingly engaged on issues that were formerly thought to be the exclusive or primary domain of government.

Isn't the concept of sustainability anticompetitive or anti–free market? No. As we've argued, sustainability produces financial and competitive advantages for those companies that embrace it, find the sweet spots, and make it work for them, not against them. In fact, companies and CEOs in some of the world's most competitive markets (such as autos, consumer products, high technology, and the extractive industries) are the most highly engaged in pursuing TBL objectives. Sustainability may be the most important competitive differentiator in the years to come, as the evidence mounts that a sustainable approach is helping these companies outcompete their business rivals. Sustainability is about turning responsibility into opportunity.

It's not surprising, therefore, that business organizations that focus on sustainability (such as the World Business Council for Sustainable

Development) tend to be strong advocates of open competition and free trade. They find that when markets are truly open, the result is often not a race to the bottom, as feared by some environmentalists and labor activists, but a race to the top, in which companies with safer, more productive, and more responsible business practices win in the marketplace. And sustainability advocates in the business world are seeking ways to use free-market mechanisms wherever possible, as with trading emissions rights (which help reduce pollution without intrusive regulation) and voluntary certification and labeling programs (which focus customer self-interest on behalf of social and environmental goals).

In a free-market economy, however, pure competition ought to give way to limited forms of cooperation for the benefit of the broader society in some cases, and this applies to certain TBL initiatives. Industry-wide codes of conduct may be necessary, for example, when it would be unfair or unreasonable to expect some companies to do the right thing (for example, voluntarily limiting the number of fish they catch) while leaving others to profit even more by continuing to act badly. Belief in free markets doesn't mean endorsing anarchy.

Don't free markets incorporate social and environmental costs in product pricing? If that's so, don't markets themselves regulate the sustainability of businesses by exacting a price for unsustainable behavior? Not yet. The idea of so-called full-cost pricing, which incorporates all the external costs of a good or service into the price paid, is an attractive one. If full-cost pricing were the norm, goods that pollute or otherwise damage society would be priced higher so as to cover the cost of repairing or eliminating the injuries caused. But in fact, full-cost pricing is rarely in effect. Many environmental and social costs remain hidden and subsidized, paid for by taxpayers or by others, rather than by those who benefit directly from the manufacture or use of the products that impose the costs.

Air pollution poses a cost to the environment, for example, but so long as companies pollute within their legal limits, society bears the costs (smog, childhood asthma, and adult lung diseases), and the companies and their shareholders enjoy the profits. Similarly, a large employer like Wal-Mart can legally shift health care costs to the public (and away from its customers or shareholders) by failing to provide health insurance to a high percentage of its employees, who then turn to hospital emergency rooms and other "free" medical services, which are paid for by taxpayers, hospitals, or insured patients, whose rates go up as a result.

Efforts to reduce or eliminate this cost-shifting are complex and difficult. The Kyoto Protocol of 2005 was designed to move signatory countries toward full-cost pricing of carbon emissions through new regulations, but the United States has never ratified the Protocol, significantly reducing the Protocol's impact on world business. In the health care sphere, the Affordable Care Act of 2010, passed with enormous difficulty, imposes limited health insurance mandates on large employers, and even these have proven to be extremely controversial and difficult to enforce.

Yet full-cost pricing works, at least insofar as it has been implemented by governments, mostly in Europe. Under new product "take-back" laws, computer and automobile companies must pay the costs associated with the ultimate disposal of their products or in some cases their packaging. These requirements put the financial burden on those who benefited from the creation of the product and who are in the best position to address the problem.

These mandates have caused companies to seek ways to reuse, recycle, or reduce the amount of material that must be taken back. European auto companies, for example, have competed to create design-for-disassembly programs to maximize the reuse of car parts. Computer companies are finding beneficial uses for their waste products, hoping to turn waste into revenue-generating feedstock for other products. Full-cost pricing can help the free market work by deploying economic incentives to protect the environment.

Unfortunately, these are isolated examples. Many environmental costs to society and most social values are harder to reflect in full-cost pricing. How do you internalize the social cost of child labor or the loss of jobs in a community that has suffered a plant closing? The reality today is that full-cost pricing, although potentially an important tool for sustainability, isn't yet an adequate mechanism for free-market governance of the environmental, social, and economic behavior of companies. Perhaps one day it will be.

Isn't sustainability just a fad in the developed world that will lead to continued impoverishment of the developing world? This is a hard one. Questions abound about how to achieve greater growth in the developing world while moving the planet as a whole toward long-term sustainability. A world in which the people of China, India, and Africa consume goods at the same rate as Americans today would be the equivalent of a world inhabited by seventy-two billion people consuming at current rates.[6] The pressure this would place on global resources is difficult to fathom.

Keeping the people of the developing world poor is not an option, either morally or economically, so it seems clear that significant adjustments will be required around the globe—especially on the part of businesses and consumers in the developed world. Some responsible companies are working to address this problem, developing goods and services that will generate profits while creating economic progress in the developing world. Others are hoping for technological breakthroughs to solve it. Meanwhile, rapidly developing countries like China and India are beginning to make significant investments in renewable energy sources and pollution-reducing technologies, creating hope for an eventual convergence between the developed world and the developing world around a new, sustainable model for long-term prosperity.

Didn't Adam Smith demonstrate that human behavior is driven primarily by self-interest, not by altruism, and that we are all better off if people and corporations just pursue their enlightened self-interest? It seems clear-eyed and perhaps reassuring to investors to assert that only self-interest is a genuine, permanent, and reliable motivating factor for human beings. But the assumption that human beings are purely rational creatures who make every decision based on a coldly logical calculation of their economic self-interest is seriously flawed. It ignores some of the most important forces shaping individual and group behavior: group loyalty, patriotism, spirituality, ideology, justice, morality, esthetic preferences, and love.

So-called behavioral economists like Robert Shiller have been busily revolutionizing the field over the past two decades by demonstrating empirically that nonrational factors like these play an enormous role in our economic choices. And popular authors like Dan Ariely (*Predictably Irrational*), Steven D. Levitt (*Freakonomics*), and Richard H. Thaler (*Nudge*) have been making these new insights widely—and entertainingly—available.

Even Adam Smith did not endorse the caricature of human nature implied in the extreme free-market position. In addition to *The Wealth of Nations*, the great economic work that founded the free-market school of economics, Smith wrote a book titled *The Theory of the Moral Sentiments*, in which he set forth his understanding of human nature and morality. He wrote passages that the followers of Friedman rarely quote, such as this one: "The wise and virtuous man is at all times willing that his own private interest should be sacrificed to the public interest of his own particular order or society. He is at all times willing, too, that the interest of this order or society should be sacrificed to the greater interest of the state or sovereignty, of which it is only a subordinate part."[7]

We needn't agree that virtue consists in being willing "at all times" to sacrifice one's private interest to the public interest. But it's important to recognize that Friedman's position—that the pursuit of private benefit is the only legitimate activity of business—is a shortsighted one that ignores many basic truths about economics, society, and human nature itself.

In the words of management thinker Henry Mintzberg,

> The argument that Milton Friedman and others use is that business has no business dealing with social issues—let 'em stick to business. It's a nice position for a conceptual ostrich who doesn't know what's going on in the world and is enamored with economic theory. Show me an economist who will argue that social decisions have no economic consequences! No economist will argue that, so how can anyone argue that economic decisions

have no social consequences? And if we train managers to ignore the social consequences, what kind of a society do we end up with[?] According to [Russian novelist] Aleksandr Solzhenitsyn ... we end up with one that rests on the letter of the law, and that's a pretty deadly society.[8]

Isn't sustainability becoming a rigid ideology to which businesspeople (and others) are required to mindlessly pay homage? Some who critique sustainability from a conservative social perspective have raised this objection. It's true that for some people, sustainability seems to meet an emotional need. It serves as a quasi-religious value system in which planet Earth itself—or an idealized vision of planet Earth whose inhabitants live in unending harmony, peace, and plenty—becomes a kind of deity. Within this system, the principles of sustainability turn into a rigid set of doctrines, never to be questioned or challenged, and discussions about the best ways to pursue sustainability goals become theological debates centered on identifying and rooting out dangerous heresies. (Some of those who question the consensus view on climate change may feel this way.) Sustainability may also become a way of escaping the "taint" of business, which is viewed as a purely selfish, destructive activity whose chief products are pollution, waste, and human exploitation.

We hope it's clear that our view of sustainability is very different. Of course, we cherish the earth and its inhabitants, and we believe strongly that businesses have a responsibility to consider the long-term interests of all in making their daily decisions. But these concerns are *practical* ones, not theological ones, and our goal is not to "save souls" or to pursue a mythical vision of a planet purified of the taint of business but simply to help create a world in which economic, social, and environmental prosperity is shared by more people, and for the long haul.

Furthermore, we believe that business offers the best hope of solving the world's most pressing challenges. We see sustainability as a way to unleash the power of the free market to do this. If free-market sustainability fails, then it is likely that governments will regulate companies to accomplish the same goals. Sustainability is about achieving balance between the interests of business and the other interests we all care about. It's as simple—and as challenging—as that.

• • •

So, having cleared away some of the distractions created by the arguments of the cynics and the skeptics, we return to what we consider the real question: How, exactly, should businesspeople carry out their responsibilities as citizens of their communities and the world so as to maximize both the long-term profits and growth of their companies and the benefits to society? Companies that find their way to the sweet spot where sustainability and profitability meet are in a much stronger position for the long haul.

6

Renewing the Penobscot
"A More Productive Use of Capital"

*We've come to realize the ecological costs of tapping
nature for our purposes, and where possible we've started
paying Mother Nature back.*

—George E. Schuler, the Nature Conservancy[1]

Giving a Voice to the Critters

John Banks, director of natural resources for the Penobscot Indian
Nation, was worried.

He was one of eight people charged with a seemingly impossible
task: to find a universally acceptable solution to the decades-old
problem of how to reopen one of Maine's most beautiful but most
industrialized river systems to salmon and other fish that needed to
use its waters as a spawning ground.[2]

The eight were gathered around a table in the office of PPL
Corporation, the utility company that managed several controversial
dams that produced hydroelectric power using the waters of the
Penobscot River. They included representatives of groups that had
long been at odds. There were leaders of environmental organizations,
officials from the U.S. Fish and Wildlife Service, sport and commercial
fishermen, and Scott Hall, chief negotiator for PPL. Banks himself
was there on behalf of the Penobscot Nation, the Indian tribe that
had lived on the banks of the river for millennia and regarded it,
along with the natural life it supported, as sacred.

The issues were deeply contentious, involving a complex mélange of property rights, tribal sovereignty, the needs of sportsmen and fishermen, concerns over pollution, the growing demand for hydro-electric power, and the future development of Maine's economy. And the odd assemblage of stakeholders around the table were unaccustomed to trusting one another, having long battled in the courts and in the news media over their differing goals for the Penobscot. Now, somehow, they had to find common ground and forge a long-term plan for the river. The only alternative was to go back to court and waste more years of effort and millions of dollars in further squabbling.

The group had been meeting regularly for weeks, gradually whittling away at areas of disagreement while leaving one huge question unresolved: Would there be any way to remove the most controversial dams from the Penobscot—a move that would cost PPL millions and reduce power production even as it revitalized the river? This was the knot the negotiators would somehow have to untie.

As the discussions wore on, moments of strain among the participants multiplied. People were arguing more, listening less, and having increasing trouble finding consensus. "I was getting worried," John Banks recalls. "So one day, I decided I would bring a couple of eagle feathers with me to our next meeting. Then I asked for a few minutes before we started to work. I didn't know what I was going to do exactly, but I knew the right thing would come to me. And it did."

Armed with his eagle feathers—regarded by Native Americans as sources of profound spiritual power—Banks began to circle the table, talking quietly and touching each participant on the shoulder with a feather as he reached that place at the table. "We have to take our egos out of these discussions," he said as he walked. "Remember that we're not doing this for recognition or praise or to get our names in the paper. Remember all the critters we're doing this for—the fish and bugs and otters and birds that live on the Penobscot and don't have a voice of their own. We're here for them, and they're the ones we need to think about."

In the annals of American corporate life, it was certainly one of the most unusual meetings any company had ever hosted. Did

John Banks's spiritual "intervention" on behalf of the wildlife of the Penobscot have the desired effect? "I don't know for sure," John says with a smile. "But everyone thanked me for the reminder. And we started having more productive sessions after that."

Within weeks, the logjam broke. The group came up with an unprecedented solution. Suddenly, there was hope for the Penobscot.

Who Owns the Penobscot?

Running some 240 miles from its source near the Canadian border to the Atlantic Ocean and fed by 467 lakes and ponds, the Penobscot River and its tributaries serve as a watershed for fully one-third of Maine and constitute the largest river system located entirely within the state. It's a beautiful river, much admired by nature lovers and those who live along its banks. But for decades, the Penobscot has also been a center of controversy among electric power companies and other businesses, environmental groups, fishermen, the Penobscot Indian Nation, and government agencies.

For each of these groups, the Penobscot has a different meaning.

For industry, it's a source of hydroelectric power, a nonpolluting, renewable form of energy that is vital to the economic growth of New England. For the utilities with hydroelectric plants, it's a source of revenue. For environmentalists, it's the natural heart of Maine and a habitat for countless species, some of them rare or in danger of extinction. For outdoorsmen, it's a former angler's paradise that now supports only a tiny fraction of the salmon, sturgeon, shad, striped bass, alewives, and other native sea-run fish that once filled its waters. For the Penobscot Nation, it's an ancestral homeland and a sacred space rich with spiritual energy. And for the government agencies, it's a headache—a shuttlecock among warring interests, each appealing to government and the courts for support.

Each of these groups has its own legitimate claim on the resources of the Penobscot River, each views the others with suspicion and sometimes hostility, and each is prepared to fight to defend its own claims with tenacity and money. Under the circumstances, it's not surprising that the Penobscot has been the focus of bitter battles with significant economic, political, social, environmental, cultural, and even religious implications—a recipe, it seemed, for endless, irresolvable conflict.

Yet in June 2004, an unprecedented agreement concerning the future of the Penobscot was reached among all the stakeholders who'd been competing for control of the river.

This agreement launched the largest river restoration project ever undertaken east of the Mississippi. Three dams that had blocked the flow of the lower Penobscot for generations—Veazie Dam in Veazie, Maine; Great Works Dam in Old Town, seven miles upstream; and Howland Dam, at the mouth of the Piscataquis River another twenty-two miles upstream—would be sold by PPL, the energy company that owns them, to the Penobscot River Restoration Trust, a not-for-profit organization that would raise $50 million for the project—half to pay PPL for the dams, half to pay for demolition and restoration work.

The trust would then demolish the Veazie and Great Works Dams. Howland Dam would be decommissioned, its entire flow shifted to a bypass channel that fish are able to navigate; at Milford Dam a few miles above Great Works, an elevator-like hydraulic fish lift would be installed. In addition to receiving payment for the dams, PPL would have the opportunity to offset 90 percent of the power lost through increases in the generating capacity at several other dams in the Penobscot system.

These changes would vastly improve access to more than five hundred miles of the Penobscot and its tributaries for the salmon and other fish that once swam far upstream to spawn. The removal of the two lower river dams would restore unimpeded access to most of the historical habitat for native sea-run species like sturgeon and striped bass, which do not travel as far upstream as salmon. Without dams slowing the current, the river's water would be colder and would flow more rapidly, providing a better environment for the salmon and flushing out pollutants that have despoiled the river.

As various species of fish returned to the river, eagles, ospreys, cormorants, mergansers, gulls, and other predatory birds would flourish, having a wider array of foods to choose from, further assisting the salmon population to increase. According to federal biologists, in time, the yearly Atlantic salmon runs on the Penobscot could increase thanks to the natural renaissance expected on the river.

The people of Maine would benefit too. The Penobscot Indians would be able once again to take the traditional journey by canoe from their ancestral homes to the sea, and would also enjoy their treaty-reserved sustenance fishing rights. Local anglers' clubs, forced to abandon fishing on the Penobscot in recent years, would return. New river rapids would support whitewater rafting and kayaking, promoting a resurgence of tourism. And government agencies, from the Federal Energy Regulatory Commission (FERC) to the U.S. Fish and Wildlife Service, would finally be able to stop spending their days and evenings in endless battles over the Penobscot's future.

In a world where long-lasting conflicts often appear intractable, how did the many stakeholders of the Penobscot manage to find common ground? A crucial role, it turns out, was played by a middle manager—a Maine native named Scott Hall, who works for PPL. Hall lived with his family near the banks of the Penobscot and was determined to find a solution for a business problem that had festered for decades.

The Industrialization of the Penobscot

Since before recorded time, the Penobscot River has been home to the Indian tribe that bears its name.

Tribal lore declares that the Penobscot Indians have lived along the river's banks for ten thousand years, and archeological evidence confirms that natives were harvesting fish from its waters between 6000 and 4000 BCE. For millennia, the Penobscots used the river and its tributaries as a natural highway for their birch-bark canoes and as a source of shad, sturgeon, salmon, eel, and other fish that they speared, trapped in nets, or caught in stone or wooden weirs.

The coming of the Europeans 250 years ago disrupted the Indians' traditional way of life. Commercial fishermen arrived in the 1760s and immediately began harvesting salmon and other fish from the Penobscot, shipping large catches to markets in southern New

England. Within two generations, logging had also become a huge industry, and the Penobscot was pressed into service as a living conveyor belt, as timbermen floated giant pine logs down the river to mills for processing and to harbors for shipping. The massive log drives produced significant pollution in the form of logs, silt, and fragments of wood and bark that clogged the river bottom.

By 1834, when Veazie Dam was constructed, the logging companies had begun to build dams on the river to power their sawmills, with sluices (gates) to permit downstream passage for the logs. Later, more dams were built to provide power for paper mills, pulp mills, textile plants, and electricity-generating stations for Maine's growing population. In time, over a hundred dams of various sizes could be found along the Penobscot and its tributaries.

Prior to 1830, fifty thousand to seventy thousand adult salmon swam up the river every year from their habitat in the Atlantic to spawn in the headwaters near the Canadian border. Countless shad, sturgeon, and other sea-run fish filled the river and its tributaries as well. Soon thereafter, damming began to obstruct the runs. In 1869, a report by Maine's first Fisheries Commission described the effects:

> When the fish came [to Veazie Dam] in the spring they found an impassable barrier across their way; they gathered in multitudes below the dam and strove in vain to surmount it; many returned down the river, and after the usual time for spawning of shad was past they were taken in weirs to the town of Bucksport, loaded with ripe spawn they could no longer contain; a phenomenon which Mr. John C. Homer who has fished with weirs at that point for forty-three years had never observed at any other time. These were doubtless shad whose natural spawning grounds lay far up the river, and who had after long contention given up the attempt to pass the Veazie Dam. A great many shad and alewives lingered about the dam and died there, until the air was loaded with the stench.[3]

To make matters worse, newly constructed paper mills and other industrial facilities in and on the river began to produce significant pollution as chemicals used in production processes were dumped into the waters. The commercial salmon catch began to decline, falling from over ten thousand fish in 1880 to just forty fish in 1947, the last year commercial salmon fishing was permitted.

For a time, sport fishing on the Penobscot continued to thrive. In 1912, members of the Penobscot Salmon Club launched an annual tradition by delivering the spring's first salmon to President William Howard Taft at the White House. For eighty years, local anglers competed for the honor of catching the presidential salmon. In 1992, George H. W. Bush became the last president to receive one of the dwindling stocks of Penobscot salmon.

Efforts were made to revive the fish population. Starting in the 1960s, the river and its tributaries were periodically stocked with salmon and other fish, and fish ladders—mechanical bypass systems that allow the salmon and other fish to swim upstream to their spawning grounds around the dams—were installed in many locations. An estimated $200 million was spent on various fish revival schemes. But continued difficulties in traveling upstream for the adults, poor rates of survival for the young fish due to pollution, and commercial overfishing of salmon in the Atlantic led to further reductions in the numbers of fish in the Penobscot system.

By the 1990s, the Penobscot still had a few sturgeon, salmon, shad, alewives, and several other species of native sea-run fish, but all the populations were substantially diminished, and some, such as sturgeon, were extremely rare. Only a thousand salmon appeared in the lower reaches of the Penobscot every spring. Removing these endangered fish from the river had been prohibited, and the aging members of the old sport fishing clubs now gathered merely to play cribbage and reminisce about their fishing exploits of a generation ago.

"We Are the Penobscot River"

As the Penobscot River changed, so did the lives of the Indians who depended on it.

When the building of dams on the Penobscot River began in the 1830s, the Penobscot Indians were in a legal no-man's-land, like most northeastern tribes. Their rights had been spelled out in treaties negotiated with the state of Massachusetts (which controlled what is now Maine until 1820), but the treaties had never been ratified by Congress. Generations of Penobscots were thus not officially recognized by the federal government.

That changed in 1975, when the Indian Self-Determination Act gave the tribes a special status as "domestic dependent sovereigns," nations within a nation with the right to manage many functions otherwise assigned to the federal government. Today the twenty-two hundred members of the Penobscot Nation have their own tribal government, not subject to state jurisdiction, headed by an elected chief and a twelve-member council. They also write their own local ordinances, which are enforced by tribal courts.

The passage of the Indian Self-Determination Act was a milestone for the Penobscots in their generations-long battle to reclaim control over lands the Indians had used for thousands of years. It led to a major land claims case against the state of Maine, in which they and other tribes sought to force the state to acknowledge its obligations under the old treaties. Under a 1980 settlement, the state formally turned over control of certain natural resources of the river to the Penobscot Nation, including the exclusive right to harvest fish, wildlife, and plants from the more than two hundred islands in the river that are part of the Penobscots' reservation. However, since 1988, the tribe has voluntarily refrained from fishing in the Penobscot, partly because of the scarcity of fish and partly because of worries about dioxin, mercury, and PCBs that pollute its waters.

Nonetheless, Indian control over the river's resources is not merely symbolic. The Penobscots harvest a wealth of plants for consumption and medicinal use. Some ignore the health warnings and eat fish they take from the river, which is one reason the Penobscots suffer from cancer rates that are double those found among the general population of Maine, according to John Banks.

The river is also more than just a provider of natural resources. As the ancestral home of the tribe, the Penobscot River is also a source of spiritual nourishment and meaning for them. John puts it very simply: "We are the Penobscot River, and the Penobscot River is us." The tribe's traditional ceremonies are held on the islands, and water from the river plays a central role in the rites, as it does in the sacred sweat lodge gatherings where meditation, prayer, and fasting lead to spiritual purification. "In 2000, my wife and I were married on one of our islands," John recalls, "but the river was too polluted for us to use it for drinking as prescribed in our ceremony. We had to bring water from a spring instead."

After 1980, armed with their new, more powerful legal status, the Penobscots began seeking to reclaim the river in hopes of revitalizing their old connection to its sacred waters. Through various means—litigation, publicity, and public protests—they began pushing industry to clean up the river, and they started forging more and more effective alliances with sporting groups, environmentalists, and government agencies to make this happen. Chief among their targets: the dams that had choked the river, contributed to its pollution, and decimated its fish population.

Warfare over the Penobscot

By the late 1990s, the problem of what to do with the dams on the Penobscot had been in Scott Hall's inbox for nearly a decade.

Scott holds two degrees from the University of Maine. Motivated by a lifelong love of nature ("I used to rush home from school so I could watch *Wild Kingdom* with Marlin Perkins on TV"), he first pursued a BS degree in wildlife management. He then held a series of conservation-related jobs in government and with NGOs, working for the state Department of Marine Resources as an entry-level field technician ("basically, a guy who pulled up nets into a boat in the Gulf of Maine") for the state Salmon Commission, and for the nonprofit Sportsman's Alliance of Maine. Having grown frustrated over the apparent disconnect between business and the environment he observed in all these positions, he went back to school to earn a master's degree in public administration. "I wanted to develop my managerial skills," Scott says. "I knew there had to be a better way to run an organization."

As his credentials suggest, Scott straddles the worlds of environmentalism and business. His ability to speak the language of people on both sides of this divide would ultimately prove to be crucial in helping him solve the Penobscot puzzle.

In 1989, Scott went to work for Bangor Hydroelectric, the utility company that owned and operated several of the dams on the Penobscot River system. As one of their resident environmental experts, Scott manned the interface between the company, the government, and the environmental community. He dealt with compliance issues; represented the firm in its negotiations with federal and state agencies, the Penobscot Nation, and NGOs; and handled applications for operating licenses from FERC and other government offices.

These were enormous, time-consuming tasks. For example, whenever the FERC license for a hydroelectric dam comes up for renewal, the process of preparing and submitting the application, developing reports, defending the application, responding to appeals from every imaginable interest group, and, if necessary, dealing with court challenges can take up to twenty years. (When we visited Scott's office in 2005, it contained a flow chart that outlined the various steps in the FERC licensing process. Printed in type smaller than the text on this page and containing a mind-boggling network of boxes, arrows, and dotted lines, it stretched across a roll of paper measuring three feet by six feet.)

Scott and his colleagues also spent a lot of time doing independent research into the technical, biological, and environmental challenges that electric utilities face around the dams—for example, radiotelemetry studies on how fish were using the passageways that had been constructed for them to help them get past the dams on the Penobscot. This work helped Scott deepen his expertise in the realities of how living things were affected by energy technology.

Of course, despite his instincts as a naturalist, Scott was duty bound as a representative of Bangor Hydro to represent the company's best interests as defined by management. And Bangor Hydro believed in taking a tough stance. When conflicts arose over resource management issues, the company pushed its legal and regulatory rights to the limit, yielding to environmental, sporting, and Indian constituencies only when forced to do so by court rulings, government regulations, or intense public pressure. Bangor Hydro's stance provoked an equally unyielding attitude from the company's adversaries. As Hall quickly discovered, his background as an environmentalist wasn't enough to soften the hostility directed against his company. Early in his tenure, an acquaintance from Scott's environmental days told him, "Now that you work for Bangor Hydro, I can't trust any report you produce."

"Once," Scott recalls, "I attended a public hearing about some environmental issue—the same kind of meeting I'd attended many times in the past while working as an environmental advocate. This time, people's reactions to me were shockingly different. As we went around the room introducing ourselves, I said, 'Hi, I'm Scott Hall, and I'm here on behalf of Bangor Hydroelectric.' The guy sitting next to me was a lawyer representing the Atlantic Salmon Federation. His head just snapped back, and he turned and glared at me. I might just as well have said, 'Hi, I'm the spawn of the devil.'"

Bangor Hydro's toughness produced unintended consequences. For example, in some dam licensing disputes, government agencies ended up imposing unusually onerous rules concerning fish passages around the dams—"vengeance requirements," in Hall's words, because "the agencies were so angry at the company" for its uncooperative attitude. Perhaps understandably, those rulings heightened the company's sense of being beleaguered by environmentalist enemies, and Bangor Hydro dug its heels in even deeper for the next fight.

Starting in the mid-1980s, the ongoing battles about the future of Maine's rivers began to focus on a proposal by Bangor Hydro to build a major new dam at Basin Mills in the lower Penobscot. It would have been one of the largest dams in the entire system, located in the portion of the river that in the eyes of most environmentalists already had too many dams. Gordon Russell, of the U.S. Fish and Wildlife Service, just shakes his head when asked about the Basin Mills proposal. "It would have been the death knell for the salmon, which we were desperately trying to restore at that time. And it would have effectively precluded future restoration of other species, like shad and alewives."

The various interest groups staked out their positions. State and federal fishery agencies, environmental groups, and the Penobscot Indians all opposed the new dam. But some of the nearby communities favored it. Increased power generation would produce new local tax revenues, and Bangor Hydro sweetened the proposal by promising to build recreational facilities on or near the river. Seeking a balance between economic and environmental concerns, the Fish and Wildlife Service proposed a trade-off: the agency would support building the Basin Mills Dam in exchange for removal of the Great Works Dam, located just upstream and less efficient in terms of both energy production and fish passage. This solution, which they felt at the time was the best they could hope for, would minimize the damage to the river and its denizens.

But Bangor Hydro was uninterested in compromise. Gordon Russell describes the company's combative attitude very simply: "They wanted to win, and in the process show us up." The controversy wound up in the courts, where it remained for years. Meanwhile, additional disputes brewed over the relicensing of the Veazie and Orono Dams, which Bangor Hydro had wrapped into its application for Basin Mills. Those battles became entangled in the overall war about the future of the Penobscot.

Caught in a thankless position between an intransigent company and its angry opponents, Scott Hall kept seeking a solution. Prior attempts to find a compromise on Basin Mills, including a major negotiating effort directed first by Maine's congressional delegation, then by Governor Angus King in 1996, failed primarily because of a lack of trust among the parties. When FERC denied Basin Mills a license in 1998 and everyone involved filed appeals, it became even more difficult to find a solution that all parties could accept.

Throughout the years of the Basin Mills controversy, the antiutility forces had grown more united. The broad-based environmental groups found common cause with the local sport fishermen, recognizing their shared interest in the health and vitality of the river. They in turn began to draw support from local businesses and governments, which saw the potential for increasing tourism and the tax revenues it would produce if recreational uses of the river could be enhanced. And as the Penobscot Nation and other tribes won new recognition for their land- and water-use rights from Congress and the federal courts, they emerged as still another ally, one with tremendous legal leverage as well as popular support among millions of Americans who recognized the fairness of their ancestral claims to the land they once owned.

Change in Ownership, Change in Attitude

In 1999, Bangor Hydro sold nine dams and power plants—in fact, practically all of its power-generating assets along with some transmission-line rights—to PPL Corporation, a utility firm based in Allentown, Pennsylvania, and formerly known as Pennsylvania Power and Light. The sale was the result of utility deregulation, which required the separation of electric generation from transmission and distribution. Over time, utilities like Bangor Hydro that had controlled power from production to sale were forced to narrow their focus to distribution, divesting themselves of production facilities.

Suddenly, Scott Hall was employed by an out-of-state corporation about which he knew very little. Perhaps, he thought, it was time for him to move on. He'd been wrestling with the environmental challenges of energy production for a long time and was fed up with the seemingly endless battles. When he heard that PPL intended to cut costs and improve efficiency in its new Maine operation, he worried that these "carpetbaggers" with their bottom-line focus might be even more rigid in their attitudes than Bangor Hydro had been.

But before Scott could decide, Jim Potter, the PPL executive who'd been put in charge of the new operation, called him. "Become part of our team," Jim urged him. "We need your knowledge, your local ties, and your links to the environmental community. There's a chance that we can make some positive breakthroughs, with your help." This is different, thought Scott, and he agreed to give the new management a chance.

To his surprise, he found that he had greater flexibility to operate at PPL Maine than he'd had at Bangor Hydro—despite the fact that PPL was a much bigger company. And the new management's emphasis on efficiency also translated into a new, more cooperative attitude toward outside stakeholders. Managers at PPL just didn't have the time or resources to waste on head-butting battles to prove a point. "Jim Potter and I agreed," Scott says, "that working to find common ground with the community rather than doing battle with them would be a better way of doing business—'a more productive use of capital,' in Jim's words. Of course, he was talking about human capital—time, energy, talent—which is actually the most expensive and valuable capital we control."

Notice the driving force here. PPL's shift toward stakeholder engagement wasn't motivated primarily by the desire to be corporate good guys or to save the planet but rather by the need to protect and maximize profits. The company sensed that a sweet spot in which both corporate and stakeholder interests could be served would be a more productive and lucrative place to do business. And the only way to find such a sweet spot would be by working with those stakeholders rather than continuing to fight them.

PPL's new attitude quickly began to yield dividends. The renewed operating license for the Milford Dam required PPL Maine to develop a plan for removing logs from the bottom of the Penobscot River. PPL developed a log removal plan and submitted it for approval to FERC. Soon, however, the Penobscot Nation announced that they weren't satisfied with the plan.

In the Bangor Hydro days, the company would probably have prepared for a protracted legal battle against the Penobscots. Instead, Scott decided to pay a call on John Banks and some other tribal leaders. "What don't you like about our log removal plan?" he asked.

"Well, we think the environmental safeguards can be improved," John told him. "But even more important, we want you to hire some members of our tribe to do the work. We know the river better than anyone, we've suffered more from its pollution than anyone, and our people need jobs. Letting us handle the assignment is the fair thing to do."

This wasn't the first time the Penobscots had lobbied for contracting work with the local utility company. Bangor Hydro had rejected similar requests, considering it a matter of principle: "We should be able to hire whoever we want, based on costs and qualifications. That's a basic rule of free enterprise." But Scott Hall and PPL Maine chose a different approach, figuring, "The best use of our people is to keep the turbines running—not to litigate."

PPL agreed to hire tribal members to remove the logs. The job was done on time and on budget, and suddenly the lines of communication between the power company and the tribe were just a little more open. It was a hopeful sign.

Swimming Upstream Together

Scott and the others at PPL Maine were determined to use the new atmosphere as an opportunity to work out a long-term plan for the future of the Penobscot. With advice and consent from Jim Potter and PPL corporate chieftains in Pennsylvania, Scott and his colleague Dick Fennelly developed a detailed proposal to settle many outstanding issues related to damming, energy production, the environment, and economic use of the river system. It included a provision that PPL would give up on its Basin Mills proposal (whose rejection by FERC the company still had the legal right to appeal). The company was also open to the possibility of decommissioning Howland Dam, rather far upriver. In return, PPL wanted the environmentalists and their supporters to agree to cooperate with the company in its upcoming dam relicensing efforts.

In October 1999, Scott invited the various Penobscot stakeholder groups to attend a meeting at PPL. Twenty-five people participated, representing all the key stakeholders, including the Penobscot Nation, the Atlantic Salmon Federation, Maine Audubon, the Natural Resources Council of Maine, Trout Unlimited, American Rivers, and an array of federal and state agencies. Individual points of view around the table ranged from the moderate to the radical, though all were suspicious, to some degree, of the goals and motives of PPL Maine. Scott greeted the assembled crowd and laid out the settlement proposal he'd labored over.

That proposal was quickly rejected. But the effort to gather everyone around the same table had not been wasted. The meeting had launched a long-term process for working out a solution to the riddle of the Penobscot that all the stakeholders could accept.

The first step was to reduce the size of the working group. Encouraged by PPL, the various environmental NGOs met with the agencies and tribal leaders over the next several months, identifying shared priorities (improved water quality, reopened fish habitats), goals (dam removals on the lower Penobscot), and assumptions (the need to minimize economic disruption for PPL and the local economies). As a strategy, PPL's approach was the opposite of "divide and conquer." The company encouraged cooperation among its erstwhile adversaries, hoping to build a broad consensus behind some ultimate solution.

In 2000, the leading NGOs formed a coalition called Penobscot Partners. It was now possible to convene manageable, productive working sessions involving just seven or eight people: Scott Hall and Dick Fennelly from PPL; Laura Rose Day, representative of Penobscot Partners; John Banks or another Penobscot Nation leader; one or two representatives of the federal government; and leaders from the natural resources agencies of the State of Maine. Nevertheless, it would take more than four years of negotiations for a workable solution to emerge.

Hammering Out Consensus

Removal of Edwards Dam from the Kennebec River in 1999 helped unite the stakeholders around a vision of what could be done, and Penobscot Partners began to focus on dam removal as the most practical long-term solution to the problems faced by the fish populations of the Penobscot. But the idea posed serious financial challenges for PPL. Finally, at one meeting, a mildly frustrated Scott Hall declared, "Look, guys. If you expect us to remove dams, you'll have to pay for them. These are valuable assets, and our company can't eliminate them for nothing." He didn't regard this as a proposal, just a candid description of economic reality.

To his surprise, at the next meeting, Laura Rose Day, the chief spokesman for Penobscot Partners and point person for all the groups not at the table, asked, "Remember what you said about us paying you to remove the dams? If we can raise the money, would you actually consider it?"

"Sure," Scott answered, "if the price were right." Suddenly a basis for a settlement began to take shape.

Penobscot Partners hired experts to analyze the economic issues involved with purchasing the dams. PPL discovered that dam removal was more financially feasible in this case than in many others. The lower Penobscot River included twin channels, the smaller back channel known as the Stillwater River itself the site of a dam. This provided the opportunity to shift power generation away from the main stem of the river, which would thereby be freed up for fish passage.

PPL and its stakeholders began to explore the business and environmental effects of reopening the lower Penobscot by removing Veazie and Great Works Dams and increasing energy production at other locations in the river complex. As the numbers rolled in from the experts, it became clear that dams could be removed without significantly reducing PPL's generating capacity, so long as a series of modest energy enhancements could be agreed to and implemented without substantial environmental studies or other regulatory requirements.

The parties now had a concept around which they could all rally. The difficulty of hammering out the specific details of an agreement, paragraph by paragraph, came next. All the negotiators were involved. "Whoever squawked the loudest about a particular clause was given the job of rewriting it," Scott Hall recalls.

Of course, throughout the process, Scott and Dick needed approval from PPL's top brass for any major business commitment. They stayed in contact by phone continually, and every few months visited Allentown to explain the current status of negotiations to the corporation's executive leadership. PPL Corporation's attitude toward PPL Maine was consistent: as long as you can make the numbers work, we're open to any environmental solution you think is appropriate. This flexibility gave Scott the leverage he needed to forge a practical agreement.

In exchange for the sale of the lower two mainstream dams on the Penobscot and the Howland Dam on the Piscataquis River tributary, the environmental coalition agreed not to contest PPL's efforts to relicense its six other dams. PPL would be able to increase power-generating capacity at those dams by raising water levels and adding or renovating turbines, thereby replacing fully 90 percent of the eighteen-megawatt capacity and revenues of the dams to be sold.

The final agreement filed with FERC was signed on June 25, 2004, by PPL Corporation; the Fish and Wildlife Service, the Bureau of Indian Affairs, and the National Park Service, all agencies of the U.S. Department of Interior; four natural resources agencies of the State of Maine; the Penobscot Indian Nation; and five nonprofit environmental organizations—American Rivers, the Atlantic Salmon Federation, Maine Audubon, the Natural Resources Council of Maine, and Trout Unlimited. The final signatory was the Penobscot River Restoration Trust, a nonprofit established one month earlier specifically to carry out the provisions of the agreement.

Promises Kept

In almost a decade since the Penobscot project was officially launched, a lot has happened—thanks mainly to vast amounts of hard work by all the signatories to that complex 2004 agreement. Laura Rose Day, now director of the Penobscot River Restoration Trust, credits the integrity of the people on both sides of the table, including the business leaders she once distrusted. "When doing business," Laura

Rose Day observes, "your word is key. They kept their word, and we've kept ours."[4]

As anticipated, ownership of the dams has been changing hands. In 2009, PPL sold most of its hydropower assets in the Penobscot region to Black Bear Hydro Partners, LLC, a subsidiary of ArcLight Capital Partners, a leading energy investment firm. Black Bear agreed to abide by the terms of the 2004 multi-stakeholder agreement, and it has done so faithfully.

Meanwhile, the Penobscot River Restoration Trust set about raising the funds needed to purchase the dams. Many private and public sources made contributions. The National Oceanic and Atmospheric Administration in the Department of Commerce, the Fish and Wildlife Service, and the state of Maine's community development office have all provided grants, along with a wide array of environmental, conservation, and sporting organizations.

In 2010, the Veazie, Great Works, and Howland dams were duly purchased at a cost of $24 million by the trust, which then set about working to raise the additional $30 million needed to remove the first two and build a bypass around the third. And in 2012, the Great Works Dam was decommissioned and removed from the Penobscot River—the first major restoration project to be completed under the 2004 agreement.

Scott Hall, now vice president of environmental and business services for Black Bear, is proud of what the private-public partnership has accomplished so far. He's also optimistic about the long-term future of hydropower in Maine. Black Bear has already begun refurbishing the existing Penobscot dams, installing two new turbines at the Milford powerhouse, creating fish bypasses at several locations, and making plans for entirely new powerhouses at the Orono and Stillwater facilities.

As of the end of 2012, the upgrades so far completed have increased the average annual power generation on the river by about 29,000 megawatt hours.[5] "We expect all of the energy lost to decommissioning will be replaced with energy that's new," Hall says, adding that this enhancement to the local economy "never would have happened" if not for the 2004 river restoration agreement.

Sitting in the headquarters of Black Bear Hydro in Milford, Maine, Hall smiles when a visitor mentions the steady thrumming sound of the turbines emanating from the nearby powerhouse. "That's the hum of money," he says, "the sound of our business."[6]

Lessons of the Penobscot Partnership

The story of the restoration of the Penobscot River is, admittedly, extraordinary. But let's see what lessons we can glean for other organizations faced with seemingly intractable TBL challenges.

Embracing accountability can unlock significant gains. Bangor Hydro thought that battling its adversaries was the best way to protect the bottom line. PPL realized that a better way to maximize profits was to bring its historical adversaries inside the tent. In fact, it was the stakeholders, not PPL, who initially advanced the ideas that allowed PPL to emerge in a far stronger financial and community relations position.

But credit PPL for being willing to engage. As a result, the company created millions of dollars of extra shareholder value. Start with the $25 million purchase price for the dams, which might well have been denied new permits and shut down without compensation. Then consider that the company would get to keep 90 percent of the lost revenues from the sold dams by increasing water flow over its remaining dams. Consider the time and money saved by obtaining the preapproval of various licenses and technologies. Then estimate the money PPL saved in terms of litigation, consultants, PR firms, and the like. PPL's calculable financial gains were all due to embracing its accountabilities to nonfinancial stakeholders.

The contrast between PPL's management of the dam issue and Hershey's handling of its proposed corporate sale could not be more stark: Hershey blew a $12 billion deal, lost share value, wasted millions in legal and consulting fees, alienated its employees and the community, and got the kind of publicity you can never live down.

There might well have been an outcome that would have worked for both Hershey and the stakeholders, but Hershey never gave itself the chance to find out.

When a sustainable solution seems elusive, search high and low for the sweet spot. Scott Hall and PPL found a sweet spot for the company—a way to continue to operate its hydroelectric dams while serving the broader interests of society. The likelihood of Bangor Hydro's reaching any such sweet spot seemed remote, given the company's reputation for intransigence and the phalanx of historically antagonistic stakeholders. But PPL demonstrated that shareholder and stakeholder demands that appear to be in conflict can often be reconciled. By comparison, Hershey faced far fewer obstacles and enjoyed more numerous options than PPL. But PPL embraced accountability and found the sweet spot, whereas Hershey chose to hide behind a wall.

Focus on mutual gain, not on short-term profits. The TBL is about creating long-term shareholder value. The Penobscot solution required four years of engagement, and the payout to the company for the dams could take years more. Getting to the Sustainability Sweet Spot would have been impossible if PPL's focus had been solely on the next quarter's numbers. By focusing on the long-term problem facing the company and the stakeholders, Scott Hall was able to create millions of dollars in extra value for PPL.

Corporate culture can be crucial. One can imagine that representatives of Bangor Hydro would have stormed out of any meeting in which the idea of dam removal was being entertained. But the new attitude of stakeholder engagement and acceptance of accountability that PPL brought to the former Bangor Hydro created an opportunity for everyone to gain, including the shareholders. In contrast, Hershey's long-standing penchant for secrecy and isolation has worked against the company's own financial interests.

Political skills matter. Scott Hall proved to be a skilled politician in the best sense of that word. He invested extraordinary time and effort in developing and facilitating a process of active engagement. He brought all the key stakeholders to the table, established an atmosphere of mutual trust and respect, and remained open to the kinds of unorthodox ideas that proved to be crucial to the solution. He engaged PPL's nonfinancial stakeholders in every way possible. The result was a win for everybody, including PPL's shareholders.

Middle managers can make it happen. The culture shift at PPL wasn't announced as part of a new corporate strategy; no one on the executive level at PPL fired a sustainability starting gun. Scott Hall wanted to solve a difficult environmental problem for his company, and he did it pretty much on his own. You don't need a budget, a staff, or a detailed executive mandate to get moving on sustainability. Scott's support consisted of a go-ahead from corporate headquarters, an admonition to make sure the numbers worked, and a commitment to support him if they did. Beyond that, the executives stayed out of his way. By contrast, at Hershey, decisions about the sale and how to handle it stayed at the highest levels of the company, executives operating with advice from a self-interested group of outside bankers and lawyers and with no involvement by midlevel employees. Perhaps Hershey would have seen the issues more clearly had middle managers been consulted.

• • •

PPL and its stakeholder partners created more than a win-win solution. They created a win-win-win-win-win solution, in which virtually every stakeholder in the complexly interwoven world of the Penobscot came out ahead—including, of course, the company's shareholders. It's a testament to what creative managers can do when they are determined to keep looking for the sweet spot and refuse to give up no matter how great the challenges may appear.

PART TWO

HOW SUSTAINABILITY CAN WORK FOR YOU

7

Where Do You Stand Today?
Your Sustainability Self-Assessment

Nothing is as difficult as not deceiving oneself.
—Ludwig Wittgenstein, *Culture and Value*

Determining Where You Stand

Regardless of your position—whether you are the CEO, a department head, or a plant manager—you can begin the process of embracing sustainability by looking at where your organization stands today: its strengths, weaknesses, opportunities, and risks in relation to the sustainability imperative.

We suggest looking at your company through three complementary lenses:

1. *Who you are:* your company's identity, which Edward Lawler, the distinguished business professor and expert on organizational dynamics, defines as "what [an organization] stands for and what it aspires to accomplish. This is part brand promise, part culture, part reputation, and part values."[1]
2. *What you do:* the social and environmental impact of the products and services your company offers as well as its business and profit models.
3. *How you do it:* the environmental and social impacts of your company's practices and processes on employees, up and down the supply chain, and in the communities where your company operates.

A company-wide self-assessment covering all three areas is a healthy step for any organization newly focused on sustainability. Consulting firms that specialize in such reviews can help you with the process. But even if your company as a whole is not involved in a formal self-diagnosis, you can review the performance of a single department or division. You can gain knowledge quickly by reading reports or scanning the Internet, and acquire additional insight over the course of several hours spent brainstorming with one or two sympathetic colleagues.

Many experienced managers are in a good position to make or assist with a TBL assessment. They know from firsthand experience how to evaluate what the company is saying and doing. They are in regular contact with stakeholders and so can serve as sources for the best information about stakeholder concerns. And they certainly know what's going on within their own departments.

In the next few pages, we'll outline the kinds of questions you need to consider when conducting a sustainability self-diagnosis.

Who You Are

One way to begin an analysis of who you are is to look closely at how your company presents itself when describing its history, values, mission, strategy, and objectives. Many companies, especially larger ones, have already planted a flag in the ground on sustainability, making a public commitment to responsible behavior as part of their broad strategic vision or mission statement. Some companies have incorporated aspects of sustainability into their branding messages to attract customers or prospective employees. Others that have not yet embraced the overarching concept of sustainability have established objectives in specific areas—environmental impacts, worker safety, diversity, or community relations—in some cases making these goals an integral part of their corporate identity.

If your company currently issues a sustainability or environmental report, this is a second important source of information about "who you are." Perhaps your firm is one of the thousands that are using the sustainability reporting guidelines issued by the Global Reporting Initiative (GRI) or some other reporting standard. If not, this may be a warning sign. The lack of a company report on social responsibility or environmental commitment may imply a lack of awareness or concern—the first big challenge you'll need to address.

Study whatever TBL reports your company has issued. Look at the vision statement, the goals and objectives, and the prescribed behaviors (such as those described in a corporate code of conduct) to see what kind of environmental, social, or economic performance your company is committed to achieving. Then determine progress by comparing the goals to the actual performance as described in the reports. Are there gaps? If so, are the gaps shrinking over time? Have company policies been adjusted as necessary to improve performance consistently from one year to the next? Answers to questions like these will help you determine how seriously your company takes sustainability.

Your self-assessment shouldn't be based solely on your company's say-so. You need to delve into the reality that doesn't appear in the reports. Some companies create "birds and bunnies reports" filled with image-boosting photographs and stories that mask a lack of real commitment. So if your company's environmental report is short on data but long on pictures of the flannel-shirted CEO standing next to a waterfall or shots of employees and their children frolicking on the beach—or if it devotes five pages to describing the environmental or community awards it has received without mentioning the fine it paid the EPA—you may begin to question the seriousness of the company's dedication to sustainability.

A meaningful TBL report is balanced, providing bad news as well as good. No company can do everything right all the time, but many companies like to report that they can. Look at the written materials: Has the company met or exceeded every target? Are all the trends moving in the right direction? Does every story shine a favorable light on the company? Does the company insist on calling every problem "an opportunity"? Such a report strains credulity and leads the sophisticated reader to ask, "What *aren't* they telling me?"

This kind of corporate image laundering in regard to sustainability is called *greenwashing*. We'll explain more in Chapter Thirteen about how to make sure the reports your company issues are credible and balanced. For now, when it comes to assessing where your company stands, you need to read your company's reports with your eyes wide open.

The clearest sign that sustainability has truly become an integral part of your company's identity is the presence of *specific* objectives, targets, and performance indicators related to the TBL, with measurement of progress based on reliable data. If expectations are explicitly described and progress toward them is objectively measured and honestly reported, then the company's commitment to sustainability is likely to be real.

You may already have a general understanding of your company's or department's major social or environmental impacts. Check to see whether there are specific performance measures in those areas—for example, targets for reducing pollution or unnecessary packaging, goals for worker training, or percentages of raw materials to be purchased from small or local suppliers. If your company outsources materials or products, find out whether it has policies that prohibit child labor, unsafe working conditions, and other unacceptable behavior by suppliers. These are quick and easy ways to see whether your organization is walking the talk.

You may also want to take a look at your competitors' reports and public statements to see what they are saying, doing, and measuring, and how you compare. You are likely to find wide discrepancies between reports from companies in your industry. You can probably get a quick overview of your company's standing in relation to its chief industry rivals by visiting your competitors' websites or that of the GRI, where you can access hundreds of reports sorted by geographical location, name, or industry.[2]

If your company does not publish any kind of TBL report, you may want to find out why not. Or simply begin the job of developing the relevant information for your part of the organization.

Finally, we suggest you complete your research into "who you are" by simply listening to people, both inside and outside the company. How often do sustainability issues get raised in staff meetings, in watercooler conversations, or in off-site motivational sessions? When people talk about "how things work around here," "what this company is all about," or "what it takes to succeed in this organization," is sustainability part of the discussion? Do employees mention the company's environmental or social performance when talking about the things that make them proud to work here?

Outside perspectives can also be illuminating—especially when they differ from those of insiders. Do suppliers, distributors, consultants, customers, and competitors think of your firm as a leader or a laggard when sustainability is mentioned? How are you viewed by members of the media, community groups, activist organizations, and regulatory agencies? Inviting opinions on this question from a dozen acquaintances—and supplementing their comments with the results of a quick Internet search—can provide you with a rough-and-ready analysis of your company's sustainability reputation.

Public sources of information about your company's sustainability efforts can also be invaluable. Hundreds of websites, most maintained by NGOs, actively monitor, report on, and rank organizations in regard to their environmental, social, and economic responsibility. Not all of these websites are equally credible, and many offer one-sided views, but you can often piece together the most accurate picture by evaluating a wide range of opinions from a variety of sources. Some of the best Web sources are

- *GreenBiz*, a news, opinion, resource, and networking site created and edited by Joel Makower, a prolific and highly regarded author as well as a lecturer and consultant on sustainability issues
- CSR Wire, maintained by a consortium of companies, NGOs, national and international agencies, and organizations interested in corporate citizenship, sustainability, and social responsibility

- Business for Social Responsibility, a member organization with corporate and nonprofit members that provides information, tools, training, and advisory services to help companies make CSR an integral part of their business operations and strategies
- The Interfaith Center on Corporate Responsibility, an association of almost three hundred faith-based institutional investors that advocates socially and environmentally responsible business policies, monitors company behaviors, and encourages shareholder resolutions on major social and environmental issues[3]

Above all, examine your company's TBL efforts with the same objective, critical perspective you'd apply when researching a rival business. We've all known individuals who cling to a self-image that's at odds with the way others view them. It's a common human foible. Some companies are subject to the same weakness. Avoid this trap when evaluating "who you are" in terms of sustainability.

What You Do

"What you do" refers to the goods and services you produce, which are the central reason you are in business. How sustainable is your product or service? What are the environmental and social impacts and implications of your business model—that is, the way you reach the market, deliver benefits to customers, and earn a profit? Is "what you do" beneficial to humankind at large and to the planet on which we live, or is it reducing the store of social and environmental goods on which life depends? These are some of the most challenging questions any company can address.

Answering them begins by considering whether or not the goods and services you offer fill a societal need. Of course, a company will quickly go out of business if it fails to produce a product or service that customers want to buy. But even a product or service that many customers buy may conflict in specific ways with societal needs or even with those of the customers themselves.

Think about home insulation made with asbestos, gasoline or paint containing lead additives, or drugs with serious undiscovered side effects. Even though these products were willingly purchased by customers who believed they met a need, they are now known to be harmful to health. They've harmed millions of people and cost society billions of dollars due to hospitalizations, lost income, premature deaths, and environmental degradation. In retrospect, society's interests were harmed rather than helped by the development and sale of these goods.

It's easy to think of other products that are associated with environmental or social evils. Many social activists and law enforcement officials believe that the manufacture and sale of handguns and automatic weapons cause grave harm to society through accidental deaths, needless suicides, and violent assaults; others consider gambling and alcohol socially and physically destructive to a degree that far outweighs their positive value as forms of recreation. And cigarettes are still being sold and smoked all over the world despite their well-known impact on health. All these products raise serious sustainability issues.

In still other cases, goods and services that are in themselves benign have harmful secondary impacts or side effects. Most people would agree that personal computers and telephones are pretty handy to have around, but not the estimated two million tons of electronic trash they create every year. We can't live without electricity, but we certainly could live without the pollution and climate-altering greenhouses gases produced by today's power-generating technology.

Examining your business through the lens of the TBL can have a profoundly disruptive effect. In 1999, Ford Motor Company's first corporate citizenship report included an interview between chairman Bill Ford Jr. and sustainability expert John Elkington in which Ford expressed doubts over the long-term sustainability of the gas-guzzling SUV—then a major source of Ford's profits.[4] The result was a firestorm of controversy that even included a rebuke of Bill Ford by his own board of directors. Perhaps the young chairman was injudicious in his language. But he was right to initiate a conversation about the kinds of changes that Ford and other car companies needed to undertake.

Today, Ford (along with the rest of the industry) is looking to hybrid and electric models as a crucial source of future growth. Unfortunately, Ford is playing a game of catch-up. Toyota remains the industry leader in hybrid vehicles thanks to the head start it gained with its launch of the Prius in 1997—based on a blue-sky research project into the sustainable car of the future that it undertook way back in 1993, six years before Bill Ford's interview with Elkington. Toyota's game-changing innovation is a vivid illustration of how farsighted thinking about "what you do" can create a long-term competitive advantage, provided you have the courage to act on the insights you develop.

Evaluating the sustainability of your product or service isn't easy. Judgment calls are inevitable. Some socially responsible investors consider the manufacture and sale of military weapons irresponsible, and screen out military contractors from their portfolios. No one wants war. But what if the presence of weapons can be shown to deter wars or limit their severity? The development and use of certain kinds of modern weaponry that significantly reduce collateral damage ("smart bombs," for example) strike us as being socially responsible, if not sustainable.

There is no bright line that clearly marks whether your company or its products are sustainable. Sustainability is an area (the sweet spot) toward which responsible businesses move in search of long-term profitability and success. Assessing the current situation of your company or your department is an eye-opening first step when you're ready to embark on this journey.

How You Do It

Quite apart from the nature of the products or services you create, the processes you use in running your business may be more or less sustainable. Think about such issues as

- How you handle chemicals in the manufacturing of your products, whether as ingredients, as waste materials, or as by-products

- Whether and how you test your products on animals
- What pollution you generate in the process of creating your products or performing your services, either directly (such as wastes emitted into groundwater by your factory) or indirectly (such as air pollution generated by the power company from which you buy your electricity or by vehicles that deliver supplies to your facilities)
- Whether labor or human rights issues exist in or around your company or its suppliers, from mandatory overtime or inadequate health insurance to child or forced labor
- The strength of your relationships with your employees and the communities in which you operate, and whether and how you take their interests into account when making key decisions that might affect them

Seeing how your company deals with existing rules and regulations related to environmental and social issues is an essential part of any "how you do it" diagnosis. Is your company generally in compliance with laws and regulations? How often has the company been subject to fines or sanctions, and for what? Do you and your colleagues roll your eyes in frustration at the mention of regulators, or do you embrace the opportunity to learn from the experiences of officials who have worked with many companies like yours? Does the company do the bare minimum required to pass legal muster, or does it strive to achieve an even higher, beyond-compliance standard when it comes to such issues as pollution, labor rights, and product safety?

Most responsible companies today recognize the value of going beyond compliance, further along the sustainability path. And this value isn't just moral—it's financial as well. For example, some companies continued to dump hazardous wastes after the environmental and health hazards they posed were obvious, waiting until the law forced them to stop. They were legally within their rights to do so. But Congress eventually passed the Superfund law, which created retroactive liability for the damages caused. Thus companies that insisted on their legal right to pollute not only hurt the environment but also ultimately hurt themselves and their shareholders as well.

By contrast, PepsiCo has gone far beyond simple compliance with the law in its efforts to achieve a high standard of sustainability. For example, the company has instituted a financial management program that requires proposed capital expenditures to pass through a sustainability analysis (designed with help from PricewaterhouseCoopers) alongside the traditional return on investment (ROI) calculation. When any project over $10 million—a new product line, a new plant, a renovated facility—is evaluated for ROI by the company's capital management committee, the project's impact on the TBL is also considered.

No law or regulation requires any company to perform a TBL review. But the benefits to PepsiCo have been enormous. The review empowers project proponents to look into the future on a whole range of issues that had not previously been systematically considered and to make appropriate adjustments to the expected rate of return. Thus PepsiCo might choose to lower the financial hurdle rate for a project with a measurable community benefit or raise it for one with a quantifiable environmental risk. The TBL requirement also strongly encourages proponents to work consciously to move their projects toward the Sustainability Sweet Spot, where benefits to both PepsiCo and the community will be greatest.

When examining how your company operates in terms of the Triple Bottom Line, don't overlook your economic impacts on the community, including jobs created; monetary flows (where money comes from and to whom it goes); local contracts generated; and local, state, and federal taxes. These can be at least as important as environmental and social impacts. As one senior manager at PepsiCo told us, "You cannot imagine the tangible financial benefits that accrue to a plant with a twenty-year history of good relations with the town. A plant that runs smoothly year in and year out is worth its weight in gold."

How Sustainability Applies to Your Industry

Many sustainability issues are highly industry specific. Pharmaceutical companies face different kinds of social and environmental issues than high-tech manufacturers or mining companies; banks and financial firms are subject to different pressures than apparel manufacturers or retailers (see the partial list in Table 7.1). Your self-assessment should include a look at where your industry stands, the driving forces affecting sustainability in your industry, and the position of your company in relation to industry-specific issues.

One place to start looking for insights into your industry is the GRI, which provides industry-specific guidelines for eleven different business sectors, including financial services, food processing, media, mining and metals, and several others. These guidelines, though focused on reporting, provide insight into significant industry-based issues and were developed with industry participation. Your industry trade association will also know whether there are any TBL initiatives under way in your sector.

Several major sectors are exploring what sustainability means to them and issuing reports on their conclusions. Much of this activity is taking place in Europe under the auspices of the World Business Council for Sustainable Development, which currently has nine such projects under way, focused on water, cement, electricity, forest products, buildings, tires, chemicals, agribusiness, and mobility (that is, transportation). Some of these projects appear likely to lead to permanent cooperative agreements.

Cooperation among competing companies is sometimes an essential element of sustainable management. As with maintaining profitable fishing stocks or eliminating questionable payments to corrupt regimes for the rights to natural resources, only joint action can solve the problem. These are situations in which the unfettered workings of competition can't solve the problem without additional help.

Unfortunately, convincing longtime rivals to cooperate can be extraordinarily difficult, even when a dire threat to their future

Table 7.1　Key Sustainability Issues in Selected Industries

Industry	Sustainability Issues
Agriculture and fishing	Sustainable production; environmental and social issues related to industrial farming; water scarcity; workers' rights; food safety
Clothing and apparel	Supply-chain labor and environmental practices, including forced labor, child labor, human rights abuses, and workplace safety; genetically modified organisms (GMOs)
Banking and finance	Widespread distrust due to fraudulent lending practices, excessive risk-taking, abusive trading, and weak regulation; loans related to projects with potentially adverse environmental and social impacts
Construction and real estate	Water, energy, and materials use; shift to solar and other renewable forms of energy; indoor air pollution; green buildings and creation and protection of green spaces
Energy	Environmental impact of drilling and of fossil fuels on global climate; renewable energy; lack of electricity for rural poor; energy availability in growing cities; energy shortages and price volatility
Food	Obesity in the developed world; malnutrition in the developing world; stress on the food delivery system based on highly concentrated, rapidly growing populations; food safety; shifting growing seasons and other issues related to climate change
Health care	Better provision of preventive, affordable, and accessible services; shifting to patient-centric, community-based care; alignment of incentives for all participants in the system; need for cost controls
High technology	Energy use and efficiency; environmental impact of electronic trash; labor issues in supply chain, as with apparel industry (see above); data security and privacy
Insurance	High cost of insurance related to extreme weather conditions; need for insurance in developing world

(continued)

Table 7.1   Key Sustainability Issues in Selected Industries (*Continued*)

Industry	Sustainability Issues
Marketing	Confusion over proliferation of labels used to promote healthy or environmentally sustainable products and services
Mining and other extractive industries	Environmental damage and resource depletion; human rights related to workforce; social costs associated with mining in war-torn or underdeveloped regions
Packaged goods	Wasteful use of materials in packaging; confusion around product labeling; truth in advertising; quality and safety of supply chain; environmental issues related to transportation
Pharmaceuticals	Access to lifesaving medicines in developing world; affordability in developed world; integrity surrounding marketing issues and relations with prescribing physicians; quality control
Retailing	Social and environmental issues related to "big box" stores; labor issues related to wages, working conditions, and benefits; environmental issues related to packaging, transportation, and disposal
Social media	Privacy abuse and misuse of information by social networking hosts and government; bullying, harassment, and other inappropriate use of media by consumers and vendors; shifting lines related to work and personal use
Transportation	Energy impacts in manufacture and use of automobiles, aircraft, and other vehicles; environmental and social effects of accidents, traffic congestion, highway construction, and parking; post-use disposal of vehicles

is involved. Journalist Michael Moss has recounted the story of a remarkable meeting in April 8, 1999, among leading executives from most of America's largest food companies, including General Mills, Kraft, Nabisco, Coca-Cola, and Procter & Gamble. The meeting was convened by James Behnke, chief technical officer of Pillsbury, who had become deeply concerned about the then-nascent problem of rising rates of obesity and associated diseases. He hoped to convince the leaders of America's food industry to take the problem seriously and to act in concert to address it—before public anger and government intervention forced their hand.

According to participants in the meeting, the effort at forging a joint solution was stymied when one of the most powerful executives in attendance—Stephen Sanger, then CEO of General Mills—flatly refused to consider any steps that might compromise his company's success in attracting and retaining millions of customers. "Sanger's response effectively ended the meeting," Moss says.[5]

Since then, obesity rates have continued to rise—along with pressure from activist groups, medical and health care organizations, government agencies, and concerned citizens demanding a change in course by the food industry. Charges of industry malfeasance have been trumpeted by a series of media exposés, including Eric Schlosser's best-selling book *Fast Food Nation: The Dark Side of the All-American Meal* (2002) and the documentary films *Super Size Me* (2004) and *Food, Inc.* (2009). Even First Lady Michelle Obama has become a spokesperson for the anti-obesity movement. The painful showdown between the food industry and an aroused public that Behnke hoped to avert seems ever more likely.

If you're active in an industry where collaboration is needed to protect some vital sustainability interest or to create a new and valuable sweet spot, you must either strive to enlighten the managers of competing firms in hopes of stimulating industry-wide consensus and action, or lobby some supra-industry body—such as a national government or an international regulatory body—to impose necessary regulations. In such cases, your competitors can also be important and valuable stakeholders.

Fortunately, many sustainability challenges are less systemic and more manageable than those now faced by the food industry. Many are capable of being addressed effectively by the actions of a single intelligently managed company. In the next chapter, we'll explain how taking advantage of the opportunities created by individual, short-term problems can be a great way of launching your business toward the ultimate goal of becoming a truly sustainable organization.

8

Sustainability Jiu-Jitsu
Turning Short-Term Challenges into Opportunities

Paradoxically, the language of shareholder value may hinder companies from maximizing shareholder value. . . . Practiced as an unthinking mantra, it can lead managers to focus . . . on improving the short-term performance of their business, neglecting . . . longer-term opportunities and issues.
—Ian Davis, managing director, McKinsey & Company[1]

Risks and Opportunities—the Yin and Yang of Sustainability

As we've stressed throughout this book, the Age of Sustainability is creating a new world for business—one in which old assumptions have been upended, new realities are taking shape, and unforeseen challenges are demanding attention. And like any birth, the emergence of this new world is an experience fraught with both excitement and danger. Companies that understand what's happening and adapt to the changes quickly and intelligently can hope to thrive and prosper; those that are too myopic or stubborn to adjust in time are likely to flounder and fail.

Thus risks and opportunities are the yin and yang of sustainability—opposed realities that are present, perhaps imperceptibly, just below the surface of a hundred consequential trends. Today's smartest business leaders are continually aware of both. And even as they struggle to minimize the risks that sustainability poses, they search for ways to transform those risks into future-enhancing opportunities—a practice we like to call *sustainability jiu-jitsu*.

Recall the Kerala water case, which we recounted in some detail in Chapter Two. As we explained, PepsiCo adroitly minimized the risk of being driven out of business by public anger over a local water-supply problem by devoting its own resources to building wells to serve the neighboring community. As a result, Pepsi was allowed to stay active in Kerala even after its chief rival, Coke, was forced to shut down. The Kerala story illustrates three important truths.

First, most companies today are running risks that don't appear on traditional radar screens. Before building its Kerala plant, Pepsi had performed its usual risk analysis of the area's water supply, which determined that the aquifer supplying the plant held enough water to produce Pepsi beverages. It never occurred to the company that its operation might be at risk because the town would run out of water from a separate supply. Now Pepsi realizes that the well-being of the community is part of the company's responsibility. "We are beginning to understand risk in a totally new way," a senior Pepsi executive told us.

Second, companies can often reduce or eliminate those risks—and sometimes transform them into business-enhancing opportunities—if they can identify them quickly and address them responsibly. By both reducing its own use of local water supplies and taking beyond-the-call-of-duty steps to improve the community's access to water resources, Pepsi demonstrated its readiness to act as a responsible corporate citizen. The result: Pepsi can produce its drinks in Kerala, while arch-rival Coke cannot—a big competitive victory for Pepsi.

Third, fostering community support and involvement can prove to be a powerful risk management tool. Pepsi could have fought for survival in Kerala by relying on traditional corporate tactics like stonewalling and legal obstructionism. Instead, the company actually *listened* to the community, worked to understand the problem, and then found an effective, inexpensive solution.

It might seem absurd that a soft drink company is required to spend its shareholders' funds to build water wells for a community where it does business, particularly where there is no legal requirement to do so. But Pepsi's actions earned the company the license to stay in business in Kerala—an act of sustainability jiu-jitsu with long-term benefits for both Pepsi and its various stakeholders.

Similar risk-opportunity conundrums are popping up in almost every industry. It takes robust, systematic, creative thinking—as well as continual, open communication both inside and outside the company—to devise innovative solutions to these puzzles. A systematic approach to the TBL and stakeholder engagement will enable forward-looking companies and managers to see beyond the horizon and eliminate new forms of risks before they strike.

Look for Low-Hanging Fruit

As the Kerala story shows, the new responsibilities companies face are creating both enormous new risks and new opportunities. In fact, many companies have discovered that the very best way to launch their sustainability efforts is to respond to today's new social and environmental challenges opportunistically—scrutinizing each one in search of ways to save money, open new markets, attract customers, create new products and services, and otherwise enhance the profitability of their businesses.

One of the best ways to take advantage of the opportunities afforded by sustainability is to first look for low-hanging fruit. Rather than searching for distant or obscure possibilities, look closer to home—at the business activities in which you're already immersed. Study what you're currently doing, in search of ways to achieve a few quick, profit-generating sustainability victories with projects that are easy and obvious and that meet an established need—an unfulfilled customer demand, a requirement to cut costs, or a needless waste of resources that can be eliminated.

This first step is often taken by a division, department, or plant led by a manager who sees a compelling business need and understands the potential value of sustainability earlier than others. This can be a brilliant way of beginning a company's move toward a more sustainable future. If the benefits of the first project or two are real, it won't be long before someone recognizes the value of a more comprehensive approach, obtains senior sponsorship, and leverages the effort throughout the organization.

Thus, forward-thinking middle managers can and often do play a critical role in the early stages of a sustainability program. 3M's Pollution Prevention Pays, an enormously effective, long-established sustainability effort that we'll describe in more detail in Chapter Nine, was driven first at the departmental level by the head of environmental quality, then by managers and engineers who identified minimization opportunities within their domains to create immediate savings. The company adroitly fostered this entrepreneurial spirit, spread the word (and the incentives), and ultimately produced the momentum that changed the direction of the entire organization.

We recommend that you emulate 3M. Don't make the common mistake of convening a blue-ribbon task force, drawing up an ambitious sustainability vision or strategy, making a grand public announcement—and then failing to follow through. A false start creates many problems, including employee cynicism that the effort is a publicity stunt or simply the "program du jour" that will soon disappear. That attitude will be hard to overcome later when you decide to get more serious about the issue.

Instead, smart small. Create a few quick, easy wins in your company's various business units, and use these as stepping-stones to a broader sustainability strategy. Here are some tips on how to get started:

- *Take a fresh look at your customers' needs.* Search for sustainability issues that will resonate with your customers—a great way to find sweet spots. Do your customers have environmental, social, or economic concerns you can address, as GE is doing with climate change and health care? Do your company's products or services have undesirable side effects you can reduce? Can your products be made easier to reuse or recycle? Can you productively use anything your customers discard? Do you know how to tackle an environmental or social issue that might be confounding your customers? Volvo followed this approach when it transformed auto safety from a social issue (a topic that only muckraking journalists and a handful of crusaders were focused on) into a competitive advantage and a sales strategy in the 1980s. Volvo recognized that a significant subset of the automobile marketplace was especially concerned with safety, felt that its needs were ignored by the major automakers, and would pay a premium for advanced safety features like airbags. In the words of one auto research analyst, "American automakers were fighting it [enhanced safety] tooth and nail. Volvo got people to pay for it."[2]

- *Work with your supply chain.* Think of your company or department as the customer. What could your suppliers do that would make your operation more sustainable? Examine your supplier code of conduct or individual contracts to see what requirements are already in place and whether it makes sense to alter them. Many win-win opportunities may become apparent. Wal-Mart has modeled this approach in its ongoing effort to collaborate with suppliers on ways to simplify, streamline, and improve product packaging. As a result, packages for everything from Cheerios to soft drinks to shoes have been made smaller and lighter, reducing costs of production, shipping, storage, and display; eliminating waste; and conserving resources.[3] Look for similar ways to partner with your suppliers to help them improve their environmental performance, reduce waste, upgrade their labor policies, enhance their community relations, and otherwise increase their own sustainability.

- *Leverage any current TBL advantages you enjoy.* If you've already moved forward in one area, create additional competitive advantage by pressuring the competition to follow suit, as Nike has done with the issue of toxins used in manufacturing. Electric companies in the northeastern United States that are required by local governments to install scrubbers and move to low-sulfur coal are using the legislative process to pressure their midwestern rivals to do the same, thereby turning their sustainability advantage into a competitive edge.

- *Build on your current skill set.* Don't try to be all things to all people. You will produce better, more meaningful results sooner if you focus your sustainability efforts around what you do and know best. If you manage a product line at a food company, the best use of your resources would probably be to assist in addressing hunger or nutrition or to deal with obesity, rather than trying to lead the way on energy conservation or the digital divide. If you have a strong supply chain, think about how to leverage it by working with suppliers to improve environmental or social performance for the extended enterprise.

- *Anticipate an impending change—and jump ahead of it.* If you can foresee where you or your customers are about to get squeezed, you may see new sweet spot opportunities. Toyota anticipated rising gas prices and the need to move beyond a hundred-year-old gasoline-based technology; in response, it developed hybrid engines years before Ford and GM. After grappling with the controversy over the Brent Spar offshore oil drilling facility (see Chapter Eleven), Shell understood that environmental groups like Greenpeace and other stakeholders would be increasingly important to its future. As a result, the company decided to master the art of scenario planning and other engagement techniques that have helped it stay ahead of the competition.

- *Empower individuals.* Scott Hall's efforts to forge a consensus between business and environmentalists on a plan to revitalize the Penobscot River illustrate how just one motivated manager can make a difference. Scott's bosses at PPL set some basic ground rules (that is, "make the numbers work, and check with us before you make a deal"), but gave him the flexibility and support he needed to get the job done. He succeeded where governors and members of Congress had failed. Other companies that have sustainability-minded managers like Scott should encourage and support their efforts in the same way.

Turn Crises into Opportunities

Beyond low-hanging fruit, there is another important way that many companies kick-start their sustainability efforts—though it isn't a method that anyone would choose intentionally. It's the path of being driven to action by an emerging sustainability problem that suddenly threatens the success of your business. As Dennis E. Welch, formerly of Northeast Utilities (NU), told us when speaking about the challenges of corporate responsibility, "If you want to transform your company, it helps to have a crisis."

Welch should know. He was given the job of transforming NU from the inside after it found itself the subject of a massive criminal investigation by the U.S. Environmental Protection Agency and the Connecticut Department of Environmental Protection. (He has since gone on to guide a second major utility firm, American Electric Power, through its own sustainability evolution.) Welch is no masochist, but he recognizes that at many companies, transformational change begins with the pain of an ad hoc response to an immediate crisis.

If your company is facing external criticism, internal rebellion, a government investigation, or potential lawsuits over such issues as the environment, community relations, employment policies, or worker safety, you should view the painful reality as an opportunity in disguise. Start your company on the path to sustainability by addressing the immediate crisis. Then use the atmosphere of heightened awareness and sensitivity as a basis for anticipating and responding to tomorrow's issues today. The sooner you can create a big-picture vision to give context to today's problem, the sooner you can begin transforming crises into opportunities.

Nike learned sustainability jiu-jitsu the hard way.[4] The use of child labor in outsourced manufacturing plants by suppliers of clothing, shoes, and sporting goods was a festering issue among social advocates throughout the 1980s and 1990s. But most American companies that marketed or retailed those goods did little to address the problem until it burst into the news in 1996. Prompted by suggestions from Pakistani human rights activists, veteran journalist Sydney H.

Schanberg traveled to South Asia to investigate charges that children were being exploited to produce products for the global market. The resulting story, titled "Six Cents an Hour," appeared in the June 1996 issue of *Life* magazine. It was illustrated with a photograph of a twelve-year-old boy named Tariq surrounded by the pieces of a Nike soccer ball that he would spend most of a day stitching together. His pay for the work: about sixty cents. The contrast with the millions being paid by Nike in endorsement fees to athletes like Michael Jordan struck many as morally repugnant.

In a matter of weeks, activists all across Canada and the United States were standing in front of Nike retail outlets, holding up Tariq's photo and urging customers not to purchase Nike products. In a movie he was shooting at the time (*The Big One*), satirist Michael Moore tried to film Nike CEO Phil Knight accepting a free airline ticket to Indonesia to witness firsthand the conditions at another substandard supplier factory. And in the popular *Doonesbury* comic strip, outraged activist Kim declared, "Do you know if you doubled the salaries of Nike's 30,000 employees here [in Vietnam], the annual payroll would be about what the company pays Michael Jordan?" Doonesbury disagreed, pointing out that if Nike did increase its factory workers' salaries, "Michael would want more. He's *very* competitive."[5]

The storm of protest over labor policies in the developing world produced business headaches for Nike and for many others in the apparel industry, including Kathy Lee Gifford and Wal-Mart. Nike's immediate response made it worse. Phil Knight took a combative stance, admitting only that "we've made mistakes in the sense that we haven't been perfect," and calling criticism of Nike "a growth industry" consisting of people who "have sort of their own reasons for the business that they're in."[6]

But the pressure mounted, and in the long run, Knight and Nike showed a willingness to learn from the crisis. Nike eventually launched a six-point reform effort, which included requirements that all new employees in factories making Nike products be at least sixteen years old, that free middle school and high school classes be provided to workers, and that independent NGOs be permitted to monitor working conditions at Nike factories.

Over the next several years, the reform effort expanded to include development of a detailed code of conduct for Nike suppliers, creation of a trained team of internal monitors to check factory conditions, and support for development of a common monitoring platform for the entire sportswear industry. In its 2004 corporate responsibility report, Nike took the unprecedented step of disclosing the names and locations of all its outside suppliers, in effect saying, "We are doing everything we can, and you're invited to check."[7] And in 2012, Nike was one of several apparel industry companies to join forces in creating the Higg Index, a new measure of sustainability (based partly on Nike's own internal Materials Sustainability Index) that includes the impacts of suppliers and that is supposed to eventually become the basis of a new system for consumer labeling.[8]

Nike has suffered setbacks in its quest to become known as one of the world's most responsible apparel companies. In 2001, Nike was sued by lawyer and activist Marc Kasky for false advertising over its claims in press releases and letters to customers that the company was now enforcing strict workers' rights policies at supplier firms. (The legal battle that ensued turned primarily on the question of whether or not Nike's statements constituted "commercial speech," which is less fully covered by First Amendment protections than other forms of speech.) When the U.S. Supreme Court refused to hear the case in 2003, tacitly upholding a California Supreme Court ruling in favor of Kasky, Nike was forced to settle, agreeing to pay Kasky's workers' rights organization $1.5 million and suffering enormous additional damage to its reputation and credibility.[9]

A decade later, in 2011, a report by the Associated Press revealed sometimes violent abuse of workers in an Indonesian factory where Nike's Converse sneakers are made. In responding to the charge, Nike spokespeople were forced to admit that two-thirds of the 168 Converse operations around the globe still didn't meet Nike's corporate standards.[10]

But despite the setbacks, the swoosh has survived. Nike has continued to push forward, spending tens of millions both to improve its image and make substantive changes in its suppliers' practices. Nike hopes to recoup its investment by gaining competitive advantage from it, portraying itself as an industry leader on environmental and social causes, forcing its competitors to make the kinds of costly investments in practices and processes that Nike has already made.

Nike has been effectively practicing sustainability jiu-jitsu— flipping an oncoming risk into an opportunity. Shell, whose executives now frankly admit they "got religion" during the Brent Spar incident, did the same thing. So did NU (Dennis Welch's company), which leveraged the impact of the federal environmental investigation to establish a corporation-wide environmental management system as well as a new attitude about compliance. The result: tighter management in almost every area.

The fast-food industry is currently trying hard to employ jiu-jitsu in defense against charges that its products are a major cause of the spreading obesity epidemic. As we saw in the previous chapter, the industry's leading companies failed to take advantage of an opportunity to address the issue through voluntary joint action as long ago as 1999. Now the companies have responded to growing public concern about the problem by changing their menus and providing more accessible nutrition labeling. However, they have acted too late to discourage the lawsuits, protests, and regulatory interventions that have popped up around the country. McDonald's fought calorie labeling every step of the way, but now provides detailed information directly on its famous overhead menus. In the meantime, snack foods are being banned from countless school lunchrooms, and the movement is spreading to Europe.

The food companies have taken very different approaches to the obesity crisis, depending on where they stand. The Whole Foods grocery chain has turned the issue to its advantage, offering its customers fresh produce and organic foods (and rewarding investors with an eightfold increase in its stock price from 2009 to 2013). Fast-food chain Wendy's has played the contrarian, offering enormous, health-defying burgers laden with bacon and cheese, seeking to differentiate itself from the competition by defying the critics. (Among the responses: a mock TV commercial by social activist Mark Dice promoting "Wendy's New Obesity Burger.")[11]

• • •

Of course, the amount of low-hanging fruit you can expect to find is limited, and no company wants to depend on a series of crises to become the engine behind any ongoing initiative. In time, you'll discover that the broader benefits of sustainability can be achieved only through a more robust, systematic approach—one that involves, and ultimately transforms, the work of every department and division within your company.

In the chapters that follow, we'll explain how to develop and implement such an approach. We'll show how the new demands of sustainability will impact several major areas of your business's activity, including the formulation of your corporate strategy; the organization and management of your business processes; your company's relationships with internal and external stakeholders; the systems by which you measure and report your results; and, finally, the underlying corporate culture and capabilities that largely shape the future of your organization.

9

Shaping Your Sustainability Strategy

You may not be interested in strategy, but strategy is interested in you.

—Leon Trotsky, Russian Marxist revolutionary
and theorist

Finding the Sweet Spot: Putting Sustainability at the Heart of Your Corporate Strategy

As we've already stressed, your sustainability approach and your overall business plan must ultimately be one and the same, not two separate programs working in parallel (or, far worse, at cross-purposes). If you take a close look at the specific strategic directions your department, business unit, or company has chosen to pursue—the business models, product and service categories, and markets that your company has identified as being ripe for growth—you will probably find that there is a recognizable sustainability component to each: an intersection between your business strategy and the interests of the wider world. This is the area we've defined as the Sustainability Sweet Spot.

The key to incorporating sustainability into strategic planning, then, is simple: *always be on the lookout for the overlap between profit and the public good.* That's where opportunities lie.

Consider the global strategy being pursued by Unilever, the $68 billion (2012) consumer products corporation known for its food, home care, and personal care products, marketed around the world under such familiar brand names as Dove, Hellman's, Lux, Ben & Jerry's, Lipton, Knorr, Sunsilk, and many others.

As defined by the company's executive leaders, Unilever's current corporate strategy focuses on five key priorities that combine to make up what they call "the Compass."[1] These five priorities are a better future for children, a healthier future, a more confident future, a better future for the planet, and a better future for farming and farmers. Each is explained and described in terms of specific Unilever products, strategies, and practices that embody it.

For example, "a better future for children" is exemplified by oral care products that encourage kids to brush their teeth, as well as Unilever's support for the FDI World Dental Federation, which works to bring access to advanced dental care to people around the world. Similarly, "a more confident future" is embodied in Dove's advertising campaigns, which use "real women" rather than ultrathin models to exemplify beauty, along with the work of the Dove Self-Esteem Fund, which supports mentoring and education programs for young women. "A better future for farming and farmers" is illustrated by Unilever's use of ethically and sustainably sourced ingredients in products like Lipton tea and Ben & Jerry's ice cream.

Thus each of these five priorities focuses on a specific sweet spot that promises both revenue and profit opportunities for Unilever and social or environmental benefits for people around the world.

At the same time, Unilever has also emphasized the importance of customers in the developing world for its future growth. In 2011, these customers already represented fully 56 percent of Unilever's revenue base, and the company estimates that this share will increase to 70 percent by 2020.[2] Here again, identifying the sweet spot isn't difficult. Selling more products in the developing world represents a clear business victory for Unilever. Those sales will not only provide immediate benefits in the form of increased revenues but also help build a base of customer loyalty that should lead to sustained growth, as the countries of the developing world continue to emerge from poverty and achieve higher levels of disposable income.

Increased sales in the developing world will also be a win for society, because anything that helps improve the standard of living for millions of the world's poorest people is clearly a socially responsible thing to do. Unilever is one of many companies that are deeply engaged in figuring out how to make their goods and services accessible and affordable to people living on less than $2 a day. Even better, many of the business activities driven by this process also spur economic growth and provide opportunities for the poor. Profits retained by local businesses, such as retailers and distributors, will help promote growth, create jobs, and launch a continuing spiral of economic benefits that can increase the market for consumer goods and lift entire regions out of poverty.

Of course, *identifying* the sweet spot in relation to this strategy is easier than *occupying* it. Many companies have written off the developing world, scared away by the relatively low incomes of most people there or the significant business risks involved in getting established in those markets. But Unilever went in with a different approach than most. Unilever has discovered that it's usually not practical to try to sell the same products that are popular in the developed world when seeking breakthroughs in the developing world. The products themselves, as well as the packaging, advertising, marketing, distribution, and pricing strategies, must all be tailored to the needs of regional and local communities.

Although rural villagers in countries like India or Kenya with modest cash incomes may be attracted by some of the same brand promises Westerners respond to, they can't afford the full-size cartons of food or health care products that Americans or Europeans are accustomed to buying. Unilever has therefore developed alternative forms of packaging and pricing designed to be suitable for customers in the developing world. In Asia and Africa, Unilever sells single-use shampoo and hair care sachets (marketed under the Sunsilk brand); small, discount-priced bars of soap (Lifebuoy); and single-serving packets of soup seasoning cubes (Knorr Cubitos). All these products can be purchased one at a time for just a few cents, which may be all the discretionary spending money that an African housewife has at a given time.

Making products of developed-world quality available to customers in the developing world represents a growing portion of Unilever's profitability, as well as a contribution to the well-being of a less advantaged portion of humankind—a sweet spot bull's-eye for the company and its stakeholders.

Unilever has also developed sales and marketing strategies for the developing world that are designed to produce benefits for the entire TBL. For example, the company's Shakti program provides training in sales, marketing, and entrepreneurship to thousands of women in rural India, giving them the skills they need to sell Unilever products to a potential market of over seventy million village-based customers. As of 2011, forty-five thousand Shakti distributors were active in one hundred thousand villages and were selling products to over three million Indian households. These women were, on average, doubling their families' annual incomes through their work. Thus Unilever's effort to expand its market penetration in India is also serving to empower women and alleviate rural poverty.[3]

It's clear that Unilever's strategic growth targets offer enormous areas of overlap with their stakeholders' natural agenda for economic, social, and environmental prosperity. Unilever illustrates a crucial principle of TBL management: start by examining your company's overall business strategy. What are the key strategic drivers of future growth that your company has already identified? What are the drivers in your part of the business? Then ask, Where is the potential overlap between these drivers and the environmental, social, and economic needs of society or your current stakeholders? That overlap is your Sustainability Sweet Spot—the greatest future source of gain for your company or department.

A Map to the Sweet Spot

To find your own sweet spot, consider that every action you take in business has two components: an impact on profits and an impact on the world. This can be represented by a four-cell matrix with two axes, which represent profitability and benefits to society. We describe this as the sustainability map (see Figure 9.1).

The northeast corner of the sustainability map is conceptually similar to the sweet spot, where stakeholders' interests and corporate interests overlap. Your goal is to get as much of your business activity as possible into that quadrant. You want every business decision to

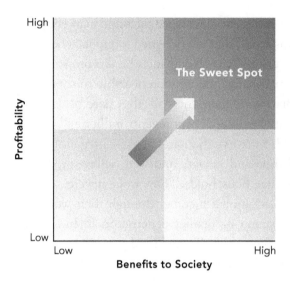

Figure 9.1   The Sustainability Map.

push you north and east. The value of the map emerges when you use it to plot the location of various businesses or activities in order to determine ways to move them in a northeasterly direction or to generate ideas for quantum strategic change.

Suppose you own a business or manage part of one that is currently located in the northwest quadrant (profitable but not sustainable). Is it possible to devise ways of moving the business eastward (more sustainable) without moving southward (less profitable)? DuPont has made such a shift by moving from the chemical business toward the soy protein business without sacrificing revenues or profits. If you have a business in the southwest corner (neither profitable nor sustainable), can you find ways to base a turnaround on moving both north and east?

Your goal should be to develop strategies and operational changes that will enable you to move toward the northeast corner of the map. For example, an energy company that profits from burning dirty coal could devote its short-term research dollars toward clean-coal technology and its long-term effort toward a future in which most energy is derived from such renewable sources as solar, wind, hydroelectric, and geothermal power. Both initiatives embody migration toward the northeast corner of the map, where both profitability and social benefit are higher.

Both small and large companies have changed their businesses to move further toward the northeast corner of the sustainability map.

Country Lanes is a tiny UK tour company that offers day trips and holiday travel, by bicycle or on foot.[4] Patrons must somehow find their way to the rendezvous point at which the tour begins. Several years ago, Country Lanes redesigned all its tours to begin at railway stations, with the result that 85 percent of their customers now use rail travel to get there. The change eliminated a million miles of automobile travel and 362 tons of carbon dioxide emissions per year. Business is up because customers now find it easier to get to the tours. Country Lanes also supports local business by encouraging its customers to spend money on snacks, drinks, and lunches from neighborhood pubs and shops. Thus the company serves environmental, social, and economic interests at the same time that it builds a growing, profitable business—the very definition of sustainability.

In the late 1990s, when Toyota revealed its intention to create a new form of gasoline-electric car, one that would capture and use braking energy, the company was derided as an environmental do-gooder that would surely lose money. "We wondered if anyone would want one," admitted Takehisa Yaegashi, the senior Toyota engineer now known as the father of the hybrid.[5] The Prius was introduced in Japan in 1997 and went on sale worldwide three years later, amazing drivers and critics with its unparalleled fuel efficiency, its quiet yet powerful engine, and its stylish design.

Today, the Prius is one of the most successful cars in the world, with sales of over three million units. The acclaim it attracted helped catapult Toyota into the number-one spot in the sales rankings for all car companies, a spot it held from 2008 through 2010 and regained in 2012. What's more, it decisively demonstrated the viability of the hybrid and all-electric segments of the automobile market, now populated with a growing array of models from practically every major manufacturer, including Ford, General Motors, Honda, and Hyundai.

Toyota made two bets at once: that both the price of gas and concern about air pollution would rise. Winning either bet might have made the car a success, but Toyota appears to have won both, making the Prius a worldwide phenomenon. Pioneering the hybrid automobile has been good for Toyota's shareholders and good for the environment—a remarkable example of finding the sweet spot.

Minimization and Optimization

Many companies, especially those that are new to sustainability, find it challenging to identify the sweet spots that will work for them and their stakeholders. One fruitful way to strategize about your business's sweet spot is to think in terms of *minimization* and *optimization*.

For our purposes, minimization means reducing the adverse environmental, social, and economic impacts of your activities. Minimization aims at reducing pollution, employee accidents, and harm to the community to the lowest possible levels. In normative terms, minimization is "being less bad" (as sometimes evoked in the corporate slogan, "The hero is zero").

Optimization is "being more good." We use the term to mean producing positive benefits in the three areas of environmental, social, and economic impact. Optimization can take you far beyond minimization. Optimization aims not just to reduce pollution but to restore the environment; not just to eliminate employee accidents but to create a healthier, happier workforce; not just to decrease harm to the community but to help revitalize it (for some illustrative examples, see Table 9.1).

The yin and yang of minimization and optimization come together in the elegant and visionary formulation of architect William McDonough, who urges a gradual redesign of all human industrial processes such that every waste stream becomes someone else's feedstock. The idea is simple: first you minimize your waste streams; then you optimize them, creating biological or technical nutrients that return to the environment or go into new products. The ultimate in eco-effectiveness, McDonough's vision of endless

Table 9.1   Minimization and Optimization

Business Function	Minimization	Optimization
Worker health and safety	Reduce workplace accidents.	Create a happy and healthy workforce.
Environmental protection	Clean up hazardous wastes.	Use waste to restore environment or create new products.
Energy use	Reduce the use of fossils fuels.	Shift energy generation to solar power.
Product packaging	Reduce the use of needless packaging.	Produce packaging that biodegrades and contains seeds or fertilizer.
Customer service	Respond more quickly to customer complaints.	Work with complaining customers to create new and better products.

reuse suggests a world in which "[d]esign can eliminate the concept of waste, producing perpetual assets rather than perpetual liabilities."[6]

Minimization: Pursuing Sustainability by Being Less Bad

Thinking about minimization and optimization can help you discover TBL strategies that you can use immediately to assist your company or department.

A company that pursues a minimization strategy is buffing its credentials as a good corporation and as a desirable neighbor and partner for the communities in which it operates. And like all sustainable pathways, minimization offers distinct economic benefits as well. Think of minimization as part of a strategy to reduce cost and risk. Minimization can cut costs (by trimming waste), reduce debt (by making your capital expenditures more efficient), lower the potential for losses (from lawsuits, regulatory and legal restrictions, and public relations disasters), and increase profit margins (by doing all of the above). Thus, by reducing the risks and costs associated with doing business, minimization can enhance your company's ability to consistently reach or exceed its profitability targets.

A few examples among the many that could be cited will show how minimization strategies can generate both financial and nonfinancial benefits.

Waste reduction is a classic, essential form of minimization. 3M is a leader in this area through its decades-old program known as Pollution Prevention Pays (3P). Launched in 1975 by Dr. Joseph Ling, a Chinese-born sanitary engineer who headed environmental responsibility for 3M's worldwide operations, 3P encourages and rewards employees who create breakthrough ideas to eliminate pollution at the source (rather than cleaning it up after the fact) and that also produce a financial payoff for 3M.[7]

Here's an illustration. 3M uses solvents in the manufacture of its products (films, fiber optics, and fuel cells, as well as the tapes and adhesives found in virtually every home and office). These solvents create hazardous air pollution when they evaporate. In 1987, the company had to spend over $200 million to reduce the emissions coming from these solvents, without addressing their source.

New technologies developed under 3P have reduced or eliminated the use of many solvents at 3M. The famous Scotch brand tape is now made using water-based (rather than solvent-based) adhesives, and 3M surgical tapes are manufactured using a patented hot-melt process that eliminates the use of highly toxic solvents. All told, 3M employees have generated over fifty-six hundred projects in the 3P program. Together they've prevented the creation of more than 2.2 billion pounds of pollutants and generated savings of nearly $1 billion for 3M, counting only the first-year savings from each project.

3P is more than just a collection of projects. It establishes company-wide targets for minimization, which currently include five-year objectives to cut energy use by 20 percent, waste by 25 percent, and volatile organic air emissions by 25 percent. The program is expanding to include life-cycle management (LCM), which anticipates environmental, health, and safety issues as part of the conception and design of products, enabling the company to eliminate problems and excess costs from the beginning. LCM is now a standard part of 3M's new product development process.

Minimization can also produce large financial benefits when applied to reducing workplace injuries and accidents as well as enhancing employee wellness and job satisfaction. Manufacturers and distributors have long understood that as injuries go down, so do lost work days, workers' compensation claims, employee grievances, lawsuits, operational slowdowns, and other costs. Even accounting firms and other professional service providers see the financial value of reducing employee distress. Internal PricewaterhouseCoopers (PwC) studies indicate that it costs the firm from two to three times annual salary to replace a manager when the full costs of recruitment, hiring, and training and of work disruption are considered.[8] Thus, whenever a manager leaves, it's as if PwC continues to pay that salary for at least two years. So the company's excellent work-life balance, employee wellness, and partner-employee connectivity programs, all of which improve employee retention, serve to boost the firm's profitability and the quality of client service while being recognized as responsible corporate behavior.

Minimization can also be a strategy for reducing negative qualities in your products. As we've already seen, public awareness of obesity has mushroomed in recent years, posing an enormous business risk for fast-food companies like McDonald's. One of McDonald's competitors, the Subway chain of franchised sandwich shops, has devised a minimization strategy around the obesity issue. For more than fifteen years, its advertising campaigns have featured spokesperson Jared Fogle, a real-life customer who lost 245 pounds while eating exclusively at Subway. (By contrast, as chronicled in the documentary *Super Size Me*, filmmaker Morgan Spurlock gained 24.5 pounds while eating only at McDonald's—for a single month.) Subway deliberately draws a sharp contrast between its most popular product, the hero sandwich stuffed with cold cuts, cheese, lettuce, tomatoes, and other fresh ingredients, and McDonald's best-known menu items, many of which contain far more grams of fat. Thus Subway is practicing both minimization and sustainability jiu-jitsu, making its offerings less bad and thereby flipping a business risk into an opportunity.

So far, the strategy seems to be working. Since Subway began showcasing the comparative health benefits of its products in 2000, revenues have surged from $5.1 billion to $15.2 billion. As a result, Subway has been expanding faster than any other fast-food chain. Today Subway has more than thirty-three thousand stores in over seventy countries and has outstripped McDonald's as the world's most ubiquitous fast-food outlet (although McDonald's still holds the lead in revenues—at least for now).[9]

Here are some ways to look for minimization opportunities that can help your company no matter what business you are in:

- *Look for processes and procedures that generate waste.* Are raw materials, energy, water, or other physical resources being discarded or spoiled, or going unused? (If you don't know, you should. Creating a program to measure, monitor, and track your inputs and outputs in all these areas is an essential first step. One good way to start is simply to ask your employees to identify waste-saving opportunities.) What about the time, energy, and talent of your employees—are these being wasted? Chances are good that an operation that generates waste can be transformed into a source of savings for your company and move you toward the northeast corner of the sustainability map.
- *Look for areas of stakeholder concern.* Think of complaints or objections as gifts: they pinpoint areas where you must improve to meet your objectives or the needs of your stakeholders. So take persistent, good-faith complaints seriously, whether they come from employees, customers, suppliers, distributors, neighbors, community groups, or any other stakeholders. Identify the cause of the friction and reduce it to save your company or department time and money and to create other benefits in the form of goodwill, improved morale, and enhanced reputation.

- *Benchmark your company against others.* Investigate how your competitors are finding and reducing waste and compare your performance. You can often find out simply by visiting their websites or reading their TBL reports. Companies tend not to view minimization as a core part of what they do and therefore are relatively free with this information—even when it offers a competitive edge.

Even in the "obvious" form of waste reduction, minimization can be challenging. Some forms of saving produce unintended consequences that largely offset the benefits you expected to gain. For example, environmentalists have long extolled the virtues of "de-materializing" (digitizing) the vast amounts of data that businesses and individuals use. It's true, of course, that storing documents, photos, music, movies, and other types of information on the Internet rather than in physical form saves enormous paper, plastic, storage, and shipping costs. But experts are now reporting that the vast data centers used to maintain "the cloud" and the many customer-facing companies that rely on it—Google, Facebook, Amazon, Twitter, and countless others—have become gigantic sources of energy waste.

"A single data center can take more power than a medium-sized town," says Peter Gross, who has helped design such centers—and at last count, there are more than three million data centers in operation worldwide. Most disturbing of all, these centers may waste up to 90 percent of the electricity they use, due to "overbuilding" by engineers who design the facilities to withstand rare, sudden surges in demand.[10]

It's obvious that Internet storage of data, and the physical facilities it relies on, are here to stay. Technology experts are now developing new designs that will help reduce the energy waste involved. But the moral of the story is clear: minimization is not a one-time-only step. It demands continual analysis and reinvention to make sure that the steps you took to improve your performance yesterday are still working as planned today—and to replace them with even better changes tomorrow.

Life-Cycle Assessment: Perfecting Business Processes

The ultimate in minimization strategy might be captured in the term *life-cycle assessment*. This is an approach that emphasizes *business as process*, examining all the activities that surround the design, production, consumption, servicing, and disposal or recycling of any good in search of ways to improve the efficiency of the flow of value from the beginning of the process through its conclusion. The goal is to reduce the use of all resources by adhering to the following five principles:

1. *Understand the value created by each product.* Identify with precision the real sources of benefit to consumers and others that are provided by any good your company offers (as opposed to physical materials or human services that do not actually contribute to value but merely deplete it).

2. *Identify the value stream for each product.* Study your company's processes to determine which activities are contributing to real value and which are depleting it, and the relative efficiency with which value is created at every stage in the life cycle.

3. *Make value flow without interruptions.* Organize all your business processes to reduce waste of time, money, energy, and other resources.

4. *Encourage customers to pull value through the entire system.* Use modern techniques of communication and information sharing so that the process of creating value can be driven by actual customer needs rather than by arbitrary schedules.

5. *Pursue perfection at every stage.* Constantly examine, redesign, and reexamine each step in the life cycle of any product or service in search of incremental improvements in efficiency as well as larger conceptual leaps that can eliminate entire processes along with the associated costs and waste.

The principles behind life-cycle assessment may sound simple, even obvious. But if each principle is applied in the broadest and most detailed way possible, the result is a complex analysis of the total operations of the company that is likely to yield (literally) *thousands* of opportunities to improve efficiency, trim costs, reduce waste, clean the environment, and further enrich all the company's stakeholders.

The auto industry was a progenitor of life-cycle thinking. From the 1930s through the 1970s, Japanese automaker Toyota experimented with production techniques designed to reduce or eliminate *muda*—a Japanese word that translates as "waste" but that includes, more broadly, "any human activity which absorbs resources but creates no value."[11]

Even after decades of development, however, life-cycle thinking in the car business is still in need of new breakthroughs. The rapidly industrializing nations of China and India are becoming the world's fastest-growing markets for automobiles. Bringing the mobility and convenience of driving to hundreds of millions of new consumers in Asia is an exciting prospect (and a fantastic business opportunity for the world's automakers). But it's also a daunting economic and environmental challenge. Where will the world get the energy to move all those new cars—to say nothing of the metal, glass, plastic, and other materials needed to manufacture them and the landfill space to dispose of them?

The smartest, most strategic way for the auto industry to respond to this planet-altering challenge is to figure out how to design and make cars that are inexpensive to manufacture and operate, produce little or no pollution, maximize the use of renewable resources, and can be completely recycled—in other words, twenty-first-century cars that *create* value (for manufacturers, resellers, consumers, and the general public) at every stage in their life cycle rather than waste value as today's expensive, polluting, gas-guzzling, dump-filling cars generally do.

This may sound utopian. But a number of companies are already pursuing this goal. One example is Sony, whose Green Management 2015 program we'll describe in Chapter Ten. A number of companies in the Japanese automotive industry are deeply involved in life-cycle assessment, not only creating hybrid cars, which enhance the efficiency of energy use when driving, but also creating cars from recycled materials, a business in which Japanese firms see both profit potential and environmental benefits for years to come. Every year, Nippon PGM Company, a subsidiary of the metal refiner Dowa Mining Company, collects the equivalent of about $130 million's worth of rare metals, such as platinum and palladium, from used automobile mufflers, which they sell back to the auto industry. Dowa is also the global leader in recycling of indium, a metal used in liquid crystal displays. Thanks to growing demand from the Chinese auto and electronic appliances industries, the price of indium has increased tenfold in recent years, making Dowa's recapturing of this metal extremely profitable—a classic illustration of improved value flow that benefits everyone.

Japanese government officials, who have long been involved in shaping and guiding national industry, see companies like Dowa as harbingers of the future direction of Japanese business. "If we make recycling a global industry, Japan could turn into a resource-rich country," says one such official.[12]

From Minimization to Optimization: The Sustainable Path to New Profits, New Products, and New Markets

As we've explained, optimization goes beyond minimization. Moving from minimization to optimization can pay rich rewards. What begins for many companies as an attempt to minimize a problem may gradually evolve into an effort to optimize by creating new and valuable solutions.

The so-called brownfields movement in the United States is a fascinating example of a phenomenon that began as minimization and evolved into optimization.[13]

During the 1980s, an estimated 450,000 despoiled and abandoned industrial locations around the United States were identified, assessed, and slated for cleanup under the federal Superfund program or similar state-based schemes. These toxic sites, usually in urban areas and often near rivers and other environmentally sensitive areas, became a nightmare for governments, businesses, and the communities in which they were located. Total estimated cleanup costs for the corporations held responsible ran into the *trillions* of dollars.

The Superfund law created unintended results. The high costs of cleaning the sites and the draconian legal liability for anyone who owned one caused developers to run at the first sign of contamination. So polluted sites, "brownfields," languished while developers rushed to pave "greenfields"—tracts of untouched land in outlying areas—ironically exacerbating problems of congestion and pollution, and contributing to unsightly exurban sprawl.

That was not what environmentalists had intended when they lobbied for the Superfund program. "We would prefer to have development occur in cities where infrastructure already exists . . . because it helps to protect green spaces, which we would like to retain as green spaces," explained Ed Hopkins, director of the Sierra Club.[14]

Seeking a solution, environmentalists began to work in concert with real estate and business lobbyists to push for changes that would relax the liabilities of brownfield owners, offer tax breaks to make developing brownfields more profitable, and create environmental insurance that would help pay for the cleanups.

As these reforms were enacted, the minimization approach to brownfields gave way to optimization. Polluted tracts once seen as huge headaches to be avoided were now sought after as sites for office buildings, supermarkets, housing developments, and parks. As the movement has flourished, over $14 billion has been invested by public and private enterprises in brownfield cleanup and development, creating some sixty thousand new jobs. As a result, thousands of communities are gaining new economic and environmental life.

Jacoby Development Company, an Atlanta-based builder that focuses almost exclusively on brownfield sites, is codeveloper of Atlantic Station, a $2 billion project located on the heavily polluted 138-acre site of an old steel mill near Atlanta. Atlantic Station includes millions of feet of office, retail, and entertainment space, including the first Leadership in Energy and Environmental Design

(LEED)–certified high-rise office building in Georgia; eleven acres of public parks; and rental apartments, condos, and hotel rooms.

By evolving from minimization to optimization, the brownfields movement has created an enormous sweet spot into which builders, businesses, and communities have rushed. Developers are cleaning the environment, saving greenfields, moving abandoned properties back onto the tax rolls, and helping create economic development in depressed areas, making millions of dollars in the process.

DuPont has leveraged technology and marketing to move beyond minimization toward optimization. DuPont's "Safety, Health, & Environmental Commitment," formally launched in 1994, outlines several specific targets, most of them clearly linked to minimization:

- Zero injuries, illnesses, and incidents
- Zero waste and emissions
- Conservation of energy and natural resources, and habitat enhancements

Yet as the concept of sustainability has permeated DuPont's culture over the past two decades, the company has moved toward more ambitious optimization goals.

For example, DuPont paints cars for Ford at an assembly plant in Oakville, Ontario.[15] By altering its contract with Ford so as to get paid based on the number of cars painted rather than on the quantity of paint used, DuPont realigned its goals with those of its customer while creating a financial incentive for its workforce to operate more efficiently. As a result of the change, hydrocarbon emissions from the plant have dropped by 50 percent.

Optimization was just a short step away. DuPont actively seeks new product lines and markets that do not rely on unsustainable processes or nonrenewable resources—investing, for example, in agribusinesses that specialize in seed, soy protein, and crop protection products as well as in West African research aimed at developing new and safer insecticides for use in cotton growing. DuPont has also developed a technique for manufacturing a critical ingredient for a polyester-like polymer using a fermentation process based on renewable corn sugar rather than petrochemicals.

Thus minimization and the new mind-set it fosters are leading naturally toward optimization, through both promising new products and more efficient processes.

Optimization can also be about discovering or creating new markets. Unilever's effort to sell low-cost products in the developing world is one example. But similar discoveries are waiting to be made even in supposedly mature markets, such as the United States. Some of the fastest-growing American companies of recent years offer examples, including Netflix (which has drastically reduced the volume of resources used in home movie viewing by transitioning its millions of members to video streaming) and Zipcar (the car-sharing company that allows city dwellers to enjoy the benefits of auto use without having to own and maintain their own vehicles) illustrate this reality.

Here are some insights to consider when your company is ready to pursue the benefits of optimization:

- *Push minimization efforts toward optimization.* When you focus time, energy, and creativity on new ways to reduce your company's footprint (whether in environmental, social, or economic terms), the process of innovation that is unleashed is likely to stimulate ideas that can lead to increased productivity, improved efficiency, and other breakthroughs.
- *Look for new product and service ideas that grow out of your sustainability efforts.* Follow the examples of DuPont and of GE's ecomagination, which are building new businesses and expanding old ones based on innovative ideas developed in the course of pursuing minimization or optimization strategies.
- *Look for new markets that are "hidden in plain sight," in the margins of the more obvious, traditional markets.* The developing markets of Asia, Africa, and Latin America offer surprising opportunities, as companies are demonstrating. But underserved markets can be identified even in the developed world, as

illustrated by the large market for low-cost health insurance in the United States. Discovering such markets can be the outgrowth of an optimization strategy that starts by identifying social and economic needs that are going unmet, then seeks to develop a business strategy to address those needs profitably.

Optimization is a powerful form of sustainability jiu-jitsu— transforming a problem into a solution by looking for the hidden opportunity. Today's most successful companies are shifting from defense to offense on sustainability, moving from "How can we minimize an environmental, social, or economic problem?" to "How can we re-engineer our product design or process to create more benefit for the world (and for us)?" That shift in thinking will represent the difference between success and failure for an increasing number of companies in the decades to come.

10

Implementing Your Sustainability Program

Begin somewhere. You cannot build a reputation on what you intend to do.
—Liz Smith, syndicated newspaper columnist

Making Sustainability Operational: Goals, Processes, and Key Performance Indicators

No matter how you decide to integrate sustainability into your business strategy, you'll eventually want to develop a management system for your efforts. This will make it much easier for you to implement your strategy, leverage your efforts, give them visibility, measure the results, and hold yourself accountable. Such a program can take several different forms. You may decide to create a formal sustainability department, appoint a senior leader, or operate a network of committed managers on an ad hoc basis—a structure we refer to as the *virtual sustainability department*.

Regardless of which way you choose to go, it will be helpful to incorporate certain foundational program elements. These include specific goals to which you are committed, defined processes to help you achieve those goals, and key performance indicators (KPIs) that will allow you to measure your progress toward the goals.

Your ultimate objective should be to incorporate a sustainability mind-set into the operational decisions being made daily by all your employees. Not that sustainability will be the deciding factor in every decision, but the economic, environmental, and social dimensions should always be considered, just as return on investment, strategic fit, and resource constraints are considered in every important business decision.

Setting Goals

You'll need to define clear and specific goals for your sustainability program or project, both to establish what you're trying to accomplish and to make it possible to measure whether you're getting there. In theory, goals should be defined with reference to your strategy. However, in the real world, you may simply be handed a goal, or you will choose one that seems to fit with where you are already headed.

One easy way to get some traction on sustainability is to consider how TBL objectives can be built into your existing business goals. For example, suppose a particular business unit has a cost-reduction goal. An energy conservation or employee retention program would further that goal. Suppose your goal is a defined increase in customer satisfaction. Perhaps you can assist your customers with health and safety issues or waste disposal costs related to your product. Or find a way to use sustainability to create more employee motivation, which is a demonstrated way to increase customer satisfaction.

For the CFO at Hershey Foods, a business goal for 2002 was evidently to sell the company so as to maximize the return to shareholders. A highly compatible social goal would have been to manage the sale in a way that would have been minimally disruptive or even advantageous to employees and to the town of Hershey. Had that objective been established and the appropriate actions taken in regard to employees and the community, the sale might have had a better chance of success.

Establishing Procedures and Key Performance Indicators

To reach your goals, you'll need procedures and KPIs that define them in clear, practical terms. How, for example, do you implement the goal of "no child labor" when many countries define that phrase in different ways? Without specific, clearly defined plans, this goal is almost meaningless and even dangerous, as you are bound to encounter situations you are not prepared to handle. PepsiCo addressed the issue by setting its own global minimum working age standard—fifteen years old—which was easy to understand and simple to enforce, avoiding entanglement in a host of local ordinances and exceptions.

Developing sustainability policies and procedures is sometimes fairly straightforward. Health and safety experts are skilled at writing procedures designed to reduce accidents, for example. But developing procedures for certain complex areas of sustainability requires a wide range of talents, backgrounds, and skills. A plan for reducing needless packaging, for instance, may require input from experts in design, manufacturing, materials science, marketing, customer service, warehousing, shipping, retailing, finance, and perhaps other fields.

As we suggested for goals, try to integrate new requirements into existing ones. Amend your human resources policies and procedures to address child labor issues; amend your standard contracting language to require suppliers to avoid child labor; and rewrite the job descriptions for all relevant personnel to make it clear that avoiding the use of child workers (as well as other inappropriate labor practices) is a core obligation.

If you must develop entirely new procedures, test their workability before you roll them out. Identify the key stakeholders and involve them in developing or reviewing the policy. Try implementing procedures on a pilot basis to work out the kinks in advance.

KPIs are critical tools that can, like the gauges on a car's dashboard, help you determine whether you're likely to reach your destination.

Successful companies often use *leading indicators* to measure their progress. For example, energy companies hold safety training sessions prior to any dangerous job. These have proved to be effective in reducing accidents, but they are often skipped or shortened by impatient workers. So a leading indicator of workplace safety might be the percentage of times the safety sessions are successfully carried out. *Lagging indicators*, in contrast, tell you about what has already happened. Money spent on workers' compensation claims would be a lagging indicator of safety.

Many books have been written about how to establish sustainability goals, procedures, and KPIs. And the topic of defining sustainability metrics for reporting purposes is one we'll address in more detail in Chapter Thirteen. But here we want to stress a few overarching points:

- *Establish goals that further the primary objectives of your business.* For a commercial bank, for example, conducting robust due diligence on the community or environmental impacts of its loans would be a far more significant sustainability goal than reducing water and waste or recycling paper.
- *Strive for simplicity.* Keep the number of goals small and mutually reinforcing. Reducing water use and eliminating your pollution of the river near your factory, for example, may be mutually reinforcing goals, as both might involve redesigning processes to minimize the flow of water through the plant. But such goals as eliminating worker accidents, reducing carbon emissions, and simplifying product packaging have little tendency to support one another. Consider tackling these one at a time, in order of priority, rather than simultaneously.
- *Make sure the goals are clear and understandable.* A goal like "no child labor" is too vague. You need to determine specific age limits; decide whether to make exceptions for part-time, after-school, volunteer, or summer employment, for student interns, or for children who are supporting others; define how far down your supply chain the rule will apply; decide what to do about local laws or customs that conflict with your policies; and determine how you'll monitor and enforce the program and how you'll handle violations.
- *Integrate goals with goals, procedures with procedures, and KPIs with KPIs.* If your operation already has existing goals, procedures, and KPIs, look to add environmental or social aspects to them. Rather than crafting a separate set of environmental procedures for a plant, for example, incorporate environmental procedures into the general operating manual wherever possible.

- *Develop clear, consistent definitions of every term and measurement unit included in your goals, procedures, and KPIs.* Don't assume that employees in different departments or locations around the world use the same words to mean the same thing.
- *Strive to define every goal and KPI in numerical terms.* Qualitative goals are inherently subjective and therefore almost impossible to verify. Only when your progress is quantifiable can you guarantee that everyone will understand and accept the validity of your analysis, results, and self-assessment.

Getting Organized

By now we hope you have a good understanding of how sustainability might affect your job and of how to get started within your own department or domain. Launching a company's sustainability efforts with a program inside a particular department or division can be highly effective, as we saw with pollution prevention at 3M. But most companies eventually look to expand those efforts and integrate them throughout the organization because of the enormous power of these ideas at the strategic level. In the pages that follow, we'll offer some advice and ideas about which individuals, groups, departments, or teams within the company are typically best positioned to tackle company-wide sustainability challenges.

Because of the wide range and interdisciplinary nature of activities that fall under the rubric of sustainability, many companies start by creating a *task force or steering committee* to define and drive their efforts. A task force includes operational managers, key department heads and divisional representatives, and other people with the power and responsibility to determine how to structure and define the effort and move it forward on a permanent basis. It also includes, or has direct access to, technical experts such as environmental or supply chain specialists.

An alternative or supplement to the task force may be to establish one or more positions within the organization that are charged with pushing the program forward. The individuals in these positions serve as *sustainability champions*. They are generally executives who are personally committed to sustainability and have the knowledge, clout, and credibility necessary to make the effort meaningful and to attract the attention and support of others in the company.

In some companies, the champion's role is played by the CEO. Chad Holliday, CEO and chairman of DuPont from 1998 to 2009, had chaired the World Business Council for Sustainable Development and written books and articles on the subject. His personal commitment to sustainability was unmistakable, and his accession to the role of CEO sent a message to the rest of the organization that no one could ignore. As of 2013, current CEOs like Jeff Immelt of GE, PepsiCo's Indra Nooyi, John Mackey of Whole Foods, and Patagonia's Yves Chouinard are playing comparable roles as highly visible advocates for sustainability.

Among other functions, the sustainability champion

- Organizes staff support, technical resources, and information on sustainability for the rest of the organization
- Facilitates and encourages communication among the various parts of the corporation around sustainability, so that innovations and solutions developed in one division are quickly spread to others
- Oversees and drives company-wide systems for measuring, reporting, and incentivizing sustainability efforts, so that there is uniformity and fairness in all these systems
- Represents or supports the organization in its dealings with other companies, the government, and the various stakeholder communities where broad sustainability issues are concerned

Under its former CEO Travis Engen (2001–2006), Alcan, the aluminum company giant, used multiple champions. Engen personally championed sustainability at the top, working with a director of sustainability and the head of corporate communications, whose efforts were aided by champions within each of Alcan's business units. Today, Microsoft has a formal Sustainability Champions program that includes 650 employees across a wide range of business units. These volunteers serve as sustainability role models, advocates, and trainers, helping strengthen the company's efforts in environmental areas ranging from energy consumption to waste reduction.[1]

A formal *sustainability department* can be an important resource for managers throughout the company, offering expertise, resources, connections, and coordination, and many companies now have such departments. But locating sustainability in its own department risks isolating it as an "add-on" to core business processes. Staffers in a sustainability department often end up fighting uphill battles with production managers, R&D departments, financial officers, and HR personnel who speak different languages, have different objectives, and see the organization and the world from different points of view. Trapped in "sustainability land," they spend most of their time figuring out how to build bridges to other people in the organization.

For this reason, we recommend a sustainability department only as a transitional step. Its role should be to help spread the values and concepts of sustainability throughout the rest of the organization, provide the needed tools and expertise, and then, eventually, go out of business.

The Virtual Sustainability Department

For many companies, the ideal solution to the structural dilemma may be to create a *virtual sustainability department*. This means linking together many employees from various departments to share ideas, insights, and tools related to sustainability. It also involves authorizing managers to seek additional support from outside sources—consultants, NGOs, business partners, suppliers, customers, and others who can contribute to the effort.

We call this a *virtual* department for several reasons. First of all, it's not a department in the traditional sense. It doesn't appear on any corporate organizational chart, it controls no budgets, and there are no employees assigned to work full-time for it. Second, the people who participate are often linked electronically, using all the communication means at their disposal—from email and texting to blogs, wikis, internal and external websites, and social media—to share ideas around sustainability. Third, this virtual department is in constant flux. New people are continually joining the network while others are dropping out (at least for a time) as projects begin and end.

The notion of the virtual sustainability department puts a high premium on networking inside and outside the company, so knowledge management methodologies, especially in a global organization, can be either a big stumbling block or a powerful lever. At DuPont, for example, engineers report wasting hours looking for environmental data or key regulations needed before they can make a decision that takes just thirty seconds once the information is available. And in the early stages of "going sustainable," the challenges can be especially acute.

Technology designed to support and facilitate collaboration among far-flung individuals can be enormously helpful here. There are software search programs that can scan people's emails to find a particular word or phrase—let's say *carbon* or *climate change*—to identify who in the company knows about a certain topic, making it possible to communicate quickly and easily with everyone in the company who is concerned about a given issue. Other programs facilitate interchange of information using social networking groups organized by topic or area of interest or expertise. Online calendars and systems designed to manage knowledge sharing and project flows can also be helpful.

How do you launch a virtual sustainability department? How does it operate? Here are some ideas.

- *Start with existing personal networks.* To identify those who ought to be included in the department, get together with two or three key people who have already indicated their interest in and commitment to the concept of TBL-based management. Then spend time brainstorming the names of people from throughout the organization who ought to be invited to participate. Think about whom you know in R&D, marketing, operations, HR, finance, and other departments who may be interested in sustainability and may have needed resources or expertise within your enterprise.

- *Survey the organization.* Augment your list of names with a general survey of the organization. Send out an email soliciting interest. Specify the key areas of focus (pollution reduction, improved worker safety, ethical management of the supply chain, sustainable package design, electronic waste, and so on) and ask employees to indicate their areas of interest and relevant background. Keep your questions brief; if it takes longer than five minutes to reply, the response rate will plummet.

- *Strive for every kind of diversity.* When drawing up your final invitation list, strive to make it reflect the diversity of the company—not just in demographic terms (gender, age, ethnicity, sexual orientation, politics) but also in business and professional terms. Be sure to include both line and staff employees, company veterans and relative newcomers, technical experts and communications specialists, "numbers" people and "people" people. Consider the various resources you might need, and try to engage at least one person who can help deliver each kind. If possible, strive to ensure that every major area of your business—in terms of geography, product line, target market, and profit center—is represented.

- *Put someone in charge.* Someone must accept responsibility for monitoring, guiding, stimulating, and controlling the activities of the department. If possible, work with senior management to write this task into the person's job description, include it in any annual list of objectives and incentives, and give it a significant chunk of assigned time (50 percent or more).

- *Use technology to facilitate your virtual community.* One of the key roles of the virtual sustainability department will be to provide a forum in which employees can address questions, challenges, problems, and opportunities; share ideas; and raise concerns. Work with your company's Web or communications team to create knowledge management systems to facilitate the kind of interaction you need. At PepsiCo, the communications department has set up an electronic bulletin board and e-room devoted to CSR; it facilitates internal communication and helps further the sustainability education and involvement of key managers. The department also produces electronic presentations on specific topics that are housed on a website and can be used by managers throughout the company for discussion and brainstorming with their employees.

- *Have periodic face-to-face meetings.* Electronic communication should be supplemented with live communication. Some topics can't be discussed in sufficient depth via email or blog, and communication is often livelier in the context of an informal get-together or structured workshop. These meetings needn't be elaborate or very frequent; they might be scheduled once a quarter or twice a year, and might vary in length from half a day to a full day. If you can meet off-campus in a convenient hotel or other conference setting, so much the better; this helps reduce the chance that people will be called away to put out fires or attend other meetings.

- *Reach beyond your company when appropriate.* Stay in touch with the people in your organization who track and respond to media and social network coverage of your company; you can help them deal with TBL issues as they arise. In today's socially networked world, it's easy to reach beyond the four walls of your company to explore shared sweet spots. For example, Hewlett Packard's sustainability and social innovation group is a small team of full-time employees that leads a larger virtual team of internal and external volunteers who work together on a variety of environmental, social, and education projects, collaborating with such organizations as the nonprofit Mothers2Mothers on programs aimed at eliminating pediatric AIDS.

- *Publicize your results.* On a regular basis, spread the word throughout the company about what you've achieved. (This is especially important when the department is virtual, as it doesn't appear on the traditional organization charts and may therefore be overlooked in the usual internal reports.) You can use existing communications media (the company newsletter or weekly email bulletin) or create a new venue of your own. Share bad news as well as good. Your credibility within the company will be enormously enhanced if you announce, "Last year, we fell short of our goal to reduce greenhouse gases associated with driving to work. Here are the details, as well as our plans to reverse the trend next year." If your company issues a sustainability report, make sure your activities are included.

- *Refresh the team as needed.* Like any working group, the virtual sustainability department will need fresh blood from time to time. Be on the lookout for new employees to add to the team, and when necessary retire others whose interest has waned or whose job descriptions have changed.

Whether you end up using a task force, champion, multiple champions, a virtual or real sustainability department, an existing department, or some other organizational model, expect to reexamine your program at least once a year. Determine what's working and what isn't, and make adjustments as needed. Like other business issues, the sustainability challenge continually evolves, and your organization must evolve with it.

Integrating Sustainability into Every Department

In the long run, integrating sustainability into every aspect of your company's operations is the only way to go. Like quality, sustainability must be built in, not added on. You can consider sustainability to be the domain of a handful of experts, but educating your operating managers about sustainability and letting them apply this knowledge to their own goals and strategies—a "train the trainer" approach—will be far more effective.

For some corporate departments, the applicability of sustainability thinking may seem obvious: for example, manufacturing, facilities management, and shipping will naturally face questions about waste management, water consumption, energy use, and other environmental issues. Managers responsible for contracting with suppliers are beginning to understand how they might be held responsible if those suppliers turn out to be socially irresponsible—abusing workers, operating unsafe facilities, or polluting the environment, for example.

But as we saw in Chapter Four, the challenges and opportunities associated with sustainability, on both the environmental and social fronts, are diverse and complex enough to affect *every* department of most organizations. Sustainability is not a specialization—it's a basic requirement for most jobs in the company. Eventually, every aspect of your business needs to be managed with sustainability in mind.

Some of today's best-run companies are striving to achieve that kind of integrated sustainability. Consumer electronics giants Sony has been pursuing this goal for at least a decade. Under Sony's pioneering Green Management 2005 program, employees from virtually every area of the corporation—R&D, procurement, product design, production, marketing, customer service, and many others—were required to integrate environmental objectives into their jobs. Each department was asked to contribute to corporation-wide environmental goals defined in specific, quantitative terms, and the job performance of managers was judged, in part, on their success in achieving those goals.[2]

Today, Sony has updated and expanded this program under the rubric Green Management 2015. The company has broken down its products' life cycles into six distinct stages—R&D, product planning and design, procurement, operation, logistics, and take-back and recycling—and established specific, detailed goals for improvement at each stage. The result is a demanding, ambitious set of expectations that apply to every one of Sony's production, management, research, marketing, sales, and service operations around the world.[3]

Sustainability and Human Resources

As we have discussed extensively in our book *Talent, Transformation, and the Triple Bottom Line*, HR often gets short shrift when sustainability is being discussed. Perhaps this is understandable, at least in

those companies that view HR primarily as a central service for transactions and compliance, with a minimal strategic role. HR staffers are
often charged with routine tasks: conducting job interviews, supervis-
ing payroll, administering benefits, and the like. HR leaders may or
may not have a seat at the table when vital strategic issues such as
sustainability are being considered.

This is unfortunate, and not only for integrating sustainability.
In today's knowledge economy, where human capital is more crucial
than ever, HR is at the front lines in your organization's battle for
talent. And the implications of sustainability for that battle for talent
are highly significant. Here are a few of them:

- *Sustainability begins with your own employees.* Many of the fundamental issues included in the Triple Bottom Line relate to
  how a company's employees are treated, such as fair labor practices, diversity in hiring and promotion, worker safety, decent
  working conditions, provision of health care and other benefits,
  and so on. Thus much of HR's traditional portfolio is directly
  related to sustainability—and the effectiveness with which it is
  managed will help determine how attractive the company is to
  talented workers.
- *Sustainability can serve as a talent magnet.* Sustainability is
  expected by many applicants and, for some organizations, has
  become an important element of the employer brand. Many
  younger workers, often grouped together as Generation Y or
  the Millennials, are concerned about the ways in which their
  employers handle environmental or social responsibility, and
  want to be part of organizations that share their values. Surveys
  show that many people place a company's reputation for social
  and environmental responsibility high on the list of factors that
  determine the attractiveness of a particular workplace. HR professionals need to understand this and must be able to highlight
  their company's sustainability commitments to attract these
  workers.
- *Sustainability alters traditional job requirements.* Sustainability
  demands new kinds of skills from workers at every level and

in every department. HR professionals need to educate hiring managers within the company to understand the array of technical and social skills involved in sustainability and to develop effective techniques for screening new hires for them.

- *Sustainable business strategies often have important HR implications.* A simple example is the company that invested in order to expand in a fundamentalist Islamic country but didn't anticipate the limitations around hiring and employing women. Or the business expanding into Asia that failed to recognize the existence of social norms that required consulting with the parents of job candidates before making hiring decisions. HR professionals need to be aware of these situations and need to be involved when business strategies are being developed that have crucial HR components.

- *Sustainability affects talent management processes.* The Age of Sustainability has important implications for policies and practices related to employee training, evaluation, incentivization, promotion, and discipline. If your organization is serious about its commitment to sustainability, that commitment must be reflected in every talent management policy. Otherwise, not only will your employees be unprepared to deal with evolving sustainability-related challenges, but your sustainability commitment will quickly be revealed as a dead letter, leading to cynicism on the part of your employees.

- *Sustainability increases employee engagement.* Studies have shown that companies with strong sustainability records not only attract better employees but also enjoy higher levels of worker loyalty, commitment, and motivation among those employees who are aware of these efforts. This leads, in turn, to increased productivity, higher levels of customer satisfaction, and greater profitability. HR professionals may want to serve as internal company advocates for sustainability in order to help the organization reap these talent-related benefits.

It's clear, then, that sustainability is already having a profound impact on the way companies recruit, hire, train, and develop employees—and that this impact is likely to increase in the years to come, as both the pressure to attract first-rate talent and the demands of sustainability continue to grow. No serious discussion about the future of your company is complete without some consideration of this vital nexus between sustainability and talent. It's a topic that calls for the thoughtful involvement of HR leaders as well as every other manager with a role in leading and motivating employees.

11

Managing Stakeholder Engagement

To understand what's going on, you have to get in a conversation with the people trying to put you out of business.
—Edward Shultz, former CEO, Smith & Wesson Holding Company[1]

Why Stakeholder Engagement Is Essential

As we've seen, the world in which we live today is more complexly interconnected than ever before. It's a world in which a growing array of individuals, interest groups, and organizations view themselves as having a legitimate stake in how you operate and a right to influence your decisions. Challenging? Yes—even scary. But stakeholders are here to stay and growing more powerful all the time.

The expanding importance of stakeholders is perhaps the single most important element in what we have called the Age of Sustainability. In fact, it's possible to examine most or all of the crucial sustainability issues you and your company will face in terms of stakeholder relationships. In most cases, the problems and opportunities you'll encounter in connection with your firm's economic, social, and environmental performance will land in your inbox because they reflect the interests and concerns of stakeholders. And as we'll see, both solving the problems and maximizing the opportunities will require communicating with and working with your stakeholders. Hence the description of sustainability that we proposed in the Introduction—a description that's not complete but, we think, quite useful: the art of doing business in an interdependent world.

Sustainability requires a detailed understanding of your interdependence in relation to those with whom you interact—whether as a company, a department, a plant, or an individual manager. It means embracing and partnering with your stakeholders rather than assuming that they are adversaries to be defeated, skeptics to be lectured to, or, at best, temporary allies to be held at arm's length. Only by making stakeholder engagement a systematic and permanent element of your management style can you hope to shepherd all the resources you and your company depend on—environmental, social, and economic—to achieve lasting success in today's interdependent world.

Stakeholders Have a Vote on Your Future

The notion that you must partner with your stakeholders may seem counterintuitive at first. Many companies maintain a distant, if not outright antagonistic, relationship with nonbusiness stakeholder groups, such as environmentalists, community organizers, social justice advocates, and shareholder activists seeking changes in corporate governance. Traditionally, these external stakeholders have been kept outside the tent. Why should business leaders and managers want to invite them in now?

The reasons may be obvious in some cases. Many stakeholders have ways to influence your decisions. In some cases, they have a direct vote: shareholders aligned with activist groups have been increasingly successful at forcing proxy votes on social and environmental issues. Outside the corporate structure, citizens in the city, state, or nation where you operate can vote for or against your company indirectly by electing or defeating government officials who are friendly to your company's interests, or otherwise seeking to influence the kinds of regulations, tax policies, and labor and environmental rules with which you must deal.

In many cases, the indirect impact of social activism on companies is significantly greatly than the direct impact. Thus, the Occupy protesters who staged demonstrations against the major banks and other financial institutions during 2011–2012 may have failed to persuade any CEO to change a single policy. But by focusing the attention of politicians and agency heads on public outrage over financial malfeasance—and perhaps by facilitating the election of sympathetic legislators like U.S. Senator Elizabeth Warren (D-MA)—they may end up winning a number of belated victories on the regulatory front.

Other stakeholders wield different forms of influence over your future. Customers can vote with their wallets by choosing to shop elsewhere when they are offended or by flocking to patronize you when they consider you supportive of their values. Activist groups can orchestrate rallies, organize boycotts, or mount Facebook and Twitter campaigns for or against you. Employees can stage walkouts or simply stop working very hard when they are disgruntled, or provide unusual levels of positive energy, creativity, and enthusiasm when they feel proud and supportive. Nowadays, many people and groups have a vote in how your business is run—and they are increasingly eager to use that vote to hinder or help you.

Stakeholders can make a real difference in your company's freedom to operate. Therefore, it's smart business to recognize their power and manage with their interests in mind. Thus the giant retailer Wal-Mart has been reaching out to environmentalists, women's rights' advocates, nutrition experts, anti-poverty groups, community organizers, NGO leaders, and others whom it previously scorned. Realizing that the attitudes of these stakeholders will influence the company's growth prospects in the future, Wal-Mart has launched expensive image-boosting advertising campaigns and created a communications "war room" to present its side of the controversies in which it periodically becomes embroiled.

But partnering with stakeholders involves more than press releases, advertisements, charitable donations, and aggressive media tactics, as Wal-Mart discovered when the global scandal surrounding its apparent use of bribery to win favorable treatment from local officials undermined the company's efforts to burnish its image. The true spirit of partnership requires trust, which in turn requires being transparent about activities that are of material interest to your stakeholders. Examples are cropping up all over the business world. Here is one.

In the rain forests of Borneo in Indonesia, logging has long been controversial. Teak and other exotic hardwoods flourish there, and the profits from harvesting them are important to the local population. But logging, like other so-called extractive industries, can be environmentally and economically destructive. Timber companies concerned more about immediate profits than about long-term growth sometimes wipe out vast stands of trees so ruthlessly that regrowth is almost impossible. Once the companies move out, they leave behind thousands of suddenly unemployed local workers and an environment denuded of the plant and animal species that once were the lifeblood of the region.[2] (As geographer and biologist Jared Diamond has documented in his best-selling book *Collapse*, deforestation has been a major factor in the economic and social downfall of a number of advanced human civilizations.)[3]

By 2003, according to an estimate from the World Resources Institute, between 73 percent and 88 percent of Indonesian timber was being harvested illegally—which means without environmental controls or socially responsible management.[4] As a result, such environmental groups as the Rainforest Action Network and Greenpeace International called for a boycott of Indonesian timber.

In response, a consortium of Asian logging companies set to work with a wide-ranging coalition of partners to establish a sustainable Indonesian logging initiative. The largest of the logging firms was Sumalindo Lestari Jaya, owned by the Hasko Group, a big Indonesian corporation. Sumalindo had been battling with the indigenous Dayak people over claims that the company had been damaging the Dayak's ancestral forest holdings, destroying cemeteries, and blocking waterways crucial to the local economy. In an effort to save its business, Sumalindo joined forces with stakeholder groups that included local village leaders; the Nature Conservancy, a Virginia-based environmental organization; and a group of major retailers of wood and wood-based products, such as Ikea and Home Depot, whose customers had been urging them to buy lumber only from sustainable sources.

The Nature Conservancy worked with Sumalindo and the Dayak people to develop mutual trust and helped negotiate a series of agreements designed to protect the interests of all sides—including the long-term viability of the forest and of the lives, human and otherwise, dependent on it. Local villagers now participate in mapping the forest, defining specific areas known as high-conservation-value forests that are off-limits to logging, and monitoring Sumalindo's activities to ensure that violations don't occur. In return, the villagers agree to abide by a complementary set of environmental rules—for example, to refrain from hunting endangered species or to use dangerous substances (such as explosives and poison) in fishing. Monthly meetings are held between the villagers and representatives of Sumalindo to raise and resolve issues.

Sumalindo employees have also received training from Nature Conservancy experts in reduced-impact logging practices. These include an inventory of forests to identify the most valuable trees so that roads can be designed that minimize forest damage while maximizing the value of the harvest; trimming vines that link tree-tops to prevent felled trees from pulling down their neighbors; and directional felling, which reduces the impact of one tree's fall on the surrounding forest.

As a result, much of Sumalindo's wood production has earned certification by the German-based Forest Stewardship Council, an influential player on the world environmental scene. Such certification opens the way for more teak and other woods produced by Sumalindo to flow freely into world markets, benefiting both the loggers and the people of Borneo, who share in the profits.[5]

This story beautifully illustrates the concept of sustainability in its original, environmental meaning: sustainable logging will help prolong the life of the forest and enhance the natural inheritance of future generations. But the partnership between Sumalindo and a range of stakeholders—from local villagers to environmental experts to the corporations that manufacture products using Indonesian wood—also illustrates how sustainable management improves a company's prospects for long-term success. Partnering with stakeholders to develop a viable, environmentally sound system of logging has enabled Sumalindo to reestablish its business on a secure footing, with the potential of being profitable (as well as politically and socially acceptable) for decades to come.

As the Sumalindo example demonstrates, the sustainable business seeks to engender trust and a true spirit of partnership with a wide range of stakeholders, including those who may seem to have little direct power over its operations.

Seeing Through Your Stakeholders' Eyes

Taking a fresh view of yourself and your company is one of the many concrete benefits you can derive from stakeholder engagement—provided that you enjoy *real* rather than sham engagement. It's not about *pretending* to listen to your stakeholders, holding occasional conversations with a couple of the more tractable activists who follow your industry, making a donation or two to a worthy cause, and issuing press releases to claim credit. It starts with *active, empathic* listening: trying to understand and accept the viewpoint of even your worst enemies and experiencing your business as they do. This is a difficult challenge.

One of the hardest aspects of accepting your opponents' point of view is bearing with a degree of tunnel vision on their part. Many advocacy groups feel that they are trying to save the world, and they view their favored issue as being of paramount importance to that salvation. This often leads to a narrow viewpoint that can be hard to appreciate or fully understand—and an unwillingness on their part to recognize the legitimacy of your opposing point of view. Furthermore, no matter how closely outsiders track your company or your industry, they almost never know the details as well as you do from an insider's perspective. So some of the criticisms you'll hear from stakeholders will strike you as uninformed and unfair. You'll find yourself saying (or at least thinking) things like these:

- "I can't believe they're still attacking *us* for that environmental damage. That mess was made by prior management, and we've been working hard to set it right." (Mistaken assumption:

that you get the benefit of the doubt because you're new management. In reality, activist stakeholders don't care; you are still the polluting corporation.)

- "Give me a break. What does the lack of human rights in the developing world have to do with us? It's not right, surely, but we haven't caused or contributed to it. We do business in many of those places, and we give our employees there the same benefits as we give anywhere. What else does the world expect?" (Mistaken assumption: that your business interest begins and ends with your employees and does not extend to their families, your customers, and the communities in which you operate—and that you have no share in the responsibility for helping fix the most serious problems these stakeholders may be facing.)
- "Sure, our company's health and safety record isn't great. But it's better than it was last year and the year before that. Don't we get any credit for improvement?" (Mistaken assumption: that you should get an A for progress. In sustainability as in other fields, only excellence earns an A from an outsider. And if other companies, especially your competitors, achieve at higher levels, why can't you?)
- "So the Internet is reporting that workers at a factory run by one of our suppliers have been committing suicide at work. We have a code of conduct our suppliers are supposed to follow; we can't control them, and we're one of their smallest customers anyhow." (Mistaken assumption: that your suppliers and vendors are separate from you and that it's OK if they operate according to different standards. In fact, your suppliers work for you, no matter how much of their business you account for; they depend for their livelihood on meeting numerous requirements that you impose—regarding quality of goods, timeliness of delivery, price, and so on. You can also enforce strict requirements on labor policies—and you're likely to be held responsible if you fail to do so.)

Your from-the-gut responses to criticisms like these may be fair, reasonable, and justified. And when you engage with NGOs, community groups, government agencies, and other stakeholders, you should always present your side of the issues frankly and nondefensively, just as Scott Hall did on behalf of PPL when debating the future of the Penobscot River. You may even receive an understanding reception, just as Hall did.

But you may not. Most stakeholders have a view of the world that is different from yours. Your stockholders and investors don't agree with you all the time, so it's unrealistic to expect your nonfinancial stakeholders to do so.

And even when environmentalists, labor activists, and community groups understand and sympathize with your point of view, they have their own reasons for doing what they do. Just as you have shareholders and a board of directors to whom you must answer, they have donors, members, and boards of their own. When they raise funds or seek other forms of support, they need to show results, just as you do. If they can't get a clear win from their encounter with you, they will at least need to show that they held your feet to the fire. The sooner you accept realities like these, the better. Once you do, you can transform your engagements with stakeholders, making them more open and mutually beneficial.

Businesspeople need to become more capable and sensitive politicians, in the best sense of that word. This includes recognizing that sometimes being right—from a scientific or technical perspective—may be valueless if public opinion is solidly against you. Look at what happened when Greenpeace took on Royal Dutch Shell, the global network of oil, gas, and chemical companies active in 140 nations around the world, over the Brent Spar offshore oil drilling facility.

Brent Spar came to public prominence in 1995, when Shell applied for permission to dispose of the giant rig in deep Atlantic waters approximately 250 kilometers from the west coast of Scotland. Claiming that the oil rig contained thousands of tons of dangerous toxins, Greenpeace ran a high-profile media campaign against the plan, including calls for boycotts of Shell service stations, and its activists occupied Brent Spar for more than three weeks.

In the face of public and political opposition in northern Europe (including some physical attacks on service stations in Germany), Shell continued to insist that deep-sea disposal was the safest and most environmentally appropriate means of disposal for the used rig. Shell stuck to its position, door closed, long after it was obvious to everyone else that the company simply needed to back off.

Seduced by the steady flow of dramatic images from the protesters, the media lapped up Greenpeace's claims, and Shell got a huge black eye in the international press, from which it took years to recover. Belatedly, the company switched its position and announced that it would abandon its plans to dispose of Brent Spar at sea.

Afterward, when independent Norwegian consultants Det Norske Veritas assessed the rig's inventory, their findings vindicated Shell. The rig was actually empty and devoid of toxins. Greenpeace issued a hasty apology, acknowledging that sampling errors had led to a substantial overestimate of the oil remaining in Brent Spar's storage tanks.

In the words of German environmentalist Dirk Maxeiner, "As we know today, the sinking of Brent Spar would have had practically no ecological impact on the marine system in the North Atlantic. In 1995, however, Greenpeace had the credibility and Shell only had the truth, so the oil company didn't have the slightest chance against Greenpeace." Shell made matters worse by being rigid and closed during the controversy, much as Hershey did with its inflexible stance during the battle over the proposed company sale.[6]

It may be unfair that a business should suffer political or financial damage when its behavior has been responsible or at least defensible. But life is not always fair. Community members may be completely wrong, in your view, about how they want you to build your plant or whether they want you there at all, but it's their community, and you can expect them to have their say—and maybe their way. Smart management is about effectively navigating the world as it is, not the world as we might wish it to be. Well-run companies and successful managers use all the clubs in their bag, including political skills, to achieve their objectives.

Sometimes, compromise with adversarial stakeholders may not be possible. Some advocates will not even talk to you, much less compromise. The Southern Baptist Convention (SBC), for instance, refused to compromise with Disney when the company began to provide equal benefits to gay partners of their employees in 1996, a concession to gay rights that conservative Baptists considered anathema. A year later, the SBC launched a boycott of Disney.[7]

How should you respond if your company is targeted by an extreme organization unwilling to engage in good faith? Disney's strategy was to stay the course, despite suffering what the Baptists claimed were "hundreds of millions in losses." The company eventually outlasted their opponents, who called off the boycott after eight years.

Win or lose, this kind of cold war can be a painful option, but it may be the only one available to you. In the vast majority of cases, however, engaging your adversarial stakeholders is possible and will be far more effective than simply ignoring or combating them. Your goal should be to head off conflicts before they arise, but in the event that they do arise, become engaged as soon as possible.

When you sit down with your adversaries, make the central agenda item (spoken or unspoken), "How can we both get something positive out of our disagreement—something we can each bring back to our stakeholders and that will benefit everybody involved?" See the discussion not as a battle of wills or a confrontation between "the good guys" and "the enemies," but as a business deal. And as with any business deal, don't assume that you know what's in your adversaries' best interest. Figuratively join your adversaries on their side of the table, looking at your business operations through their eyes, and see whether you can find ways to respond to their legitimate concerns by modifying and improving your operations without harming your own interests.

Who *Are* Your Stakeholders, Anyhow?

Stakeholder mapping, a technique for identifying and prioritizing your stakeholders, is a powerful diagnostic tool. It helps you identify your current position in relation to the various interest groups, community organizations, economic and financial interests, government agencies, and others who take an interest in and can affect your activities. It is important to note that not only does the company as a whole have stakeholders, but so does every division, department, business unit, plant, and facility. And understanding who they are and what they want is a prerequisite to effective stakeholder engagement.

An easy way to start is by putting your stakeholders in three categories: those within the company (internal), those with whom you do business (value chain), and those outside the company (external). This type of stakeholder mapping is often called a *target analysis*, simply because the chart it yields resembles an archery target with your organization at the center (see Figure 11.1). Most stakeholders will fall neatly into one or another of the three circles shown on this diagram. On occasion, however, a particular stakeholder may fit into two or even three categories (for example, by being both a shareholder and a community activist), which would typically give this individual or group greater impact on your organization.

To start mapping, make a list of individuals and organizations in each category. The more specific you can be, the more effective

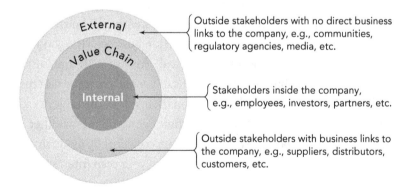

Figure 11.1　Categories of Stakeholders: Target Analysis.

the mapping. Name names and take time to brainstorm these lists; some stakeholders who may be important may not be immediately obvious—for example, the local television news reporter who covers business news (and likes to present occasional exposés about alleged corporate malfeasance); the unaffiliated, self-appointed gadfly who posts critical tweets about you on the Internet (and has somehow accumulated several thousand avid followers); the sustainability guru who has just signed a consulting contract with the retailer that is your biggest customer (and may be working on an array of tough new environmental standards that your company will be expected to meet). Individuals like these have no official relationship with your company—yet they may end up having significant impact on you in the coming months or years.

Identifying and segmenting your company's (or your department's) stakeholders will generate further insights into how you might interact with them and how they may perceive you from their particular perspectives, all of which can easily become part of your self-assessment (see Chapter Seven). For each stakeholder, consider these questions:

- How do we communicate with this stakeholder? Do we have open lines of communication that permit both sides to express needs, concerns, and problems easily and honestly?
- What are the stakeholder's interests as they affect our company? How are we addressing those areas of concern?
- Are we already in a debate or conflict with this stakeholder? If so, how are those conflicts being managed? Are we moving toward a mutually satisfactory resolution? Are we headed toward a sweet spot where both the stakeholder and our company can enjoy benefits? If not, can we find one and head in that direction? If we can't, what is the best way to minimize the damage to both sides?
- Who within our company is responsible for this stakeholder relationship? What policies, procedures, and principles are in place for guiding the relationship? What objectives, explicit or implicit, has the company set, and what incentives are in place that affect the management of this relationship?

What Do Your Stakeholders Care About?

A second technique for stakeholder mapping is known as an *impact chart* (see Table 11.1). It's an easy way to organize your insights into how specific sustainability issues affect particular stakeholders.

To create this type of chart, draw up a table in which every possible stakeholder group is listed in its own row. (The list shown in the sample chart is illustrative only; your own list is likely to be much more detailed and specific.) In the vertical columns, list the key issues, or impacts, relevant to your company. Then examine each cell in the chart and ask, Does this group of stakeholders have an interest in and an impact on our activities in relation to this issue? If so, put a check mark in that cell. In some cases, the stakeholders will be connected to issues that are not on your list, and these too should be recorded. The resulting pattern of checked and empty cells will help you answer such questions as the following:

- Which issues or impacts affect the broadest array of stakeholder groups? (It's likely that these issues will present the most complex challenges for stakeholder relations.)

Table 11.1   Sample Impact Chart

Stakeholders	Issues and Impacts					
	Human rights	Privacy	Lobbying and Legislation	Economic Effects	Safety Impact	Environmental Effects
Customers	✓	✓	✓		✓	
Suppliers	✓			✓	✓	✓
Community	✓	✓		✓	✓	✓
Environmentalists			✓			✓
Regulators	✓	✓	✓			✓
Labor unions	✓			✓	✓	
Employees	✓	✓			✓	✓
Media	✓	✓	✓		✓	✓
Competitors		✓	✓			

- Which stakeholder groups have an impact on the largest number of relevant issues? (These are groups that deserve the most consistent and thoughtful nurturing by managers from within your organization.)
- Specifically how do our impacts and the interests of this stakeholder overlap? (This will identify either sweet spot opportunities or areas of conflict.)

How Do You Prioritize Your Stakeholders?

A third way to look at your stakeholders is to prioritize the many individuals and groups vying for your attention, interest, and resources in terms of their potential impact on your organization. To do this, you can create what we call a *priority table* (see Table 11.2).

Like the impact chart, the priority table begins with a list of all your key stakeholder groups. (Again, the list shown in the sample table is illustrative only.) For each stakeholder, estimate its possible impact: its ability to help or harm your company in whatever way it might act—lobbying, making statements to the media, purchasing your product or boycotting it, contacting other influential third parties, or taking other actions. Rate help and harm, each on a scale of 1 to 5, with 5 being the greatest ability to help or harm, 1 the least.

Table 11.2   Sample Priority Table

	Ability to Help Us	Ability to Hurt Us	Likelihood of Acting	Overall Priority
Customers	4	1	0.3	1.5
Community	2	3	0.5	2.5
Environmentalists	1	3	0.7	2.8
Regulators	1	4	0.6	3.0
Labor unions	4	5	0.8	7.2
Employees	3	4	0.5	3.5
Media	1	3	0.4	1.6
Competitors	1	2	0.6	1.8

These ratings for each stakeholder will depend entirely on your company's current situation and challenges. Suppose your company is facing a financial crisis due in part to costly commitments for employees' future retirement benefits. Your financial health may depend on whether you can negotiate a reduction in those liabilities with the leaders of the employees' unions. The ability of the unions to help or harm you right now would be unusually high, possibly critical to your company's future, whereas at some other time, the unions might have had a much lower priority. At the moment, environmentalists or customers would not rate as high in terms of their ability either to help or harm you.

The third column in the table is labeled Likelihood of Acting, and it should contain decimal fractions ranging between 0 and 1. A rating of 0, of course, would reflect *no* possibility that a particular stakeholder will take action to influence your company; a rating of 1 would reflect the *absolute certainty* of stakeholder action. (Both of these extremes are likely to be rare.) In the example, the unions are shown as most likely to act, with a rating of 0.8 (the equivalent of an 80 percent likelihood), whereas the customers are least likely to act, rated at just 0.3 (30 percent).

To determine the relative priorities, you'll add up the two help-or-hurt columns to come up with a total, which will range between 2 (least) and 10 (most). Then multiply this total by the rating for likelihood of acting. The resulting numbers serve as a guide in prioritizing your stakeholders. Those individuals and groups with the highest total scores are the ones that demand the most immediate and focused attention from your organization.

Using each of the three systems we've illustrated in the last few pages, you should be able, at any given time, to sketch an accurate map of your most important stakeholders. If you can do this, it means that you can identify the most influential people in the life of your organization and develop at least a broad-brush strategy for managing your relationships with them.

Advanced Stakeholder Strategy

We've looked at who your stakeholders are, what they care about, and which ones might be the most important in terms of their ability to affect your agenda and their likelihood of doing so. The question now is, What do you do about it?

You can use all the information you've acquired (and laboriously mapped) as a means of developing strategies for managing a specific program or initiative, such as a plan to expand your factory in an environmentally sensitive region. One way to plot strategy is by creating an *influence grid* (see Figure 11.2).

This grid consists of a vertical axis representing the degree of support for the particular program or initiative, and a horizontal axis representing the degree of influence each of various stakeholders might have on your initiative. This grid is just a more highly focused version of the priority table, created in the same way.

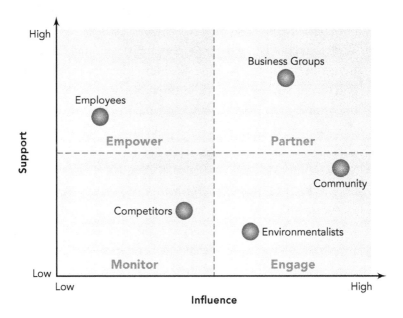

Figure 11.2 Sample Influence Grid.

Having created the influence grid, you then map each of your key stakeholders. You can begin to develop your strategy according to where each stakeholder group falls on the grid:

- With stakeholders whose support for you is high but whose influence is low (as with Employees in the sample grid shown in Figure 11.2), your strategy should be to *empower* them. Work with these stakeholders to enhance their influence by supporting their efforts to attract members, communicate through the media, and spread their message to the larger world.

- With stakeholders whose support for you is low and whose influence is also low (as with Competitors in the sample grid), your strategy should be to *monitor* them. Under normal circumstances, you should have little to fear from these stakeholders. But you should track their behavior and communications so that if the dynamic should change such that these stakeholders gain greater influence, you will be prepared to work with them or oppose them, as necessary.

- With stakeholders whose support for you is high and whose influence is high (as with Business Groups in the sample grid), your strategy should be to *partner* with them. Look for opportunities to work together in support of your shared goals, thereby augmenting your own influence and increasing the chance of achieving your goals.

- With stakeholders whose support for you is low but whose influence is high (as with Environmentalists and the Community in the sample grid), your strategy should be to *engage* them. Keep the lines of communication open, seek areas of agreement (however minor these may appear), and look for ways to influence their thinking to be more favorable toward you (or at least less intensely negative).

The utility of an influence grid and especially the importance of ensuring its accuracy can be illustrated by contemplating what might have happened if the board of the Hershey Trust had attempted to

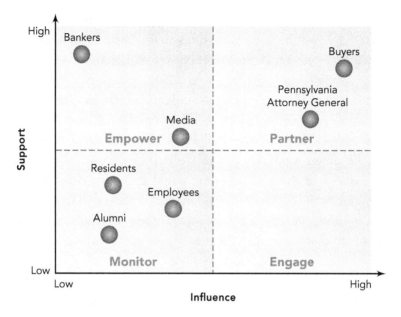

Figure 11.3 Influence Grid as Viewed by the Board of the Hershey Trust (August 2002).

map their own stakeholders onto such a grid before announcing their plan to sell Hershey Foods (as described in Chapter One).

Figure 11.3 shows how the board apparently viewed the attitudes and influence of their key stakeholders. In the upper right-hand corner of the grid, we see two stakeholders the board probably viewed as significant: potential buyers of Hershey Foods (such as Nestlé, Cadbury Schweppes, and Wrigley) and the office of the Pennsylvania attorney general.

As of August 2002 (prior to the sale announcement), the Hershey Trust would have considered both of these stakeholders highly influential. Potential buyers were influential because their readiness to make attractive offers for the company was critical to any sale, and the attorney general would be influential because, under state law, the actions of trusts are overseen by his office.

The board also had reason to believe that both would be supportive of the possible sale: buyers, because of the opportunity to expand their market base and sales by snapping up a major competitor; and the attorney general, because the board believed that his office favored greater diversification of the trust's assets, which, in their view, mandated a sale of their Hershey Foods stock holdings.

The board would have placed place three other stakeholders in the lower left-hand corner: the residents of Hershey, Pennsylvania; the union representing Hershey Foods employees; and the alumni of the Milton Hershey School. The board assumed that local residents and the union would have negative attitudes toward the proposed sale because of the uncertainty it would introduce concerning the economic future of the town. And the board could well have assumed that at least some of the school's alumni would vehemently oppose any action that would alter the ninety-plus-year relationship between the trust, the company, and the school.

But the board would also have believed that these three groups had minimal influence over any sale. Community and worker protests are common when corporations are put on the block, but they rarely manage to derail a sale. And, as Hershey resident Kathy Taylor pointed out at the time, history suggested that any protests would probably be muted: "There wasn't much outcry in town when the discount drug store was taken away or they shut down the junior college. So the board must have figured there would be no outcry when they decided to sell the company."[8]

Unfortunately for the board, it badly misgauged the realities on the ground.

As we explained in Chapter One, soon after the proposed sale was announced, protests erupted from many quarters. Within weeks, it became obvious that the actual attitudes and degree of influence of several of the key players in the Hershey drama were quite different from what the board had assumed (see Figure 11.4).

The influence of the attorney general *was* high; indeed, he turned out to be the most important stakeholder of all, as revealed by his ability to win a court order temporarily halting the sale altogether. But his supposed support for the sale, if it had ever existed, had evaporated. Mike Fisher, attorney general at that time, later claimed that the board of the trust had misinterpreted his deputy's recommendation

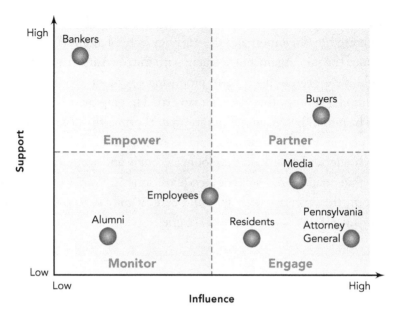

Figure 11.4   Influence Grid as Revealed During the Hershey Sale Controversy (September 2002).

about diversifying the fund's holdings; Fisher would have favored a partial sale of Hershey stock, but not sale of a controlling interest. Had the board members understood this, they could have engaged the attorney general in a discussion about how to accomplish their objectives without crossing swords with him.

Most crucially, the residents of Hershey (and to a lesser extent the employees) proved to be far more influential than the board anticipated. Not only did they mount far stronger protests than they had over previous unpopular steps, but they succeeded in mobilizing public opinion around the country behind them, making skillful use of the town's image as America's beloved Chocolatetown in their public relations campaign. By presenting the board's actions as callous and ill-considered, they probably reduced the eagerness of potential buyers to make generous offers for the company (which is why we've moved the Buyers circle slightly south in the revised influence grid).

Even more important, the residents helped motivate the attorney general to take his strong legal and political stance against the sale.

The confluence of forces that the residents helped put in motion (supported by the union and the Hershey School alumni) ultimately doomed the sale. Again, engagement with the town and the employees would have been a much more promising course of action than the steamroller strategy that the company tried to employ.

The moral? Before launching any major corporate initiative, gather the people who are most deeply knowledgeable about your key stakeholders, and work on developing a timely and accurate influence grid that maps those stakeholders' positions in your world. If you perform this exercise with skill and care, it may save you and your company resources—and a world of grief.

12

Dealing with Special Stakeholder Challenges

We can either dance with you, or dance on you.
—Greenpeace slogan

The Many Faces of NGOs

Nongovernmental organizations (NGOs) are the stakeholder groups that businesspeople most frequently misunderstand and mismanage, often with painful results. They include a wide range of lobbying organizations, citizens' interests groups, environmentalists, labor and human rights activists, and many other organizations that sometimes operate as if making life difficult for your business were their only objective.

But business leaders who assume that NGOs are all fundamentally hostile to business are making a big mistake. These organizations are as varied as companies themselves and just as numerous: according to the State Department, an estimated 1.5 million NGOs are operating today in the United States alone.[1] Recognizing the many and sometimes subtle differences among them is crucial for any business that wants to forge a mutually beneficial relationship with an NGO or simply get the NGO out of its hair. The attitudes and approaches taken by advocacy organizations toward business have been evolving rapidly in recent years, and savvy businesspeople are altering their thinking and behavior to suit.

The fact is that many NGOs are more open to cooperation with business today than ever before. One reason is a shift in attitude on the part of the NGOs themselves. A growing number of NGOs have come to see the power of the free market as a source of energy for improving our world. Many NGOs are largely giving up on government regulation as the solution to environmental, social, and economic problems and instead are working directly with companies and consumers to find Sustainability Sweet Spots in the form of market-based win-win solutions. George Carpenter, former director of corporate sustainable development for Procter & Gamble (P&G), liked to describe his work in leveraging stakeholder connections as being about "corporate social *opportunity*," and the phrase expresses the potential for positive outcomes that exists when businesses and NGOs can find common ground.

Oxfam America is an example of how NGOs are evolving. One of the world's most aggressive and effective advocacy organizations for the poor, Oxfam created a private sector team that has been working cooperatively with companies—for example, collaborating with Coca-Cola and SABMiller to examine their impact on poverty and with Swiss Re to create microinsurance programs to protect Ethiopian farmers from the threats posed by unusual weather patterns. At the same time, Oxfam reserves the right to campaign publicly against companies that they believe are exploiting the poor or neglecting their needs—even against companies they may be working with.

Greenpeace, the Rainforest Alliance, PETA, Oxfam, the Sierra Club, and other globally prominent advocacy organizations once considered antibusiness have embarked on partnerships and alliances with a number of global corporations. In the words of Stephen Tyndale, executive director of Greenpeace, "We need companies because companies are in a position to deliver the solutions. And when they engage, they can move faster and be more dynamic and creative than government. With the right company, it enables you to get things done that you could never possibly do on your own."[2] Hence, for example, Greenpeace's collaboration with Unilever to ensure that suppliers of palm oil for the company's products are protecting ecologically valuable forests and peat lands in Borneo.

The Rainforest Alliance is another NGO that is working cooperatively with business. Its mission is to preserve the rain forest along with the diverse strains of plant, insect, animal, and human life that depend on it. In the past, the Alliance has clashed with many businesses that sought profit through activities that harmed the rain forest.

Today the Alliance is emphasizing market-based activities that can both protect the rain forest and facilitate the search for profit. Working with companies like Chiquita that have been heavily criticized for poor environmental practices and human rights abuses, the Alliance has developed certification programs that assess the way companies are growing crops and timber or how tourism is being managed. The organization uses market-based conservation mechanisms, and conducts audits that track some two hundred criteria to verify that coffee growers, banana farmers, and pulp and paper companies are operating sustainably.

•••

When businesspeople are scanning their environment to evaluate stakeholders that may have an impact on their companies in the years to come, they need to understand the kinds of NGOs that are out there and the specific organizations they are dealing with, and approach each engagement accordingly.

When dealing with an NGO that is likely to turn aggressive (or become "riled," as Greenpeace says), proceed with caution. Stakeholder mapping and analysis are called for, as is a consultation with those in your organization whose activities might be targeted. Also speak with your attorneys and your PR professionals. Before pursuing any strategy, triple-check the accuracy and completeness of every document you file and every public statement you release, and leverage all your resources of goodwill, media connections, and social support to publicize your side of every controversy in order to stay off the defensive.

Avoid the temptation to "go negative" on an adversarial NGO. You may be convinced that your opponents are misguided, politically motivated, even venal or corrupt. But coming from you, such charges will generally ring false and may even backfire. Most people generally assume that any controversy pitting business against an NGO is a David-and-Goliath battle, with business as the powerful bully and the NGO as the heroic underdog.

Under these circumstances, the best media strategy is to appear statesmanlike while being honest and responsive. Spend time, energy, and money presenting your side of the argument in a positive light. And when it's plain that you are *wrong* on a particular point, don't dig in your heels. Concede the issue promptly and completely, if possible going beyond what your adversaries demand in offering transparency, reparations, and an appropriate change in policy. If you take this approach, what could have been a weeks-long drip-drip-drip of negative news will be transformed into a short-lived story that few people will notice or remember. And if you move quickly to admit and fix the problem, you might even come out a winner.

Managing Partnerships with NGOs

Partnerships with NGOs can provide enormous business benefits when properly managed. What are the keys to managing partnerships for maximum corporate benefit? Here are some important tips:

- *Do your homework to accurately identify allies and opponents.*
  Use the stakeholder mapping techniques described in Chapter Eleven to identify and prioritize opportunities for collaboration and partnership. Note that the "environmental community," the "social justice community," or the "human rights community" is not monolithic. Nuclear energy has long been anathema to environmental groups, for example, and many still strongly oppose it. Yet concern about global warming has caused a rift on this issue, because nuclear power doesn't contribute to climate change. British scientist James Lovelock, who helped found the European Green movement, was one of the first environmentalists to go pronuclear. He has since been followed

by a number of others, including Barry Brook, George Monbiot, and Stewart Brand.

- *Study potential partnerships to determine the likelihood of success.* Part of your homework is to look at how the NGO connects with other organizations. How does it spend its money? More important, from whom does the NGO raise it? What are its objectives in general and in working with you specifically? The specific personalities of NGO leaders can make a big difference in your ability to work with them. It helps greatly to have the right personal chemistry, as Scott Hall of PPL had with the environmental and Indian leaders in their negotiations over the Penobscot River dams. Don't make the mistake of thinking that you can get advocates to change their minds, and don't send as your emissary someone who is set on getting his or her own way; you are looking not for victory but for common ground.

- *Create a network of stakeholder organizations.* Use your networking skills and social networking platforms to link from one NGO leader or organization to other groups with related interests. P&G is masterful at working though NGOs to gain access to communities and to community-based groups it might otherwise not be able to contact.

- *Focus on the long haul and be prepared for continuing challenges.* Most NGOs that are willing to work with business are looking for marriage partners, not one-night stands. You may be able to strike a particular deal relatively quickly, but you build credibility and trust with advocates only over the long haul. Envision what a long-term relationship would look like and where it might lead. And don't assume that working closely with a specific group makes you immune from criticism by the same group on a different issue. Thus Greenpeace criticized Unilever for creating mercury pollution in India at the same time that it was working with the company to develop a climate-neutral refrigerator.

- *Remember that NGOs can be marketplace allies or marketplace adversaries.* Some NGOs have become increasingly sophisticated at using the marketplace to inflict pain. You may face direct action from a disaffected NGO—for example, a forty-foot banner denouncing your company, flying over your headquarters. But you are just as likely to hear about an action aimed at your customers, suppliers, or investors. "We attack the weakest link in the company's value chain," says Kert Davies of Greenpeace.[3]

- *Set specific expectations, then lower them.* Partnerships with NGOs and other stakeholders may be highly formal, with memoranda of understanding that define all the terms of engagement: the purpose, scope, and duration of the project, and how disputes are to be resolved. Or they may be based on handshake agreements, shaped and maintained on an informal basis. In either case, the best way to ensure success is to clarify expectations from the beginning and avoid overly ambitious goals. Partnerships with NGOs are usually harder to manage, more costly, and more time-consuming than expected, and it helps if everyone understands and acknowledges that reality. Many NGOs do not operate on strict schedules as businesses do, and they are often far more resource constrained than they let on. Both factors can make dealing with them difficult; be patient and try to avoid becoming frustrated.

- *Have an exit strategy.* Just like commercial partnerships, partnerships with NGOs can fail or fall apart for any number of reasons. Some NGOs will react badly and seek to retaliate, even if you think it's their fault. The best way to avoid a fight is to acknowledge the possibility of failure at the beginning and agree on how it will be handled by all sides. This discussion will serve the added benefit of lowering expectations appropriately and increasing trust.

Some companies see engagement with NGOs as a sideline, relegated to someone as a fourth job if he or she can get around to it. That is a big mistake. NGO relationships should be an explicit part of your strategy and receive all the resources and attention they require.

Pfizer, for example, provides funding to its local operations groups that are trying to develop NGO relationships. Alcoa establishes key performance indicators that it uses to measure the progress of its managers toward achieving important goals related to NGOs and stakeholder engagement. And Anglo-American, the global mining and natural resource conglomerate, monitors its success by having the relationships scrutinized, analyzed, and reported on by the same outside auditors who examine the company's other TBL practices.

Creating Your Own Stakeholders

It's sometimes advisable, even necessary, to *create* stakeholders—that is, to encourage or facilitate the formation of a group of company stakeholders to provide a forum in which issues can be raised, discussed, and, one hopes, resolved. We aren't suggesting that you foster conflict where none exists; we are advocating for an open channel for dialogue through which existing concerns can be managed constructively.

Nike used this technique to get back on its feet after allegedly failing to follow through on its own labor rights promises. The company had been in a bunker during the Kasky lawsuit (discussed in Chapter Eight), failing to address the still troubling issue of child labor. However, Nike had joined Ceres, a dynamic and highly effective advocacy organization of investment funds and environmental and public interest groups that originated the Global Reporting Initiative (GRI) and works with companies in support of sustainability. Nike asked Ceres to create an independent panel to assess and, where necessary, challenge Nike's TBL reporting policies and evaluate its next report.

The review panel was designed to represent many of Nike's key stakeholder groups. Members included Neal Kearney, general secretary of the International Textile, Garment and Leather Workers Federation; Vidette Bullock-Mixon, director of corporate relations and social concerns for the investment board of the United Methodist Church; and Liz Cook, director of the Sustainer Enterprise Program of the World Resources Institute.

The assessment was time-consuming and in some ways risky for Nike, but it led to a positive result. According to the panel's unedited public statement, which appeared as a three-page insert in Nike's 2004 corporate responsibility report, the company made "significant improvements" after the first critical review of the report. The panel praised the company for its candor while also listing eight ways in which the report could be substantially improved.[4]

Nike thus preempted the possibility of another effective attack on its practices by engaging with some of its harshest critics and by agreeing to an open and uncensored collaborative process. In today's interdependent world, the way to gain control of a difficult situation involving stakeholders is often by giving up some control to them, working cooperatively rather than trying to dominate. Other companies have set up similar independent review programs.

Bringing NGOs to the table to provide independent views or to work with you on initiatives or projects can be a powerful way of transforming hostility into positive energy for change. But it can backfire if not handled with a high degree of attention and integrity. Here are some important dos and don'ts to remember if you plan to try this strategy:

- *Do* seek stakeholder partners with real credibility and strong credentials, whose independence and integrity are unquestioned in the stakeholder communities you are trying to reach.
- *Do* give the stakeholder organizations you create or work with genuine independence, allowing them to set up their own policies and procedures and giving them the opportunity to communicate with the outside world freely and without censorship.
- *Do* offer the stakeholder groups as much corporate transparency as possible, giving them open access to company records, employees, and facilities as consistent with genuine issues of legal liability, privacy, and trade secrets.
- *Do* involve your own key leaders who are in a position to make and keep commitments on behalf of the company.

- *Do* be candid about your role in helping create and, if necessary, fund a stakeholder group; if the connection is exposed against your wishes due to investigative work by the media, it will seriously damage both your credibility and that of any stakeholders involved.
- *Don't* create an "Astroturf" organization—a phony grassroots group that masquerades as an independent NGO while secretly serving your corporate interests.
- *Don't* renege on any commitments you make; the damage to your company's reputation will be doubly serious if you first boast about, then try to eliminate, any moves toward dialogue and partnership with outside stakeholders.
- *Don't* assume goodwill or your own entitlement to receive the benefit of the doubt if conflicts arise. If there is any question about whether something you are doing violates the letter or the spirit of your collaboration with stakeholders, reconsider it—or run the risk of shattering the partnership.

Of course, even a sincere, consistent effort to engage with stakeholders is no panacea—as the multistate electric company American Electric Power (AEP), based in Columbus, Ohio, recently discovered.[5]

Beginning in 2009, as part of an ongoing program to improve its sustainability performance, AEP asked Ceres to help organize meetings of relevant AEP stakeholders. Ceres did an excellent job of convening a wide-ranging group of stakeholders. It included AEP company shareholders, labor leaders, experts from government and academia, and representatives of such NGOs as the Environmental Defense Fund, the Sierra Club, the Natural Resources Defense Council, the Clean Air Task Force, and the Great Plains Institute.

The process provided for AEP to share advance copies of its TBL report with the Ceres stakeholder team for feedback via an initial teleconference followed up by an in-person meeting at the company's corporate headquarters. AEP and the stakeholder team continued on this course through 2010, at which time both parties mutually agreed that the process had matured and that it was time for more issue-focused engagement. In these meetings, the group provided extensive, detailed feedback about many elements of AEP's sustainability efforts, including the company's continued reliance on coal, its role as a major producer of carbon emissions, its efforts to encourage greater energy efficiency on the part of its customers, and ongoing programs to improve worker safety and integrate sustainability into the supply chain. The judgments and recommendations offered by the stakeholders were frank and specific—for example, urging that AEP set more aggressive energy-saving targets and move to "phase out" its use of coal derived from mountaintop mining.[6]

AEP took the recommendations to heart and made a number of commitments in response, including providing a detailed description of its public policy positions and agreeing to survey its coal suppliers about their environmental and safety practices. Most important, AEP's willingness to engage with its stakeholders, to devote a significant amount of its executives' time and energy to prepare for and meet with such a diverse collection of stakeholders, and to take seriously the business recommendations generated by the group, all enhanced AEP's reputation as a leader in the utility industry's movement toward sustainability.

But then in 2011 an unfortunate misunderstanding occurred that deeply strained AEP's good relationship with the environmental community and largely reversed its hard-won reputational gains.

The company had made known its strong disagreement with the stakeholder group about how new environmental regulations should be implemented. However, it had failed to make it clear that, in addition to working with the regulators, AEP was also trying to get Congress to modify the Clean Air Act to take their concerns into account.

When news about AEP's lobbying efforts became public, some environmental advocates felt blindsided and believed that their trust had been violated. They ended discussions with AEP and began a vocal and visible campaign against the company, which included picketing and press releases suggesting that the company was willing to "sacrifice lives" in pursuit of its business interests.[7]

For their part, AEP executives acknowledged that, in retrospect, they should have been more transparent about their legislative agenda when meeting with the stakeholder group. Yet they seemed startled by the intensity of the reaction—a testimony to the depths of misunderstanding that are possible between people from very different perspectives, even when communication appears to be at its best.

The lesson for business leaders: your relationships with stakeholders are like investor relations, labor relations, customer relations, or any other relationships—complex, challenging, ever evolving, and unpredictable. The moment you think you have your relationships "solved" is the moment when disastrous miscommunication is most likely.

Engagement with Your Value Chain

Sustainability involves issues of communication, shared vision, and the balancing of interests with all your company's stakeholders, both inside and outside your company. Among the most crucial of your stakeholder relations—and the most challenging to manage—are those with the various members of your value chain. These include companies both upstream (those who supply you with raw materials, finished products, skilled or unskilled labor, and services of all kinds) and downstream (distributors, shippers, marketers, retailers, middlemen, and others who help you deliver goods and services to customers).

The value chain also includes (on the downstream side) the consumers or other customers who buy and use your goods and services, as well as those responsible for the ultimate disposal or recycling of your products. And, perhaps most critical, it includes your own employees, who of course play the single largest role of any stakeholder group in creating value. (This is one of the reasons why, as we discussed in Chapter Ten, sustainability begins with your employees. Maintaining high standards for your relationships with your workers is one of the most important steps any company can take to ensure that it has a positive social impact on the communities where it operates.)

Managing most of these value-chain relationships may seem fairly straightforward. They are generally traditional business relationships, in which each party is primarily focused on its own interests and in which shared objectives, obligations, time frames, incentives, rewards, and penalties are spelled out in contracts or established in the course of dealing. The terms of engagement are negotiated by the parties, with each side seeking its own best interests and with the comparative bargaining power of the organizations playing a major role in determining which side will enjoy more favorable treatment. Thus, when a powerful retailer like Wal-Mart is negotiating with suppliers, the retailer holds the upper hand and can usually dictate terms; when a supplier like the De Beers Consolidated Mines has near-monopoly control of a valued commodity—in this case, diamonds—the supplier can dictate terms to retailers.

But once sustainability is on the agenda, the nature of the relationship changes. Now profit may no longer be the defining consideration in mapping out contract terms. Thus when Nike, newly focused on sustainability issues, negotiates contracts with supplier factories in Asia or Latin America, the discussions are not solely focused on timing of delivery, increasing profit margins, reducing costs, improving efficiency, and guaranteeing quality. Now Nike also pushes its suppliers on such issues as worker safety, factory conditions, overtime wages, and, of course, child labor and human rights.

Nike's commitment to sustainability is thus transmitted to its supply chain almost like a beneficial virus. Policies, procedures, and guidelines that Nike has developed to govern its own behaviors become part of the management systems of Nike suppliers, which are required to share the TBL responsibilities Nike has assumed. Even Nike's corporate commitment to transparency is being shared by its suppliers: Nike's 2004 sustainability report listed all its suppliers—the first time any major company in the shoe or apparel industry had made this information public.[8] Today this level of transparency has been increased to include a public listing of all eight hundred or more factories manufacturing Nike products, sortable by geography, brand name, and product type.[9] Nike has in effect opened its supply chain to global scrutiny, inviting NGOs and interested members of the public to examine every link in the process by which Nike products are designed and manufactured, whether those links are technically inside or outside the company.

It may seem arbitrary and even unfair for a company to impose its own TBL commitments on its suppliers. But in today's interconnected world, it's inevitable. Stakeholders and the general public no longer recognize strict lines of separation among closely linked businesses. In the eyes of the world, if you're making a profit from a particular product or service, you're responsible for its design, creation, distribution, sale, and even, in some cases, its ultimate disposal. You can't disavow responsibility for a product or package that bears your logo just because it spends most of its lifetime outside your direct control.

When companies try to distance themselves from a problem they participated in creating—no matter how fair or unfair it may be to blame them for the problem—the public quickly recognizes that buck-passing is taking place, and soon every involved party ends up with a soiled reputation. In 2000, both Ford and Goodyear looked bad during several months of public debate over which company was responsible for rollover accidents in Ford Explorers. By 2001, the mutual reputational damage was so bad that the two companies ceased doing business with one another, ending a century-long supplier-customer relationship.

You cannot hope that downstream or upstream problems will go unnoticed or remain unlinked to your company. The public, the media, government agencies, and advocacy organizations are now accustomed to following the value chain to uncover the ultimate sources of problems that threaten the environment, public health, or community interests. Thus, for example, when horse meat was discovered in some food products sold by the giant retailer IKEA, investigations into other European food companies were quickly launched and publicized, using the latest methods of DNA analysis to verify the contents of packaged meats (adding a newsworthy touch of detective-show science to the embarrassing media coverage).

Complexities of Responsible
Value-Chain Management

It would be easy if value-chain management were simply a matter of applying your company's internal policies up and down the chain. The reality is complicated by a range of factors, including the following:

Varying legal and regulatory regimes. Laws covering environmental protection, labor rights, worker safety, child labor, and other issues vary widely from one country to another. Many companies that adhere to local laws have been harshly criticized when those laws permit them (or their suppliers) to pollute or to maintain factory conditions that would not be tolerated in their home countries. Even progressive companies have been criticized for offering different pension or health benefits to similar workers in different countries, charged with valuing employees in one country more highly than those in another. Finding the right balance among business realities, political and PR pressures, and the desire to "do the right thing" can be difficult and complicated, all the more so in a global economy.

Social and cultural differences. In certain countries, bribery is a traditional cost of doing business, but most companies refuse to pay, and prohibit their suppliers from asking for or soliciting bribes. Many companies have been flummoxed by cultural restrictions in the Arab world concerning women.

P&G's commitment to diversity and women's rights was tested in 2000 when the company hired four women for its office in Jeddah, Saudi Arabia. Local regulations, clearly discriminatory by Western standards, required that the women be designated as contractors, paid less than males, and given offices in a separate building. P&G pursued the responsible path, exerting constant, low-key pressure to lessen the restrictions. Eventually the women became official P&G employees with strong career-path management positions, and, as P&G proudly noted in its 2004 TBL report, "Progress this year has been so great that the four women attended a major strategy meeting in the same room with the men." This was a small step, but a significant one, especially for the women involved.[10]

Similarly, to support its women employees in Pakistan, in 2009 P&G launched a new tradition called Sponsor Day, in which a family member (mother, father, or mother-in-law, for example) is invited to visit the office. The shared experience, and the sense it creates that P&G honors family connections, has helped female employees win sympathy for their career goals from conservative relatives who might otherwise be opposed to such a nontraditional lifestyle.[11]

Difficulties of enforcement. Many companies want to impose sustainability requirements on their suppliers, but these are difficult to enforce. Some have established rigorous auditing programs, paid for by the suppliers themselves, as a contract condition, under which independent verifiers make scheduled and unscheduled inspection visits to factories. Others rely on self-certification or a simple commitment to meet their requirements. But almost every company complains about the difficulty of enforcing against suppliers who are intent on evading the rules.

Tracing responsibility through a complex network of contractors and subcontractors can sometimes be confoundingly difficult. In the case of the tragic 2012 garment factory fire that killed 112 workers in Bangladesh (mentioned in Chapter Two), inspectors had discovered safety violations at the factory months earlier. As a result, Wal-Mart had removed the company, Tazreen Fashions Ltd., from its list of authorized suppliers. However, it's not clear whether or how Wal-Mart communicated the deauthorization to its other suppliers, one of which appears to have subcontracted production of goods for Wal-Mart to Tazreen. When garments bearing Wal-Mart brand labels were found in the charred wreckage of the factory, the world blamed the giant retailer for the tragedy.[12] As this example illustrates, clear, timely communication and effective enforcement of supplier policy decisions aren't just bureaucratic niceties—they may be matters of life and death, and can certainly have a major impact on your company's global reputation.

Unintended consequences. It's often extremely difficult to anticipate all the potential upstream impacts of decisions you make in company headquarters. In an interview we conducted, Dan Henkle, senior vice president of HR at Gap, explained a typical example. When a particular Gap product began to sell in expectedly large quantities, it was once routine procedure for the company manager to simply place an order for additional units with the supplier for that product. Unfortunately, faced with unanticipated demand to quickly produce, say, an extra hundred thousand units of a garment, the contract manufacturer might have been forced to resort to such unacceptable business practices as demanding excessive overtime, recruiting underage workers, or cutting corners on safety—all without Gap's knowledge or approval. Today, having recognized this phenomenon, Gap includes education about it in its Retail Academy training program. Now managers understand the need to anticipate the upstream implications of their actions and, when necessary, work around them—for example, by splitting up a rush order among several suppliers so that demand can be met without violating sustainability principles.

Because of these and other challenges, pushing your entire value chain toward greater sustainability can require thoughtful analysis of complex, changing circumstances. In 1993, Levi's closed its manufacturing operations in China because of that country's human rights record.[13] Fifteen years later, satisfied that significant progress had been made, it returned to China. In other countries where child labor provides a family's only income and where human rights are protected, Levi's pays contractors to keep the children in school to age fourteen. Like many companies, Levi's varies its tactics to address human and labor rights issues as they arise in different situations.

Customers as Stakeholders: The Power of Information

You probably don't need to be reminded about the importance of customers to the future of your business. They're the source of your revenues, and without them, your business simply wouldn't exist. But thinking about customers as stakeholders in the context of your quest for sustainability is a different matter. It's not about marketing and selling your goods and services effectively; it's not even about providing a fine product and excellent customer service at a fair price. It's about enlisting customers as partners as you strive to improve your and their environmental and social impact on the world. And that means respecting their values, sharing their concerns, and responding to their demands—even when these have no direct bearing on your buyer-seller relationship.

If you sell directly to consumers, then many of your customers will also be members of other stakeholder groups. Some are shareholders in your company; others are your employees or employees of companies in your value chain; some are residents of the communities in which you do business; and some are supporters of NGOs with strong feelings about the ways in which you operate. But even customers with none of these affiliations may have definite opinions about your TBL efforts—and a readiness to back up those opinions with action. They are increasingly "voting with their pocketbooks" to support companies whose products and policies they consider consonant with their values. The evidence is popping up everywhere—in the growing popularity of hybrid and plug-in electric cars (even those with a higher sticker price or shorter range than conventional vehicles); in the growing willingness of consumers to pay more for sustainable foods, from free-range beef and chicken to organic milk and ethically sourced products like jewelry and coffee; and in the expanding retail shelf space being devoted to sustainable product lines offered by packaged goods giants, from Clorox's Green Works to Tide's energy-saving Coldwater detergents.

For companies that are serious about pursuing sustainability, this is great news. It means that the marketplace is likely to increasingly reward you for the social and environmental efforts you are making. But it also means that a growing number of customers are expecting you to treat them as sustainability partners—which means keeping them fully informed about your products and about the way you operate as a company.

One of the liveliest arenas in which companies are competing to win the hearts of customers-as-stakeholders is the world of labeling.

Honest disclosure of sustainability information on product packaging or in other easily accessible locations (such as restaurant menus) has proven to be a surprisingly powerful tool for enlisting customer support. Consequently, labeling has also become a battleground, with companies jousting to shape disclosure systems that will give them an edge over their rivals in the battle for credibility and customer loyalty.

Labeling systems often originate with private efforts by individual companies responding to consumer demand for information about the environmental or social impact of their products. Over time, as the number and variety of company-designed labeling systems grow, customers, retailers, and other stakeholders may become confused about to how compare and judge various offerings; some grow cynical, suspecting that the array of contradictory labels is actually designed to mislead them.

This predicament has been resolved in varying ways in different industries. In one common scenario, businesses organize themselves around a single standard, usually with one or a few major companies leading the way. In a second scenario, two or more standards coexist for a time, contending in the court of public opinion for legitimacy, credibility, and dominance. In still other cases, government steps in to mandate a labeling standard, often motivated by demands from both customers and business leaders for the simplicity and predictability of a single system.

An example of the first scenario is the standard-setting process for consumer goods being developed for retail giant Wal-Mart by The Sustainability Consortium (TSC), which is designed to measure and report the sustainability of specific products and suppliers in over one hundred product categories. Wal-Mart has pledged to buy 70 percent of its goods only from suppliers that use TSC's Sustainability Index, and the retailer's marketplace clout ensures that the index will be taken very seriously by manufacturers of consumer goods.[14]

Another such effort that is currently gaining traction in the world of apparel is the Higg Index, created by the Sustainable Apparel Coalition to measure the sustainability of clothing brands, products, and manufacturing facilities according to specific environmental and social criteria. Wal-Mart and other retailers are part of the coalition, but so are many major apparel manufacturers and marketers, from Nike and Levi's to Patagonia and Timberland. In time, the Higg Index is expected to form the basis of a labeling system that will enable customers to judge and compare the sustainability of particular products, from jeans to hiking boots, as part of their shopping routine. And because preexisting rating systems used by Nike and Levi's are being incorporated into the index, it's likely that those two companies will gain at least a modest edge over the competition when it comes to earning a favorable score. It's a good example of how subtle political gamesmanship often lurks just below the surface of intra-industry debates over labeling.[15]

A good example of the second case is the battle between two certification schemes for labeling environmentally responsible forest and paper products. The Forest Stewardship Council (FSC) program was launched in 1993 by a collection of environmental organizations and human rights advocates working with socially concerned timber users and traders. A year later, the Sustainable Forest Initiative (SFI) was created as an alternative to the FSC by members of an industry group, the American Forest and Paper Association (AFPA).

For a number of years, these two certification programs competed for business support and public credibility on an almost equal basis, with many timber products companies applying for both FSC and SFI labeling. Over time, however, the FSC scheme emerged as the more widely recognized and respected of the two. The FSC had several advantages, most notably the greater independence and credibility enjoyed by environmental and human rights NGOs as compared with industry representatives. SFI tried to counter this advantage by formally separating itself from the AFPA in 2007, but it still has not fully shed its reputation among environmentalists as a mere "front group" for loggers—or, in the words of one activist, "a fake eco-label of, by, and for the forest industry."[16] When seven companies, including four members of the Fortune 500, announced in March 2011 that they would phase out their use of the SFI label, it was widely viewed as a decisive victory for FSC in the "forestry labeling war."

The third approach to labeling—intervention by a government regulatory agency to mandate a particular labeling regime—took place in the world of organic foods in the 1990s. The driving force was growing consumer unhappiness over the proliferation of confusing, contradictory, and misleading labels in which words like "organic," "natural," "ecofriendly," and many others were bandied about without clear definitions or rules. In 2002, after extensive study and enormous input from food industry advocates and the general public, the National Organic Standards Board, a division of the U.S. Department of Agriculture, issued specific labeling guidelines that define precisely three levels of "organic" claims—100% Organic; Certified Organic; and Made with Organic Ingredients.

The burgeoning sales of organic foods in all three categories suggests that consumers appreciate the clarity this labeling system provides. Far from representing an example of burdensome government intrusion, the system establishes a level playing field where businesses and consumers can interact with confidence.

There are many areas of business where such clarity, consistency, and simplicity have yet to emerge. Battles among businesses, consumer groups, and government agencies at every level, from federal departments down to state and local authorities, have led to confusing and frequently shifting labeling rules that are difficult for companies and customers to track and apply.

Consider, for example, the ongoing conflicts over calorie-count information in fast-food restaurants. For years, health care organizations and consumer groups concerned about the obesity epidemic among children have demanded that this information be made readily available to customers. Responding to this pressure, cities like New York and Philadelphia eventually passed ordinances requiring the posting of this data in restaurant chains of specified sizes. Now a similar rule, long advocated by health care organizations, is expected to take effect at the federal level sometime during 2013 (though the specifics have yet to be announced).

It's fascinating to see how industry giant McDonald's has dealt with the mounting pressure for greater transparency about calorie counts. Originally, this information was simply not made public by the company in any form. Then a chart of calorie data was made available online (where few customers were likely to see it). In time, the information was offered to in-store customers who specifically requested it from a manager; later still, it was provided in a loose-leaf binder mounted on a stand in a corner of the store; finally, it was printed directly on product packages (which customers would not see until after they'd already chosen and purchased the product).

In September 2012, with federal regulations looming, McDonald's announced that it would post calorie counts on all its store menus. At the same time, it presented several new food items designed to be more healthful than its traditional burgers and french fries, including an egg-white McMuffin and a selection of seasonal fruits and vegetables—a classic bit of sustainability jiu-jitsu.[17]

The story illustrates one of the more subtle yet significant implications of the labeling wars. Information, whether mandated or voluntary, often leads to substantive change. Companies that share data about their TBL performance with the public tend to find themselves driven, either by outside pressure or internal aspirations, to improve that performance. Thus (as we'll detail in the next chapter) federal "Right to Know" laws mandating the release of information about toxic pollutants helped drive a huge reduction in such pollutants—and the prospect of having to post calorie counts on its menus helped convince McDonald's that it was time to expand its list of less-fattening food alternatives.

This story and the others we've shared also underscore the power of customers to drive companies toward greater sustainability. This dynamic can be seen in the world of business-to-business selling as well as in the consumer marketplace. Wal-Mart's success in pushing many of its major suppliers to reduce unnecessary packaging and otherwise improve their environmental practices is a clear example. Another took place at PricewaterhouseCoopers (PwC), when a couple of managers questioned the value of the company's ongoing efforts to achieve greater diversity among its professional staff. In response, Andy Savitz, then a partner at the firm, suggested that these efforts be highlighted in future contract proposal packages. To the surprise of Andy's colleagues, a number of potential clients were favorably impressed by the firm's diversity achievements, which helped win PwC several major consulting contracts.

Information is power. The more information about your TBL efforts you provide to your customers in their role as stakeholders, the greater your ability to attract their loyal patronage. In the long run, it's a winning combination for everybody.

Employees as Stakeholders

Employees are often overlooked in their roles as stakeholders. Some companies still manage their workforces in the mode of "Employees work and they get paid," assuming that this financial transaction constitutes 99 percent of the so-called give-and-get defining the employment relationship. But in fact, employee stakeholders have a substantial impact on a company's sustainability in two major ways. First, working men and women increasingly expect businesses to help solve the world's big problems. Thus, like many other stakeholder groups, employees are helping create the pressure for sustainability that smart companies are responding to. Second, by their choices and actions, they can dramatically advance—or significantly retard—the company's efforts to create value from sweet spots.

Studies show that employees have a growing desire to be inspired by what their companies stand for. They want and expect opportunities to be involved in efforts to help make the world a better place, not only through personal activities like financial contributions and volunteer work but also in their daily tasks and activities on the job. As a result, employees pay more attention to their company's TBL reports than any other group. They know what is really going on inside the company and can be counted on to recognize when greenwashing is taking place. And many surveys have shown that today's younger employees in particular share serious concerns about environmental and social causes. As these socially engaged employees increasingly integrate their personal lives into their work environments—for example, by following the action on Facebook, YouTube, and Twitter on the laptops and cell phones they bring into the office—the expectation that they will check their personal values at the door is coming to seem increasingly unrealistic and outmoded.

Consequently, sustainability is becoming a bigger and bigger part of the employer brands of many companies, and organizations that find ways to unleash this passion are reaping major benefits. We noted in Chapter Three the impact that GE's ecomagination and healthymagination initiatives have had on the corporation's employer brand; HR leaders at GE report that the company's growing reputation as a sustainability leader is helping attract the brightest young people from college campuses and business school programs around the world.

Coffee chain Starbucks, whose business model is built around creating pleasant environments staffed with friendly, caring employees, has designed its sustainability efforts specifically to attract its ideal workers. As Rick Badgley, the company's vice president for global staffing, told us in an interview, "If your values aren't in line with ours, then I don't care how good you are; this isn't the right place for you. We try to be very thoughtful in our selection process to make sure we're aligning those values."[18] The values alignment process includes designing the company's employee recruitment Web pages to focus on Starbucks' programs to buy ethically sourced coffee, support local farmers, and stimulate economic growth in customer communities.

For Starbucks, the sweet spot is where sustainability as a way to benefit society overlaps with sustainability as a strategy for attracting great workers. The company has found it to be a remarkably large and profitable spot to occupy.

Having used their sustainability programs to attract talented, like-minded employees, many companies are now encouraging those employees to initiate, participate in, and help spread sustainability projects throughout the organization. We've seen vivid examples in previous chapters, from the creativity of middle manager Scott Hall in devising a hugely profitability solution to the Penobscot River dilemma for PPL Corporation (Chapter Six) to the numerous ecofriendly innovations devised by 3M employees under its 3P program (Chapter Nine). When employees understand that they are working for a company that shares their environmental and social values and is willing to empower them to express those values on the job, the Sustainability Sweet Spot discoveries they can generate are almost limitless.

Using Social Media to Enhance Your Stakeholder Relationships

The growth of social media is transforming the field of stakeholder relationships. In the age of Facebook, YouTube, and Twitter, almost anyone with a laptop or cell phone can become a friend or foe of your company, with the opportunity to articulate social, environmental, and economic concerns that millions of others may share and that your company can't afford to ignore. Focusing a significant fraction of your public outreach efforts (whether under the heading of marketing, public relations, shareholder relations, or corporate communications) on social media is now an everyday necessity.

One strategy being used with great success by many companies is to have full-time social network ombudsmen who monitor all Internet chatter about the company and respond if and when necessary. The most effective have broad latitude to respond truthfully and candidly to valid criticisms and proactively address possible areas for improvement. This strategy allows unhappy stakeholders, from dissatisfied customers to disgruntled community activists, to vent their frustrations while enabling the company to manage complaints before they go viral. When handled adroitly, this approach can significantly enhance your company's reputation for transparency, responsiveness, and credibility.

In addition, it's important to encourage managers from many departments and levels of your organization to get involved in social media on your behalf. Getting to know the interests, objectives, and motivations of stakeholders who are active in and around your industry can give you important advance notice of the issues that are likely to explode next. The most effective way of hearing about and understanding those stakeholders is to engage in continual, open dialogue with them—and in today's world, that often means through social media.

Achieving a balance between maintaining company oversight of individual social media activities by employees and encouraging open, freewheeling engagement can often be tricky. Of course, legal and regulatory restrictions on public communications apply on Facebook just as they do in newsprint or on television—so, for example, inappropriate disclosure of "material information" by a leading executive of a publicly traded company via social media can lead to serious legal consequences. It is also true, however, that when employees are restricted to disseminating messages that strictly "toe the company line" on social media, their blog posts, Facebook entries, and tweets tend to lose credibility and interest. The best company policy is one that empowers employees to "be themselves" online while always remembering that they represent the face of the organization and should comport themselves accordingly.

Thom Lytle is senior manager of social media at EMC Corporation, a leading supplier of cloud computing and other IT services (as well as the husband of Devon Long-Lytle, the talented researcher and consultant who helped us write this book). Lytle uses social media success stories to encourage his company's middle managers to get involved. He also emphasizes the value of a clear, well-articulated overall corporate strategy in helping employees strike the right balance between freedom and control when sending out social media messages. Lytle explains, "I spend a lot of time trying to help teams understand that social media is just one piece of a larger marketing plan. When social campaigns are planned in the absence of a larger strategy, the result is often a series of disjointed activities with little affiliation to the larger story. So the next time someone asks you to build a social media plan, I give you permission to ask them for the marketing plan first."[19]

The effectiveness of this approach may be suggested by the fact that EMC has garnered more than 1.2 million fans and followers via Facebook, Twitter, and LinkedIn—a huge base of friends and supporters that the company can call on when it has an important message to broadcast.

The ability to communicate with your stakeholders and work with them rather than against them represents a significant competitive advantage for responsible companies that are open to stakeholder engagement. Companies that do this are likely to enjoy increased goodwill as well as public and political support, two forms of capital that are particularly valuable in our interdependent world. Equally important, they will be able to fend off attacks from potential adversaries that could otherwise cripple their ability to grow, expand, or even simply remain in business in a world where a public commitment to sustainability is increasingly demanded.

To quote management guru Peter Drucker, "In the next society, the biggest challenge for the large company—especially for the multinational—may be its social legitimacy: its values, its missions, its vision."[20] The sustainability movement will be addressing this challenge in the years to come.

13

Measuring and Reporting
Your Progress

*It takes twenty years to build a reputation, and five
minutes to ruin it.*
—Warren E. Buffett, chairman and CEO, Berkshire
Hathaway Inc.

Sustainability Metrics—the Unacknowledged Driver

The classic question from high school, "Will this be on the test?"
continues to shape the psychology of most people long after they've
graduated and joined the world of work. When people know that
their behavior is being observed, measured, recorded, and published,
they change that behavior to meet the expectations, whether those
expectations are expressed or implied. When they know (or believe)
that their behavior is *not* being measured, they tend to slack off. Hence
the well-known rule of organizational behavior: what gets measured
gets done.

No wonder that the burgeoning movement to observe, measure,
record, and publish data on companies' behavior in regard to corporate social responsibility has become a key driver—though often an
unacknowledged one—of progress toward sustainable business. The
very establishment of a reporting mechanism—the TBL—creates
pressure on companies to improve their behavior.

It may seem odd, perhaps even counterintuitive, that the pressure
on companies to *report* should be one of the key drivers in making
them want to *perform*. But in fact, the sustainability metrics movement

is simply an outgrowth of the stakeholder rights movement and the critical lessons learned by environmentalists during the pollution control era.

Perhaps the simplest and most effective environmental law ever passed in the United States was the "Right to Know" (RTK) provision of the 1980 Comprehensive Environmental Response, Compensation, and Liability Act, commonly referred to as Superfund. Added in 1986 as Title III of Superfund and technically known as the Emergency Planning and Community Right-to-Know Act, RTK simply requires companies to report annually on the amount of hazardous chemicals they have within each company-owned facility. Nothing in the law requires *removal* of these dangerous materials, but companies suddenly faced with the simple disclosure requirement immediately began to take dramatic, unprecedented steps to redesign their processes to eliminate the need for these chemicals at all. No CEO or manager wanted to have to explain to the neighbors or employees or, worst of all, his children why his company was on the year's "Dirty Dozen" list of the worst polluters.

Between 1988 and 2003, the RTK law drove a 59 percent reduction in the amount of hazardous chemicals stored on-site by U.S. companies, by far the most dramatic voluntary environmental improvement in history—all because of a simple disclosure requirement.[1] And more recent data suggest that in the following decade, an additional reduction of about 17 percent has occurred, indicating that the benefits are both long term and persistent.[2]

It's not surprising that environmental and other advocates have seized upon sustainability reporting as a tool for promoting socially responsible management. From the advocates' perspective, a disclosure requirement is often the fastest way to get a company to clean up its act.

Call it the tail wagging the dog, but one company after another is now finding that the pressure to report is driving it to create sustainability programs simply to have something *positive* to report. Wal-Mart's interest in sustainability appears to have been driven in part by demands from some of the company's shareholders, including the United Methodist Board of Pension and Health Benefits, that the company issue a TBL report.[3] Similarly, PepsiCo's sustainability initiative started with a shareholder resolution by the New York City comptroller (who votes the thousands of PepsiCo shares held in the city's five public pension funds), asking the company to start using the Global Reporting Initiative (GRI) guidelines for sustainability reporting. Endorsing this trend, stock exchanges in France, the United Kingdom, South Africa, Australia, India, Malaysia, and many of the Scandinavian countries now require or strongly recommend broad nonfinancial disclosure as a condition of listing.[4]

We are firmly opposed to dog wagging. If you've decided *not* to pursue sustainability, then don't let yourself get pushed into publishing a TBL report. If you don't care what you weigh, don't waste your money on a bathroom scale. But if you do care, then you need a scale to measure how you are doing.

As with every aspect of sustainability, the business case should drive and define your reporting effort. What kinds of information will be useful to your business in pursuing its strategic goals? What data will help your company enhance efficiency, spark innovation, and increase productivity? Which information do you need to know in order to reduce waste and minimize the risks from lawsuits, regulatory run-ins, and PR disasters? What TBL information do investors want, and what information will they be seeking in the near future? Questions like these should determine what you report and how you report it.

Knowing what to report and how to report it poses a number of practical challenges, especially considering that the most widely used sustainability reporting framework, the GRI, includes 152 individual performance indicators, not all of which are equally relevant to every business. Your choices should be dictated by business considerations after identifying the data that are most relevant to making your business more efficient, profitable, and sustainable.

The Global Reporting Initiative

In 2011 (the last year for which complete data are available), more than fifty-one hundred corporations issued an environmental or social responsibility report using the reporting guidelines developed under the auspices of the GRI.[5] That includes more than 80 percent of the 250 largest corporations in the world. The GRI has clearly become the world's leading benchmark for measuring, monitoring, and reporting corporate sustainability efforts. Whether or not your company opts to use the GRI system, you need to understand it, as GRI's reporting categories and terminology are now the lingua franca of sustainability reporting around the world.

The GRI initiative was conceived by Ceres in 1997 and developed in close cooperation with the Tellus Institute, a nonprofit research center in Boston. Cosponsored by the United Nations Environment Program during the lengthy development process, the guidelines were officially released at the 2002 World Summit on Sustainable Development in Johannesburg, South Africa. Ceres continues to be a driving force behind the GRI, representing a large number of socially responsible investment groups and funds, many of which were using different, homegrown systems for measuring sustainable business practices. Those investors wanted a shared set of universal protocols, so that each new fund wouldn't have to keep reinventing the wheel.

Ceres and Tellus understood the power and logic of making corporate reporting of nonfinancial information widely available and comparable from company to company. These organizations correctly predicted that companies and investors would begin to change their behaviors as comparable, objective information became available. The GRI was thus modeled after GAAP—generally accepted accounting principles—which were established as a way of codifying, simplifying, and unifying disparate and occasionally conflicting accounting methodologies. The GRI attempts to put environmental, social, and economic reporting on the same plane as financial reporting in terms of rigor, clarity, accuracy, usefulness, comparability, and influence with investors.

Hence the idea of the Triple Bottom Line. For many, the ultimate goal is to merge GRI and GAAP information so that companies eventually issue one integrated report containing all the financial and nonfinancial information that investors need and want to know. (We'll discuss this important trend in more detail later in this chapter.)

The most recent version of the GRI guidelines (Version 4, issued in 2013) sets forth ten reporting principles designed to help reporting companies achieve transparency in sustainability reporting. The principles are stakeholder inclusiveness, sustainability context, materiality, completeness, balance, comparability, accuracy, timeliness, clarity, and reliability.[6]

The 152 indicators currently included in the GRI framework are grouped in categories to reflect the three parts of the Triple Bottom Line—environmental, social, and economic. Within each category, a series of "aspects" is outlined, with specific indicators grouped by relevant aspects. For example, within the environmental category, the following aspects are listed:

- Materials
- Energy
- Water
- Biodiversity
- Emissions
- Effluents and waste
- Products and services
- Compliance
- Transport
- Overall
- Supplier environmental assessment
- Environmental grievance mechanisms

If we drill down into one of these aspects—say, energy—we find the following five indicators listed:

- Energy consumption within the organization
- Energy consumption outside of the organization
- Energy intensity
- Reduction of energy consumption
- Reductions in energy requirements of products and services

The social category includes thirty aspects, grouped under the headings of labor practices, human rights, society, and product responsibility. Finally, the economic category includes four aspects pertaining to the economic impact of the company on society, including economic performance, market presence, indirect economic impacts, and procurement practices.

Some of the GRI indicators require quantitative responses—for example, "Energy consumption within the organization" (under the environmental category), "Financial assistance received from government" (under the economic category), and "Average hours of training per year per employee by gender, and by employee category" (under the training and education aspect of the social category). These indicators present technical hurdles, such as defining, gathering, and checking the data and making sure that information drawn from facilities, divisions, and departments in various geographical areas can be rolled up into one number for the entire enterprise. In large companies, GRI information may be found in over forty different corporate departments, from investor relations to human resources, from the supply chain to the office of the CFO. A great deal of information must also be generated by field operations.

Other indicators require descriptive verbal responses rather than quantitative ones. In the economic category, for example, the aspect referred to as "indirect economic impacts" asks companies to describe "significant indirect economic impacts, including the extent of impacts," and offers illustrative examples that include "economic development in areas of high poverty" and "availability of products and services for those on low incomes." It's up to individual companies to decide whether these impacts apply to their operations and, if so, to describe them clearly and accurately. In the environmental category, under the biodiversity aspect, companies must describe "significant impacts of activities, products, and services on biodiversity in protected areas and areas of high biodiversity value outside protected areas," including activities such as "construction or use of manufacturing plants, mines, and transport infrastructure" and "introduction of invasive species, pests, and pathogens." Once again, individual companies must determine whether they've engaged in such activities and, if so, how to describe them correctly.

As you can see, these nonquantitative indicators demand careful thought, an effort to define your company's relevant activities clearly and consistently, and, above all, a high degree of the quality of "balance"—unbiased information that includes both positive and negative aspects of your performance. In other words, you shouldn't try to spin your responses. It's far better to report information straightforwardly.

Developing a sustainability report that follows the GRI guidelines is challenging, especially for any company that is new to the process. However, the GRI offers a great deal of flexibility and can be adapted to your industry or to your company's strategic or management needs. Under the guidelines, you can choose which indicators to report, how to define the scope of your operations for reporting purposes, the degree of accuracy and reliability of the information, and any plans you have for future reporting. The guidelines also define an incremental approach that your company can use to begin the process. Companies using only a portion of the GRI guidelines can declare themselves as having prepared a "core" report, and those who use the entire framework can say they have created a "comprehensive" report. There's no stigma attached to the core level (although of course particular stakeholders may urge your organization to "graduate" to comprehensive reporting as soon as possible).

Because GRI reporting is largely about disclosure and stakeholder engagement, transparency is key. If there are data you feel you must withhold because of privacy issues, confidentiality commitments, or other concerns, your report should explain the reason for the omission. As long as you are clear about the reasons behind your choices and can manage stakeholder expectations accordingly, the guidelines provide the best framework for capturing and reporting your Triple Bottom Line.

The GRI guidelines offer many benefits to businesses. One is the availability of a uniform set of indicators that define how sustainability should be measured by companies around the world and that is widely accepted by the global advocacy community. A reasonably well prepared report following GRI guidelines is a valuable document to use when explaining or defending your sustainability efforts.

Another benefit is that studying the GRI reports developed by companies you admire—especially those in your own industry or in related industries—is an effective way to identify your sustainability strengths and weaknesses and to create performance benchmarks. Even if you choose not to use the GRI indicators as a basis for your own reporting, you may want to use them as a valuable tool for assessing risk—to identify potential problem areas your company ought to be examining before a problem arises. At a minimum, the GRI and its continuing evolution should be on your corporate radar.

If your company is thinking about TBL reporting, we urge you to use the GRI guidelines. If the entire package strikes you as too ambitious, complex, or costly, take an incremental approach. Identify the most important GRI indicators for you—the ones that drive *your* business—and work on developing accurate, up-to-date reporting on those.

Then see what kind of data you already have. If your management and information systems are well designed, you should have access to most of the necessary information already—provided that the indicators you select are as vital as you believe. It is perfectly acceptable to start by reporting only the information to which you already have ready access, as long as you are open about that. You want to make sure that your report is not misleading, and the best way to ensure that is to disclose all the limitations on the information, whether that information is partially complete, somewhat inaccurate, or reliant on outside sources. It's also a good idea to report on your plans for improving the quality of the data in subsequent reports.

Ultimately, you may or may not decide that the complete GRI framework is useful and necessary for your company. But whatever you decide, remember that your reporting practices should be driven by your business needs, not vice versa. Don't think of the GRI as an inquisitor's rod; instead, look at it as a tool for running your business more effectively.

The Costs and Benefits of Reporting

Some internal advocates for sustainability reporting have encountered serious pushback in their companies because of the costs and difficulties of collecting and analyzing the data needed to issue a credible report. Perhaps this is understandable. Public companies have traditionally devoted serious time, energy, and money to gathering and reporting financial, managerial, and other data for the benefit of investors. Since 2002, the Sarbanes-Oxley law has dramatically increased the reporting burden, requiring companies to report additional details on the quality of their financial and antifraud controls, whistleblower protection, code of conduct, and other programs to identify and control financial malfeasance and fraud. Various tax and regulatory regimes impose further obligations to report data; in the case of a large corporation, this includes rules from numerous state, national, and international regulatory bodies. It's not surprising that some companies resist calls for yet another set of complex and costly reports to satisfy yet another constituency. "With all the reporting we have to do," they say, "when are we supposed to get any actual work done?"

TBL reporting can be difficult and expensive, but it is easy to overestimate the time and cost involved. Most companies are already gathering and disclosing enormous amounts of TBL information, though some may do so in a largely uncoordinated fashion. If you were to survey your company and list all the various kinds of accounts, surveys, questionnaires, and other reports you already create for stakeholders—customers, business partners, banks, insurers, industry organizations, government agencies, employees, and shareholders—you would probably find that much of the data you need in order to create a comprehensive TBL report exists right now, somewhere within your company. If you haven't already done so, it's time to organize this vast array of chaotic information and make it work for you.

Most companies face the immediate challenge of obtaining global information rolled up on an enterprise-wide basis. This can be difficult even with financial reporting, where money is the common denominator. With TBL reporting, it takes time and resources to develop metrics for dozens of different denominators—from water use to product regulation noncompliance data to use of locally based suppliers—that are uniform across company divisions and geographies while also flexible enough to make business sense when applied to widely varying operations. Very few companies have written procedures on data collection and roll-up outside the financial area. And the sheer effort of requesting information in language that everyone understands, collecting that information, verifying its accuracy, and compiling and publishing reports that convey it in a meaningful fashion can be costly.

Nonetheless, most companies have found the benefits to be worth the effort. When driven by business imperatives, reporting often leads quickly to better management and enhanced value creation. Knowing the total amount of fuel your company consumes, the number of accidents your workers have, or the amount of government subsidies you receive—and tracking how these indicators are changing over time—enables you to recognize trends, problems, and opportunities, and puts you in a position to develop and strive for long-range, enterprise-wide goals. Simple, shared goals and measurements motivate employees and trigger conversations across divisions, departments, and business functions, leveraging best practices and promoting the spread of valuable ideas and innovations.

TBL reporting is also a way to organize a vast amount of internal and incoming information about a variety of risks and opportunities. If properly and aggressively used along with stakeholder engagement, the GRI can enable you to spot emerging economic, social, and environmental issues before they become crises.

Finally, being able to communicate with the world about your sustainability efforts has enormous business benefits. Companies that don't identify or capitalize on their sustainability activities are leaving value on the table, a serious mistake in today's hypercompetitive business marketplace. A legitimate effort to conserve natural resources or to do something positive for the community is of interest not only to the participants and to environmentalists or the neighbors but also to other stakeholders, including your employees, investors, customers, and suppliers. If the company doesn't capture those benefits by spreading the news, it has neglected an opportunity to create valuable social capital.

Furthermore, in today's wired world, it's likely that most of what you are doing is going to come out eventually. When *you* report, choosing your own time, place, manner, and style of disclosure, you build credibility and reduce negative feedback if the news you report isn't completely positive (as should usually be the case if you are being transparent).

A TBL report will assist you in expected and unexpected ways with the advocacy community. If the report is credible, it defines you as a company that "gets it," that takes its responsibilities to society seriously. This can sometimes provide a protective aura that deflects negative attention elsewhere.

Many companies have discovered the concrete benefits that a commitment to increased transparency can provide. One typical example: Andy was working with a company that faced a shareholder resolution from a religious pension fund. The trustees of the fund were demanding a report on the impact of HIV/AIDS on the company's business. The company responded that it had just signed up to issue a sustainability report using the GRI framework, and that its report would include information on the company's HIV/AIDS programs. Mollified, the leaders of the pension fund withdrew their resolution.

The Hidden Risks of Sustainability Reporting

Costs and benefits aside, sustainability reporting presents some risks that many companies do not see or evaluate until they are too far into the process to change course. These risks can be minimized or eliminated if you proceed with your eyes open.

Sustainability activists and socially responsible investors share one trait with the general public: they've learned to be highly skeptical about corporate claims of virtue. Trust in business remains low—a fact of life in today's world. Credible reporting is part of the trust rebuilding process, and you should therefore expect your sustainability reports to be challenged—particularly if they paint an unrealistically rosy image of your company. Certainly any prose that smacks of greenwashing is likely to hurt your credibility unless you are able to back up your claims with irrefutable evidence. And you may come under pressure to do so from a shareholder resolution, a lawsuit, or some other challenge.

Interestingly, any *negative* news you report is generally accepted at face value, even by antagonistic groups and individuals who normally treat every word your company utters as a falsehood. Hence this paradox: *bad news is good news.* One of the best ways to improve your company's image and its credibility among activist stakeholders and the public is to publicize your mistakes and failures—along with the corrective steps you are taking, of course. Don't report only your environmental and diversity awards or the fact that you've been named a "Best Company to Work For." You should also report that you fired a dozen employees for taking bribes, shut down a manufacturing line because of its terrible pollution record, and are working to improve the monitoring of your suppliers' unsatisfactory labor practices.

This may sound like unnecessary risk-taking, but it's more like money in the bank—an investment in credibility that will more than compensate for any short-term criticism you may receive. Any criticism that does come will be muted (and media interest dampened) by the simple fact that *you* are breaking the news. In the long run, you'll win respect for your honesty—and the next time you have good news to report, the skepticism will be just a little less intense.

One way of enhancing the accuracy and credibility of a TBL report is through the use of outside sources—something that the GRI refers to as *external assurance.* Although there are a variety of methods for achieving external assurance, two approaches are particularly popular. One is the use of an accounting firm or environmental consultancy with a dedicated program for checking the information and claims contained in company TBL reports. These analyses have the formality and feel of *attestation,* which in the world of financial reporting means that the information contained in the report (whether quantitative or not) is "fairly presented." However, fewer than one-tenth of reporting companies provide this highly rigorous type of independent verification.[7]

As we discussed in Chapter Twelve, other companies have been using a second method of pursuing external assurance. Companies like Nike and Shell have taken to inviting stakeholder panels—including environmental leaders, community activists, scientific and technical experts, business and economic analysts, and others—to evaluate their sustainability efforts and comment on them in the companies' own reports. This approach provides readers with a meaningful assurance of accountability, while giving the company the benefit of stakeholder engagement to help improve the quality of its report.

A large part of the pressure for accuracy is coming from inside companies themselves. In the post-Sarbanes-Oxley era, many managers and executives want to be sure that any number that goes outside the company is bulletproof. Advocates for TBL reporting within companies have encountered highly concerned CFOs, lawyers, and others who worry about the legal and reputational risks if an environmental or social report has a wrong number in it.

Although the focus on accuracy is to be applauded, an excessive concern with exactness can impede forward progress on reporting or result in an unduly expensive, belt-and-suspenders approach that, although possibly appropriate for financial reporting purposes, may be unnecessary for TBL reporting.

Managers should understand, as most responsible advocates certainly do, that if you are in the early stages of sustainability reporting, obtaining an exact number for global water or energy use, employee accidents, or government subsidies may be impossible and, in most cases, unnecessary. The cure for slightly inaccurate or incomplete information is disclosure and an honest effort to improve over time.

In its 2004 sustainability report, for example, Coca-Cola stated that its water and energy data covered only 68 percent of the company's operations, explaining that this was the best the company could offer at that time.[8] By the time the 2012 report was published, water and energy data covering nearly all of the company's activities were available, with the sole exception of greenhouse emissions created during the packaging process.[9] As this example illustrates, partial reporting that would be unacceptable for financial data may be acceptable in the world of TBL reporting—at least with proper disclosure. When it comes to most of the quantifiable data requested by GRI, the perfect is the enemy of the good: publish the most reliable information you have, disclose its shortcomings, and pledge to do better next year.

However, you do face a serious risk if you fail to follow through on the claims, commitments, promises, and programs you set forth in your sustainability reports. To borrow a phrase from Nike, if you've promised stakeholders that you will do something, *just do it*. The Kasky lawsuit against Nike (see Chapter Eight), which resulted in payment of $1.5 million to a workers' rights organization and the cessation of reporting by the company for three years, was sparked by the company's failure to follow through on claims it had made related to workers' rights at its supplier firms. The years of negative publicity generated by that case underscore an important lesson: before you publicly identify a particular area of sustainability as important to you, be certain you're prepared to mount a real effort to improve it, to measure and report your progress, and to substantiate your claims.

As a practical matter, most companies should devote more energy and effort to accurately describing their own policies and practices than to precisely measuring the number of gallons of water they consumed in a particular year. We know of one company that had a widely publicized "no animal testing" policy. Imagine its embarrassment when it suddenly discovered that two major divisions "hadn't gotten the memo" and were, in fact, conducting product tests on animals. Be clear and accurate when describing your policies and procedures—and make sure you practice what you preach.

Finally, you run the risk of being disappointed if you assume that doing a conscientious job of launching a sustainability program, measuring and monitoring progress, and reporting it honestly will earn you universal accolades and support from your stakeholders. Eventually, if you keep at it, you will gain credibility and win their trust. But in some cases, even well-intentioned efforts to be transparent and responsible may not be enough to keep stakeholder relationships positive. We recounted an example of this in Chapter Twelve, in describing how American Electric Power ran afoul of its erstwhile partners at Ceres and other environmental organizations due to an ill-timed, undisclosed lobbying effort. Here's another, even more disturbing example of what can happen even to companies with the best intentions.

Talisman Energy, Inc., Canada's largest independent oil company, got caught up in the tragic civil war in Sudan. Over two million people have been killed in this war since 1983, which pits the northern-based, largely Arab government against rebel groups from the predominantly non-Arab southern part of the country. The Greater Nile Petroleum Operating Company, one-quarter of which was owned by Talisman (in partnership with government-controlled companies from China, Malaysia, and Sudan), was producing oil extraction fees of up to a million dollars a day in 2001 for the Sudanese government.[10]

Outraged that a Canadian firm was helping support a murderous government, church and public pension funds (such as the influential California pension fund known as CalPERS) divested from Talisman; and Presbyterian, Episcopal, and Catholic groups began demanding that Talisman sell its interests in Sudan. In a public relations nightmare, groups of nuns began showing up at Talisman's facilities in Sudan to demonstrate, accusing the company of supporting genocide.

Talisman responded by following all the rules of stakeholder engagement, transparency, and reporting. They sent officials to attend the Sudan Catholic Bishops' Conference, met with refugee groups and NGOs, and issued detailed sustainability reports (prepared with assistance from PricewaterhouseCoopers) highlighting how their operations in Sudan were benefiting the country's people and especially their own Sudanese employees, all of whom received health and educational benefits as well as wages far higher than the national average. The company was also vocal in advocating for better human rights policies on the part of the government.

Talisman's efforts at engagement and reporting were to no avail. The nuns kept on the attack, demanding that Talisman stop paying extraction fees to the government or get out of Sudan entirely. As a result of the constant negative publicity, Talisman's stock price fell, suffering what internal and Wall Street analysts began to refer to as "the Sudanese discount," an estimated 10 percent reduction off what the company's value should have been. In October 2002, after years of unfailing efforts to be responsible, Talisman succumbed to the pressure, selling its stake in the Sudan oil operation to an oil company owned by the Chinese government.

Did the transfer of ownership improve the lot of the Sudanese people? Unfortunately, it probably made matters worse: a company trying to do the right thing was replaced by one far less committed to human rights, labor rights, employee issues, and government reform, and far less vulnerable to political pressure from the nuns.

Some businesspeople may conclude, on the basis of this story and others like it, that sustainability reporting—even the idea of sustainable business itself—is a futile delusion, and that trying to communicate and reason with stakeholders is a waste of time, money, and energy.

It's true that a strategy of transparency and stakeholder engagement offers no *guarantee* of success, either for your business or for society. But what business strategy does? The challenge is to find an approach that will improve your odds of victory—and the overwhelming evidence is that transparency and stakeholder engagement do just that. For every Talisman, there's are several cases in which a long-term commitment to sustainability has carried a company successfully through a crisis.

The Rise of Online and Integrated Reporting

The quantity of information contained in company financial reports has grown dramatically over the past few decades, especially since Sarbanes-Oxley. Now the calls for more comprehensive disclosure on the financial bottom line have clearly spilled over to the Triple Bottom Line. As we've noted, stock exchanges in several countries now require listed companies to publish TBL data. Under SEC rules established in 2003, mutual funds must now disclose how they vote their billions of shares on shareholder resolutions—many of which are about additional disclosure.

One natural response to this trend is the rise of online reporting—providing up-to-the-minute data about a company's environmental, social, and economic performance on an interactive Web page as a supplement to, or replacement for, a printed report. In 2013, for the first time, American Electric Power (discussed in Chapter Twelve) has chosen not to publish a hard copy of its TBL report, instead putting all the relevant data on the Web.

This approach offers a number of advantages, including instant updates (so that information is always current rather than lagging reality by months or even years) and live links to other relevant information (so that a reader studying the environmental performance of a company's manufacturing plants, for example, can quickly click on links that connect to air, water, waste products, employee safety, and other related topics rather than having to scroll through many pages of a report). The interactive nature of the Internet can even allow readers to easily compile their own "personalized" TBL reports by selecting charts, tables, and explanatory material from many Web pages that relate back to a handful of specific concerns.

The move toward online reporting can be seen as an outgrowth of the trend toward a networked world that we discussed in Chapter Three. If we extrapolate a bit further—factoring in the recent emergence of "big data" as a major force in shaping corporate strategies and capabilities—we can imagine a world in which corporations are becoming more and more "virtual," embodied in networks of participants and stakeholders who are continually in touch with one another and with the information that defines their shared concerns. It will be fascinating to see whether this virtual corporation is characterized by a more democratic and responsive system of governance than the traditional company, or whether it actually turns out to be more prone to manipulation and control by those with their hands on the "download data" button.

In the short term, the trend toward online reporting is driving other trends in turn. As more companies move to online reporting, the quantity and detail of information expected or even required are likely to increase—sometimes, perhaps, beyond what seems reasonable. In a rule adopted in August 2012, the Securities and Exchange Commission (SEC) began requiring companies to report purchases of metal from suppliers in countries whose governments support violent armed rebels—so-called conflict minerals.[11] It's a topic directly related to the sustainability agendas of companies like Apple and Boeing, whose products may use such metals, but it seems only tangentially connected with the financial disclosure principles that are the SEC's central mandate.

Perhaps most important, mainstream investors and financial auditors are also calling for far broader disclosure, suggesting that the information available today is not sufficient for investors to make fully informed decisions. These trends point to one natural outcome: in time, most or all businesses are likely to integrate the TBL into their traditional performance reporting, tracking environmental and social impacts alongside economic and financial results in the same quarterly and annual reports that all investors scrutinize. Companies will eventually cease to issue separate environmental or sustainability reports and will instead integrate all material information in one form that presents the complete picture that a prudent investor or other stakeholder would want to see. As GRI cofounder Allen L. White told us, "Why even bother to distinguish between what is financial information and what is nonfinancial information? It's all information. Ultimately, the important distinction is whether it is something a reasonable investor or other stakeholder would want to know."

This new reporting paradigm is already taking shape. Some companies in Europe, such as Novo Nordisk, the Danish biotechnology group, have begun to drop the distinction between sustainability and other data entirely, moving from incorporation of TBL data to full integration. The *2011 Global Responsibility Report* issued by Starbucks includes data on the company's financial performance and corporate governance along with information on environmental stewardship, ethical sourcing, and community engagement. And American Electric Power and Southwest Airlines have been producing annual reports that integrate TBL data with traditional financial results since 2010. That year, 163 companies self-identified their reports to GRI as integrated; in 2011, the number rose to 183.[12]

In support of this trend, GRI and a collection of other business, investment, and accounting organizations cofounded the International Integrated Reporting Council (IIRC) in 2009. IIRC is now working to develop a broadly accepted framework for integrated reporting, supported by a group of more than eighty worldwide businesses that form what's called the pilot program business network. Members of the network range from such industrial powerhouses as Microsoft, Clorox, Coke, and Unilever to Deloitte LLP, Grant Thornton UK LLP, and other leading accounting firms. By the end of 2013, IIRC hopes to publish its first integrated reporting framework—undoubtedly just the first step in a multiyear process by which the framework will be gradually expanded and improved through feedback from a growing number of companies.

The implication: today's Triple Bottom Line may simply be a transitional phase from an older to a newer theory of how business works—one in which environmental and social concerns are no longer relegated to a sideshow but rather inextricably intertwined with fundamental business strategies, goals, and reporting. We'll look at this possibility in more detail in Chapter Fifteen.

14

Aligning Your Culture to Support Sustainability

Things don't change. You change your way of looking,
that's all.
—Carlos Castaneda

Sustainability and Corporate Culture

By now you've probably begun thinking differently about how your business intersects with society and are looking to find ways to improve your profitability while doing the right thing for your stakeholders. That's a great start. But becoming a sustainable enterprise isn't just a matter of placing an overlay on top of your conventional business thinking. It entails making a shift from an old way of thinking to a new one—a new set of beliefs and attitudes that subtly or dramatically alter everything you see and do.

Here's an analogy. At a certain point in the last two decades, many managers learned to see fellow employees as their customers. One day, your colleague was bothering you for something he needed to do his job, not yours; the next, that same person's satisfaction with you was part of your performance evaluation—so meeting his needs became part of your job, and rightly so. Seeing and treating your colleague as a customer required a change in your underlying attitude about his or her relative importance—perhaps from "She doesn't matter, so I'll get to it when I can," to "I want her to be a satisfied customer, so I'd better do this right now and as well as I can."

This change in viewpoint was a foundation of the quality movement, a transformation that vastly improved performance within companies. Similarly, the sustainability movement is now changing the way that executives, managers, and line employees relate to their jobs and to those inside and outside the organization, with consequences that will be even more far reaching. Sustainability demands a new perspective, one that is embedded in the culture of your company.

When conducting the organizational self-assessment we described in Chapter Seven, you may have begun to notice aspects of the business that resist easy classification according to our "who you are, what you do, and how you do it" system. These are likely to include certain deep-rooted psychological and social realities that embody what is often called *corporate culture*.

Many business leaders talk about culture, but few have a systematic way of thinking about it, understanding it, or measuring it, let alone managing and changing it. The fact is that organizational culture is intangible, difficult to define precisely, and often resistant to change. Yet it is a vitally important influence on the health of the entire organization. Thus, understanding the role of corporate culture and the challenge of changing it is crucial for any leader who hopes to support an organization's movement toward greater sustainability. Any attempt to make your company more sustainable is likely to stall if it doesn't take into account your cultural strengths and weaknesses.

Yet if you are successful, the payoff can be great. Research has shown that a company with a culture that promotes sustainability is also more likely to be profitable, particularly in the long term. For example, the study by Eccles, Ioannou, and Serafeim that we cited in Chapter Two as evidence of the stock market advantage enjoyed by sustainable businesses focused specifically on companies with a sustainability *culture*.[1] So a lively awareness of the impact of your culture is a crucial element in launching any sustainability initiative.

Why Corporate Culture Resists Sustainability

Unfortunately, many companies have cultures that resist the transformation to sustainability. There are understandable reasons why this should be so.

Most successful companies were started before sustainability began to gain acceptance as an operating principle. The need to comply with laws and regulations has existed for a long time, but the idea that companies have an obligation to preserve and nurture the world has not. Almost all companies in the United States and other free-market countries were founded with the primary goal of maximizing profits while operating within the law. The measure of success was based on generally accepted accounting principles that measured financial gains in narrow terms based on a snapshot in time, which encouraged short-term profit maximization. Thus it's only natural that corporate culture at most companies has evolved to support profit maximization as the central objective. Sustainability, though growing rapidly in importance, is not yet accepted by many companies as essential to the pursuit of profit.

But even in companies that have found their sweet spots, opposition exists in terms of a resistant culture. Evidence of this can be seen when leaders require internal advocates to "prove" the business case for sustainability beyond a shadow of a doubt or demonstrate that it will produce a return on investment far higher than that required to justify other kinds of investments. In other cases, employees may not openly reject such goals as environmental stewardship or social responsibility—they may even pay lip service to them—but they quietly, perhaps even unconsciously, sabotage any efforts to change their business behaviors in order to pursue these goals.

In the long run, no company can continue to be profitable without becoming more sustainable, and no company can become sustainable without changing its culture to support sustainability. Of course, corporate culture change—though essential—is easier to describe than to create. Here are some of the most important principles to consider when you need to mount an effort to change your company's culture.

The Three Levels of Corporate Culture

Edgar H. Schein, professor emeritus at the MIT Sloan School of Management and an authority on corporate culture, defines organizational culture as "a pattern of assumptions, values, and beliefs that shape individual and organizational behavior."[2]

He goes on to identify three levels of culture, all of which must be examined if you hope to truly understand the factors that influence your organization's behavior.

The first level includes what Schein calls *artifacts*—a company's visible behaviors, organization, programs, processes, activities, and rituals. It's possible for a thoughtful observer to study these artifacts as they appear in the daily life of an organization and deduce from them certain basic conclusions about the corporate culture—the things it emphasizes or disregards, the ways resources are invested, the behaviors that are rewarded or discouraged, and so on.

The second level is made up of *espoused values*. These are revealed through explicit organizational messages (such as slogans, speeches, presentations, posters, and ads) as well as strategies, goals, and plans that embody values and serve to guide the organization. For example, when a company announces a program designed to cut greenhouse gas emissions by 30 percent, it is expressing the espoused value of minimizing environmental damage and helping to slow climate change.

The third level of culture is that of *underlying assumptions*, which Schein describes as "unconscious, taken for granted beliefs, perceptions, thoughts and feelings . . . [that are] the ultimate source of values and actions." Because these assumptions are impossible to observe directly, they often go unrecognized, even by those within the organization.

You might summarize these three levels as *doing, thinking,* and *believing,* or, as your employees might say it, "what we do," "what we say," and "what we believe" (see Figure 14.1). For culture to change,

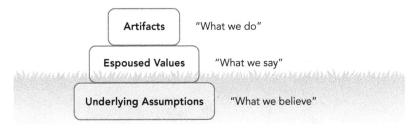

Figure 14.1   The Three Levels of Organizational Culture.

all three levels need to change in a consistent, mutually supportive fashion.

Evaluating Your Existing Culture

To formulate a plan for shaping a company culture that is aligned with your sustainability efforts, you need to understand the current situation. Begin by asking, What is our organization's *existing* culture, and how well can it support an effort to make sustainability a high priority? Answering this question may require an in-depth analysis of the explicit and implicit values, goals, attitudes, and worldview that shape the behavior of employees, based on input from people throughout the organization.

Then ask: What are the gaps or impediments between our existing culture and the sustainable culture we want to attain? In particular, try to examine the unspoken assumptions about business, work, and the company mission that underlie your daily decision-making processes and those of the people you work with most closely. You may want to consider using employee focus groups, surveys, and informal conversations to reveal the kinds of hidden beliefs employees are harboring around sustainability.

Finally ask: How does our culture need to be changed to support a move toward greater sustainability? What must we do to alter our behaviors, activities, and programs (artifacts of corporate culture), our statements of espoused values, and, above all, the underlying assumptions we take for granted every day?

As we'll see, when corporate culture is resistant, even the best-intentioned and most heartfelt commitment to change is likely to prove ineffective. So any organization that is serious about traveling the path toward sustainability needs to study the cultural barriers that may stand in the way, and develop a meaningful plan for overcoming them.

Identifying and Overcoming Underlying Assumptions That Hold You Back

Underlying assumptions that conflict with the values of sustainability are often the crucial factors that impede progress on environmental and social goals. A change initiative of any kind is unlikely to succeed if employees cling to conflicting underlying beliefs—and this is emphatically true of a change program aimed at movement toward sustainability. In our experience, identifying and systematically addressing underlying beliefs that impede progress is often the single most crucial step required in organizations that are trying to become more sustainable.

How do you go about uncovering and then challenging the underlying assumptions that impede your sustainability initiatives? This can be a challenging task. Employee surveys, focus groups, informal gatherings, one-on-one interviews—all can be helpful in ferreting out widespread beliefs that conflict with sustainability values.

When the leaders at American Electric Power (AEP) decided to transform their corporate culture into one that made worker safety the number-one priority, they first had to expose the underlying assumptions that hindered them. Through countless conversations with employees at every level, they gradually discovered that while workers heard the management speeches and "pep talks" urging adherence to safety procedures, they also believed that the company's *real* priority was to maximize speed and production. At the same time, workers also believed that safety was up to the individual and that accidents were inevitable—a matter more of luck than of safety rules violated. Assumptions like these were found to underlie many of the unsafe behaviors that AEP workers practiced.

It took time and consistent effort for AEP executives to gradually change these worker assumptions. One effective strategy was sharing the stories of individual AEP employees who had held risky jobs for decades without experiencing a single accident. The real-life examples set by these safety-minded individuals began to change the underlying belief that accidents are inevitable. The company started a program called My Brother's Keeper, which began to break down the assumption that safety was a personal matter. AEP leaders seized every opportunity to talk about the new assumptions about safety that they wanted to inculcate, and they publicly praised and rewarded employees who exemplified the changed approach. Employee training programs, evaluation systems, and financial incentives were aligned with the new emphasis on safety. Little by little, employee attitudes and the culture they supported began to change.

Over time, the effect of all these culture-shifting efforts has been significant. The number of accidents has fallen dramatically. As a result, AEP has saved over $30 million in worker's compensation and other costs between 2004 and 2011. It has also moved from the lowest quarter of the electric utility industry in safety to the top quarter, with the goal of reaching the top 10 percent by 2015.[3]

When you tackle culture change patiently and systematically, changes in underlying assumptions, values, and behavior will begin to reinforce one another. At AEP, as workers began to accept the assumption that accidents were not inevitable, some of them began to behave differently—for example, they started pointing out unsafe actions by their peers. As behaviors changed and safety results improved, an upward cycle of positive reinforcement was established. This kind of cycle is essential to a successful program of culture change. Doing, thinking, and believing are intimately related; the more energy you can bring to creating change at each of these levels, the greater your chances of shifting the entire culture to new ground.

Above all, accept the reality that culture change is complex, difficult, and slow. Don't expect the process to be completed in a matter of weeks or months. More often it involves change over years, or even generational evolution driven in part by the gradual process of employee turnover. Try not to be discouraged. Keep "working the culture" at every opportunity you get, expect resistance, and learn to celebrate small signs of improvement. Eventually you'll reach a tipping point at which positive changes begin to reinforce one another. Then and only then is it safe to anticipate victory in your company's version of "culture wars."

Corporate Capabilities That Nurture Sustainability

In addition to a supportive culture, a number of specific supporting capabilities seem to be important for companies that hope to enjoy a prolonged period of sustainable growth. *Capabilities* are talents that are widely shared among the employees of the organization and have become integrated into the daily thinking, decision making, and behavior of the company. Many of the capabilities we refer to here are widely recognized as important tools for success for almost any twenty-first-century business. They include *innovation, collaboration, long-term orientation, outward focus, interdependent thinking, learning,* and *adaptability.*[4]

We could easily dedicate an entire book to discussing each of these valuable capabilities (and some fine books have been written on each of them). However, in the remainder of this chapter, we'll focus on just four capabilities that we view as particularly crucial in relationship to sustainability: collaboration, long-term orientation, interdependent thinking, and adaptability. All of these characteristics have appeared in the stories we've shared, but they're important enough to bear further emphasis and explanation.

Collaboration

Many of today's biggest business challenges are too complicated to be met by any one person or even a single team, no matter how talented. Instead, they require the shared efforts of many people and teams with a variety of experience, knowledge, skills, and tool sets—often from multiple departments or divisions and, in many cases, from outside the organization. And this applies particularly to sustainability, which often requires multiple disciplines and perspectives.

Consider, for example, the social challenge faced by packaged goods companies accused of promoting snacks that are exacerbating the childhood obesity crisis. Fixing this problem isn't a simple matter that can be handed off to a single department within a company. Instead, it will require the combined efforts of numerous professionals: chefs, cooks, nutritionists, flavor and texture specialists, and others capable of designing new, healthier products with the taste appeal of traditional snacks; manufacturing, packaging, and shipping experts who will know how to adapt existing processes to meet new requirements (such as maintaining freshness with less use of preservatives); and perhaps most of all, marketing and advertising experts—including psychologists and anthropologists of food—who can devise ways of convincing kids to fall in love with the new goodies.

This irreducible complexity is one reason that sustainability is highly focused on working cooperatively with often demanding stakeholders: customers, suppliers, advocacy organizations, regulators, potential litigants, the news media—and your own employees, of course. The ability and willingness to learn from *anyone* who may be able to help address a crucial challenge are essential elements in any sustainability program.

Recognizing this reality, many companies have started their sustainability initiatives by creating committees near the top of the organization to steer and coordinate the effort. A committee structure creates an immediate need to collaborate, at least among the members; to share ideas and information; and, often, to establish common objectives, a vision, and a shared purpose. Getting committee members from various departments who may not regularly work together to discuss the company's activities in terms of the TBL can be a powerful catalyst, not only for creative and innovative thinking but for focused and effective collaboration.

Unfortunately, impediments to collaboration exist in many organizations; strong-willed departmental managers intent on building fiefdoms, defending turf, or maintaining what they consider necessary levels of autonomy and independence may resist efforts to encourage openness and teamwork. Managers engaged in intense feuds or rivalries with their peers in other divisions are unlikely to reform their behavior merely in response to calls for collaboration. Recognizing the existence of such impediments to collaboration and patiently, painstakingly working to reform the underlying attitudes that produce them will be a crucial element in the culture change program of many companies.

Long-Term Orientation

Understanding sustainability means seeing how the corporate world—and your industry and company in particular—works within the larger social and natural world. This is big-picture thinking: How is the world enriched or diminished by your products or services? What are your major impacts on society, and how does your overall business strategy reflect those impacts? How are stakeholders included in your decision making, and how are the costs and benefits of what you do shared among them? How do you take into account the needs of society and of future generations? Leaders of sustainable businesses will be able to answer future-oriented questions like these, and doing so requires the ability to think beyond the next quarter or two and instead to articulate a vision for the long-term future of your company.

Many companies find it useful to summarize their sustainability vision or mission in a sentence or two. DuPont's vision, for example, is to be "the world's most dynamic science company, creating sustainable solutions essential to a better, safer, and healthier life for people everywhere." PepsiCo's is to "continually improve all aspects of the world in which we operate—environmental, social, economic—creating a better tomorrow than today." Caterpillar envisions "a world in which all people's basic requirements—such as shelter, clean water, sanitation and reliable power—are fulfilled in a way that sustains our environment," and the company has taken as its mission "to enable economic growth through infrastructure and energy development, and to provide solutions that protect people and preserve the planet."

It's valuable to put your vision down on paper. A brief, well-crafted statement provides employees and stakeholders with a set of clear, broadly stated principles against which your efforts can be measured and that can be used to develop more specific guidelines, including your strategy, goals, and key performance indicators.

But developing a vision that includes sustainability is more than catchy words. It requires you to see how to incorporate the TBL and its emphasis on long-term environmental, social, and economic prosperity into every decision made throughout the organization, and to think about how it takes hold at the operating level.

Many of the stories we've told in this book involve trade-offs between short-term costs and long-term benefits. The word *sustainability* itself implies long-term thinking, because it focuses on how your company can survive and thrive in the long term, and includes consideration of future generations. It's a time frame that most American businesses—unlike many of their counterparts in Asia and Europe—aren't used to, but one that is increasingly important to businesses today.

In recent years, millions of people in the United States and around the world have been gradually coming to recognize that we live in an age and on a planet of genuine limits, and that as world population approaches nine billion, there are some problems we simply can't solve fast enough. And as this happens, the wisdom of longer-term thinking is becoming more apparent.

Much will have to change for long-term thinking to supplant quarter-by-quarter thinking in American business. U.S. business leaders need to learn from their counterparts in Asia and Europe the wisdom of planning for decades in the future, not just the next three months. Wall Street will need to learn to reward long-term growth, not just beating expectations for a quarter or a year. This will take time—but it will happen. We want to be living together here on planet Earth for a long time, and to do so, we will eventually have to change our way of looking at things.

Interdependent Thinking

A natural corollary of the capabilities we've already described is inter-dependent thinking—the ability to consider the direct and indirect results of your actions and how those might cause consequences for others. Working closely with stakeholders is one way to help see and understand more of the nonobvious connections and linkages.

Without stakeholder feedback, it's often far easier, for individuals and for organizations, to see the positive consequences of their actions and to overlook or ignore the negative ones.

Here's a striking example. In 2011, Oxfam America, the anti-poverty NGO, worked with beverage makers Coca-Cola and SAB-Miller to examine the impact of their operations on poverty in Zambia and El Salvador. Although most companies understand the connection between their organizations and economic growth, far fewer realize that they can inadvertently *create* poverty through their actions. A small detail from the Oxfam America study illustrates the point:

> For a number of years, a pipe on the outside of the Zambian Breweries plant [a subsidiary of SABMiller] was leaking treated wastewater. Community members began to use this water on their subsistence farm plots. When Zambian Breweries later installed upgrades to its water efficiency processes, it repaired the pipe and the water supply was shut off. As a result of the repair, the community no longer had access to the water that they had been using from the leaking pipe. Many community members had depended on this water to grow maize and bananas for their families. A community leader interviewed for this study stated that Zambian Breweries did not consult with the local community prior to fixing the pipe, thereby inadvertently depriving the community of an important water supply.[5]

In creating more wealth for the company (and protecting the environment), Zambian Breweries unintentionally caused economic harm to many specific members of the community.

Developing the habit of interdependent thinking empowers organizations to identify unknown but potentially important cause-and-effect relationships—positive and negative—between their behaviors and the communities in which they operate. And this is a habit that can be learned. As we saw in Chapter Twelve, Gap's employee training program now includes a deliberate effort to encourage purchasing managers to anticipate and plan for the unintended consequences of their decisions. The goal is to minimize the social and environmental harms—and maximize the benefits—caused by the interdependent relationships in which Gap is inextricably bound.

Interdependent thinking is closely linked to the reality that sustainable businesses must recognize and respond to the demands of multiple stakeholders, somehow balancing the needs and wants of shareholders, employees, customers, suppliers, communities, interest groups, and others with a legitimate interest in the organization's impacts, even if those impacts turn out to be indirect. Thus the capacity for interdependent thinking is close to the heart of sustainability. In fact, it's difficult to imagine one without the other.

Adaptability and Agility

The sustainable organization is, above all, an adaptive and agile one—one that recognizes, understands, prioritizes, and responds quickly to changes in its natural, social, and economic environment. When an organization loses the ability to adapt, it can't stay healthy for long.

Working on being able to thrive under future environmental and social conditions, while at the same time trying to optimize their own impacts today, is a high priority for sustainable organizations. Many are already dealing with such future-oriented challenges as climate change, eventual limits on the use of fossil fuels, population growth, and urbanization of the developing world.

Companies that lack the capacity for adaptability often develop sustainability programs only when a dramatic event forces them to act—and even then, they are often slow to respond effectively. Consider, for example, the relatively long reaction time of Google and Yahoo to the emergence of political censorship issues in China as key concerns of human rights activists.

Nike, for another example, first reacted to news reports about the abuse of child labor in their supplier factories with a dismissive, "Those aren't Nike facilities or Nike employees, so that isn't our problem." The resulting firestorm was exacerbated by Nike's lack of nimbleness. (As we've seen, Nike awoke in time to make the necessary adjustments and has, to its credit, worked hard to become a leader in managing the social and environmental challenges of a global supply chain.)

In a world where outside circumstances are constantly evolving in ways that are difficult to predict, companies should strive to operate according to the maxim, "Change before you get changed." Adaptability and agility give you the capacity to do just that.

• • •

Modifying your company's culture and working to develop or strengthen specific organizational capabilities represent two essential systemic responses to the challenges of sustainability. But there are signs that future trends in the relationship among business, the environment, and society may demand even more far-reaching changes than these—changes that may affect the very nature of the corporation. In the final chapter of this book, we'll examine these changes.

15

The Emerging Multipurpose Company

Sustainability: An Evolving Concept

Twenty-five years after the idea of sustainability was introduced, the theory and practice continue to evolve. As more and more companies explore its implications in their own businesses and among their own networks of stakeholders, new ways of envisioning and creating the sustainable company are being imagined and embodied. Eventually, today's idea of sustainability is likely to be viewed as simply one stage in a long journey that all of us—business leaders, consumers, community members, scholars and students, and government representatives—have embarked on together, and whose end is not yet in sight.

As the evolution of sustainability continues, the idea seems to be splitting into two parallel forms. The first views sustainability primarily as a way to maximize shareholder value. It focuses on exploring how companies can become more profitable while also becoming more responsible by finding their sweet spots—that is, by doing business in those areas where profit and responsibility overlap.

This approach to sustainability has been the central focus of this book. We've seen how PPL's management, by working with its longtime adversaries rather than combating them, was able to find a way to save the salmon and the local economy by removing two dams voluntarily—and get paid millions to do it. By contrast, the Hershey trustees failed to consider the social and economic impacts of their plan to sell the company and the powerful opposition they would encounter. Missing the sweet spot meant blowing a twelve-billion-dollar deal.

Both PPL and Hershey illustrate the first idea of sustainability as a new, more enlightened way of pursuing the traditional goal of businesses—to maximize profits.

The second idea is a more radical one. Those who embrace it raise a fundamental question: Are companies simply profit-maximizing machines whose every action needs to be directed toward the goal of increased profit for shareholders, as many business thinkers today assume? Or can companies pursue other purposes that may be just as important as profit—even goals that may not be measurable in financial terms?

Supporters of the second view of sustainability argue that maximizing shareholder value need *not* be the sole purpose of a business—or even the primary one. And in the latest phase of the Age of Sustainability, they are growing in numbers and influence.

One leader in promulgating this new approach to sustainability is Dr. Allen L. White, cofounder and former CEO of the GRI and the organization's first acting director. In White's view, mainstream business thinkers have erred in viewing shareholders—those who contribute capital in exchange for equity in business—as the only "investors" in a company. White told us, "Financial capital providers are not the only investors in the company. Other parties invest nonfinancial capital and incur risk. Communities invest their natural and social capital. Employees invest their human capital. Suppliers invest their organizational and technical capital. Yet our concept of the corporation—embodied in securities law, charters, fiduciary duty, and principles of governance—largely focuses only on financial investors. Such a perspective is both myopic and untenable in the long term for both companies and society at-large."

If financial investors are not the only ones with a legitimate claim on the value created by the corporation, then it logically follows that profits as traditionally defined should not be the sole measure of business success.

White is doing more than merely talking about his unorthodox vision of capitalism. He cofounded and heads an NGO known as Corporation 2020, which is working with business leaders, investors, scholars, economists, social activists, and many others to explore and advocate shifts in corporate purpose, design, ownership, capitalization, and governance that align with this new, broader view of the role of the corporation.

Meanwhile, the first, less radical view of sustainability as the most effective way to maximize profitability has come to be widely accepted. No company is more closely aligned with the business mainstream than the global consulting firm McKinsey & Company. So it's significant that in an opinion piece in the *Economist*, Ian Davis, the firm's former worldwide managing director, has written about the weaknesses of what he calls the "business of business is business" mind-set, part of the skeptics' response to sustainability we discussed in Chapter Five.[1]

One of these weaknesses, in Davis's view, is that a narrow-minded focus on shareholder value can lead companies to overlook crucial economic, political, and cultural trends that will have a major impact on the future of their business, involving both risks and opportunities. We quoted his words at the head of Chapter Eight, but they bear repeating: "Paradoxically, the language of shareholder value may hinder companies from maximizing shareholder value in this respect. Practiced as an unthinking mantra, it can lead managers to focus excessively on improving the short-term performance of their business, neglecting important longer-term opportunities and issues." With these words, Davis is endorsing our basic argument that in the long run, the sustainable company is likely to be a more highly profitable one as well. Davis doesn't quite join Allen White in proclaiming that maximizing shareholder value should no longer be considered the main purpose of business. Davis writes, "Shareholder value should continue to be seen as the critical measure of business success. However, it may be more accurate, more motivating—and indeed more beneficial to shareholder value over the long term—to describe business's ultimate purpose as the efficient provision of goods and services that society wants." Notice the powerful implications of Davis's reformulation. If the "ultimate purpose" of business is "the efficient provision of goods and services that society wants," then an array of stakeholders has a legitimate interest in how a company uses its resources. The "society" Davis invokes is simply a shorthand way of describing those other stakeholders: employees, business partners, neighbors, environmentalists, community leaders, and so on.

So when a company is managed wisely, it provides goods and services in ways that offer greater and greater benefits for shareholders *and* other stakeholders, with fewer and fewer adverse impacts on society and the environment and more and more positive ones. Davis sees this as a noble purpose, and we fully agree.

Companies that share this vision may ultimately define their missions so as to make them synonymous with the public good, finally arriving at Davis's view that "profits . . . [are] a signal from society that their company is succeeding in its mission of providing something people want." In other words, profit and the public good share the spotlight as equally important purposes of business. Companies that operate in this way are, in effect, moving their entire businesses inside the Sustainability Sweet Spot.

Is this vision of business merely a pipe dream? Far from it. When one of the world's most venerable and successful corporations publicly redefines itself as "a company that solves big problems for customers and the world," it is tacitly accepting Davis's formula. This is the real significance of GE's self-redefinition (which we described in Chapter Two). It quietly acknowledges that there is more to business than business—that society at large has as valid a claim on GE's creativity, productivity, and value as those who own shares of GE stock.

The Multipurpose Business: Merging Private Profit and Public Good

When we survey the rapidly changing landscape of global business with White's new definition of sustainability in mind, we quickly discover that thousands of organizations are now emerging that embody this new approach to business. They take a number of forms, but all share one fundamental understanding: organizations that produce and sell goods and services in the free market using the best techniques of contemporary capitalism may serve a variety of goals beyond profit. Thus we refer to these varying types of new enterprises as *multipurpose businesses*.

Social Entrepreneurship

One reflection of the spread of this new approach to business is the rapidly growing phenomenon of *social entrepreneurship*. The social entrepreneur is someone who uses business tools, structures, and methods to pursue social goals—reducing poverty, protecting the environment, reforming education, providing health care to the disadvantaged, and so on.

Social entrepreneurship is not entirely new. Scholars, students, and practitioners of social entrepreneurship point to a number of pioneers who illustrate how melding business disciplines and social objectives can lead to powerful, even world-changing results. One of the best known is Muhammad Yunus, who created the microfinance movement when he launched Grameen Bank.[2] By providing loans in tiny amounts (the equivalent of $5 to $100) for start-up capital to poor women in rural Bangladesh, Grameen Bank has helped jump-start hundreds of thousands of small businesses and lifted countless families out of poverty. The bank is a profit-making institution, but it has created more social benefits through its innovative financial methods than have most NGOs. It has also sprouted a network of Grameen companies that provide services such as health care and renewable energy to rural Bangladeshis.

Today, new ventures in social entrepreneurship are sprouting up all over the world. Some, like Grameen Bank, are organized as for-profit businesses; others are nonprofits that use business methods (such as producing and selling goods or providing services to paying customers) to create social benefits.

The appeal of social entrepreneurship has proven to be enormous. The concept has found its way into the MBA curriculum; the first course in the subject was offered at Harvard in 1995 by Dr. J. Gregory Dees (now at Duke University's Fuqua School of Business), and courses on social entrepreneurship are now taught at more than thirty U.S. business schools. Organizations like the Skoll Foundation and Ashoka are providing encouragement, seed money, and intellectual capital to support promising ventures in social entrepreneurship; *Fast Company* magazine covers social entrepreneurship in a continual stream of features and interviews and in an annual conference; and at Harvard Business School, sometimes dubbed "The West Point of American Business," the social enterprise club has become one of the most popular student groups, with over four hundred members.[3]

The B Corporation

Some of today's leading social entrepreneurs have been experimenting with new structures for multipurpose businesses that blend aspects of the traditional for-profit and nonprofit models. In the United States, the structure that is growing fastest is the *B corporation*.

The idea of the B corporation (B corp for short) was created by an organization called B Lab, which was founded in June 2006 by a young social entrepreneur named Jay Coen Gilbert. Sensing the need for a descriptive term for a business that has social goals as well as financial ones, Gilbert came up with the designation on the analogy of C and S corporations, which are named after specific provisions in the U.S. tax code. The B in B corp stands for "beneficial," because a B corp is supposed to provide benefits to the community in which it operates.

When Gilbert launched the concept, the B corp had no real legal status. Today, that has changed—and in a big way. As of mid-2013, California, Illinois, New York, Pennsylvania, and nine other states have passed laws defining and authorizing B corps, making this a viable option for newly minted businesses. According to these statutes, a designated B corp must include language in its governing documents (for example, its articles of incorporation, partnership agreement, or company bylaws) that specifically states that company directors may consider not just the financial interests of shareholders but also the welfare of other stakeholders, such as employees, customers, the community, and even the natural environment. The idea is to formally acknowledge the company's responsibilities to society alongside its economic responsibility to make a profit for investors.

B corp rules also typically call for publication of an annual benefit report. Gilbert's B Lab also offers a rating system that allows companies to measure their own environmental and social performance by answering a series of survey questions. As of 2013, over 770 corporations in sixty industries have opted for the B corp designation, including such well-known companies as Ben & Jerry's (a division of Unilever), Cascade Engineering, the online retailer Etsy, and the maker of ecofriendly cleaning products Seventh Generation.[4]

Perhaps the most famous is the outdoor clothing firm Patagonia, which on January 3, 2012, became the first company in California to take advantage of the state's new B corp law. Founder Yvon Chouinard, a longtime leader of the sustainability movement, believed that the certification would help Patagonia remain true to its social and environmental goals and discourage some possible future owner or manager from abandoning them.

There are currently no tax or other benefits associated with B corp status, which makes their growing popularity all the more noteworthy. Business owners and managers are opting to become B corps not because of any financial edge they may gain but simply because they want to create multipurpose companies with goals beyond profit in mind—a clear sign of the growing importance and mainstreaming of the concept.

Other Structures for Multipurpose Businesses: L3Cs, CICs, and Social Businesses

Other business structures are emerging in the United States and elsewhere that are variations on the B corp theme.

One is the *low-profit limited liability company (L3C)*. A variation on the familiar business structure known as the limited liability company (LLC), the L3C idea was originated by Robert Lang, CEO of the Mary Elizabeth and Gordon B. Mannweiler Foundation. As of the end of 2012, the concept had been legally recognized by the states of Vermont, Michigan, Utah, Wyoming, Illinois, Louisiana, Maine, North Carolina, and Rhode Island. Legislation permitting the formation of L3Cs is also being considered in more than twenty additional states.

The L3C is fundamentally a for-profit company that pursues a social purpose. Like other businesses, an L3C has one or more owners, which can include individuals, charities, or for-profit companies. An L3C can pay dividends on any financial surplus it generates. These dividends are expected to be low, as the laws creating L3Cs specify that "no significant purpose of the company is the production of income or the appreciation of property." However, there are no written guidelines limiting the size of profits, and no public regulator is designated to pass judgment on whether a particular L3C is earning profits that are "excessive." As of April 2013, there are more than eight hundred companies registered as L3Cs in the United States, most of them small, community-oriented businesses.[5]

Another new business structure is the *community interest company* (CIC), a designation available in the United Kingdom since 2005 for what the British government refers to as "social enterprises." As of 2012, there were over six thousand CICs registered in the United Kingdom.[6]

The emergence of these new legal structures, from the B corporation to the CIC, suggests the enormous ferment in the business world around issues of corporate purpose. It also reflects an issue that Muhammad Yunus of Grameen Bank has been focusing his attention on: existing legal formats in most of the world may not do justice to the needs and objectives of multipurpose businesses. In Yunus's view, neither existing for-profit structures nor the tax-advantaged nonprofit structure is entirely appropriate for the new array of organizations that are using business methods to tackle social and environmental problems.

To address this gap, Yunus has been promoting his own vision of what he refers to as *social business*. As Yunus defines it, a social business has one or more owners, generates revenues, and uses business methods, much like a traditional for-profit company. It may, like a publicly traded company, even attract funds from outside investors. But it explicitly disavows the intention of generating profits, dedicating itself solely to creating social benefits and reinvesting any surplus generated so as to spread those benefits more widely. Yunus believes that governments need to pass legislation that officially recognizes, codifies, and encourages the existence of social businesses, and he has been traveling the world addressing national leaders about this issue.

However, as we'll discuss later in this chapter, even in the absence of enabling legislation, a number of social businesses have already been launched with help from Yunus and his acolytes around the world.

Big Business and the Multipurpose Model

Having read about so many giant corporations in this book—GE, Wal-Mart, Procter & Gamble, and so on—you may think that this chapter is anomalous; the largest business we've mentioned so far, Patagonia, has annual revenues of just around $500 million. We believe that the time will come when some large publicly held company decides to formally join the ranks of multipurpose companies, perhaps by applying for B corp certification. In the meantime, however, it isn't difficult to imagine that big companies will begin to find other ways to experiment with the multipurpose model—perhaps by buying an existing B corp, partnering with one, or creating one either as a wholly owned subsidiary or as a joint venture.

When this happens, it will recapitulate a familiar pattern from sustainability history. A number of pioneering companies that helped introduce the concepts of sustainability into mainstream business were purchased by Fortune 500 companies that were seeking, implicitly or explicitly, to learn the "secrets" of sustainability in this fashion. Thus, ice cream maker Ben & Jerry's was purchased by Unilever (in 2000), yogurt maker Stonyfield Farm by the French multinational Groupe Danone (2003), health care product maker Tom's of Maine by Colgate-Palmolive (2006), and the Honest Tea Company by Coca-Cola (2011).[7]

Supporters of sustainability vigorously debated the merits of this buyout trend. Some denounced it as a series of sellouts or even betrayals, while others lauded it as a way to inject sustainability into the bloodstreams of some of the world's biggest and most influential companies. In fact, however, the corporations that made the purchases were already relatively advanced from the standpoint of corporate social responsibility, so the impacts of the buyouts were not particularly striking in either direction—more a matter of evolutionary change than revolutionary upheaval.

Might similar evolutionary change be the result if a giant company like GE or Procter & Gamble were to buy a B corp? It's possible—but the culture shock caused by absorbing a B corp into the structure of a traditional profit-maximizing company may well be significant. After all, the concept of a multipurpose business calls into question the central purpose of a company and the basic framework within which daily management decisions are made. How would a B corp subsidiary be treated when the time comes to set annual financial goals for a corporation's various divisional operations? Would credit be granted for social benefits created, or would the B corp be pressured to produce profits comparable to those generated by other divisions with no social goals to meet? What will happen when a business turndown or stock market decline leads to demands for larger financial contributions from every company unit—including the B corp? Only time will tell.

The possibility of a happy marriage between a large traditional enterprise and a multipurpose subsidiary is suggested by the experiments in social business launched by a number of corporations operating in partnership with Muhammad Yunus and the Grameen family of companies in Bangladesh. Empowered by his success at Grameen Bank and his prestige as a Nobel laureate, Yunus has persuaded the leaders of a number of important global corporations to launch social businesses to benefit the people of Bangladesh. These social businesses include Grameen Danone, which manufactures and sells vitamin-fortified yogurt at affordable prices to combat childhood malnutrition; Grameen Veolia Water Ltd., which provides clean drinking water for villagers whose local supplies are contaminated by arsenic and other toxins; and BASF Grameen, which manufactures treated mosquito nets and sells them at low prices to help prevent the spread of malaria.

Each of these social businesses is a joint venture between one or more Grameen companies and a particular corporation (Groupe Danone, Veolia Water, and BASF). The Bangladeshi companies and their international partners both contribute investment funds and expertise, and they share an understanding that, although the joint venture should be self-supporting, no contribution to the profits of either parent company is expected.

What benefits do the leaders of Danone, Veolia, and BASF derive from this arrangement? There are several: the prestige of a partnership with a widely admired business and philanthropic leader; the satisfaction of participating in a project that will benefit the people of one of the world's poorest countries; and an opportunity to learn about customers and business conditions in South Asia, one of the world's most underserved but rapidly growing regions. For now, those motivations appear to suffice.[8]

New Ways to Finance Multipurpose Businesses

Over the centuries, many mechanisms have developed to finance traditional profit-maximizing businesses, including commercial and investment banks, stock exchanges, mutual funds, and venture capital funds. All are based on the assumption that the companies financed will produce competitive financial rewards in return for the funding they receive.

But what about the multipurpose business? If a company is not focused primarily on maximizing profit, how will investors or lenders be found to provide the money needed to start the company and help it grow? On the surface, this might appear to be an unanswerable question. Why would anyone invest with no hope of earning at least a market rate of return? Isn't the sole motivation of investors to make a good return on their money?

Further thought, however, suggests that the situation isn't as black-and-white as this. Not all investors are dedicated solely to maximizing their own returns. The existence and growth of socially responsible investing (SRI), as discussed in Chapter Three, demonstrates that many investors want their money to create social benefits as well as economic returns. As SRI continues to grow and gain influence, the funds it generates may begin to flow toward multipurpose businesses, helping fuel their future growth.

SRI funding alone, however, may not suffice to fund all the multipurpose businesses needed to address the world's many complex social problems—especially those multipurpose businesses that explicitly disavow any intention of earning profits or paying a return on investments.

New funding mechanisms are emerging in response to this need. These new financial enterprises have entered the marketplace to provide financing to enterprises whose goal is to provide social or economic benefit to communities in need.

A leading example is Acumen Fund. Founded in 2001 with philanthropic contributions from the Rockefeller Foundation, Cisco Systems Foundation, and three individual donors, Acumen Fund funds early-stage multipurpose businesses that address specific areas of social need: health care, water, housing, alternative energy, and agricultural development. The money provided is in the form not of grants like those given by foundations but rather of loans or equity investments, much like the seed money invested by venture capital funds. And just as a venture capital fund takes partial ownership of the start-ups it supports, providing technical, management, and marketing expertise, Acumen Fund takes an equity position in the social ventures it funds as well as providing access to expert guidance and advice to enhance their performance. Any profits are reinvested in the fund.

Because the money that Acumen invests derives either from charitable donations or from its past investments, the fund can afford to make longer-term investments than the typical for-profit venture capital firm. The expected payback or exit term for an Acumen investment is seven to ten years. As the fund's website observes,

"Patient capital is a third way that seeks to bridge the gap between the efficiency and scale of market-based approaches and the social impact of pure philanthropy."[9]

In its decade-plus of operations, Acumen Fund has invested in more than ninety organizations in eight countries, ranging from a Kenya-based company that manufactures malaria-fighting medicines made from the extract of the artemisia plant to a chain of hospitals that treats preventable eye diseases in Andhra Pradesh, the fifth most populous state in India. Some are for-profit businesses; others are non-profits. All, however, are evaluated according to strict set of financial, operational, and social metrics. They are also benchmarked against a real or hypothetical nonprofit alternative known as the best available charitable option, as the leaders of Acumen Fund are determined to ensure that the initiatives they fund outperform traditional charities.

Acumen Fund is not the only organization that is experimenting with innovative ways of funding multipurpose businesses. Echoing Green, a nonprofit founded in 1987 with support from General Atlantic, a leading growth equity firm, supports both for-profit and nonprofit organizations that meet its definition of social entrepreneurship. Its best-known program is the highly competitive Echoing Green fellowships, which provide up to $90,000 in seed money to assist social entrepreneurs in launching new organizations.[10]

New Profit is a "venture philanthropy fund" that, like many foundations, supports only nonprofit organizations. However, the New Profit model differs from that of the traditional foundation in its use of rigorous metrics (which track both the revenue growth and social benefits created by the organizations funded) as well as in its provision of cutting-edge business and management advice through its partnership with Monitor Group, a leading consulting firm.[11]

The success of Acumen Fund, Echoing Green, New Profit, and similar organizations shows that multipurpose businesses are attracting significant financial support. It seems that many deep-pocketed institutions and individuals agree with us that the multipurpose business is likely to be an important source of social, environmental, and economic progress in the years to come.

New Ways of Measuring Value

With so many business leaders recognizing the potential for sustainable business strategies to enhance shareholder value, there's a growing demand for new ways of measuring business value that take environmental, social, and economic factors into account. One response to this demand is the growing trend toward including TBL data in traditional financial reports. As we saw in Chapter Thirteen, online reporting and integrated reporting are two increasingly popular features of TBL reporting that are making it easier for company observers to find both traditional financial measures and TBL data and to instantly draw connections between the two.

Mainstream sources of financial information are also moving to provide more TBL information. An example is Bloomberg ESG, a data service launched in July 2009 by the eponymous company that is the world's leading source of business and financial information. It was the brainchild of Curtis Ravenel, Bloomberg's director of sustainability, who repeatedly pointed out to his colleagues that environmental and social forces are having a growing impact on the financial performance of virtually every company. Now Bloomberg ESG (which stands for "environmental, social, and governance") is channeling news about the importance of TBL performance into every office on Wall Street.

Today, when Bloomberg's customers turn on their terminals in the morning, they can see ESG data—greenhouse gas intensity per sales, water usage, employee fatalities, toxic discharge, and more than one hundred other indicators—as part of their basic package alongside the rest of the Wall Street alphabet soup. (The ESG data does not cost extra.) And investors are using it: in the second half of 2010, five thousand unique customers in twenty-nine countries accessed more than fifty million ESG indicators via Bloomberg's screens—a 29 percent increase over the first half of the year. "We expect that trend to continue," Ravenel says. Recently, Goldman Sachs, Deutsche Bank, UBS, Merrill Lynch, and Credit Suisse launched divisions to analyze ESG data from Bloomberg and its ESG competitors. (A number of these competitors have bought one another or merged in the wake of Bloomberg's entry into the field.) "We feel there's enough quality data out there now that we place it on our platform in a variety of ways and from a variety of different vendors," says Bruce Kahn, senior investment analyst of Deutsche Bank Climate Change.[12]

An even more innovative and potentially important example of how traditional management systems are adapting to the new world of sustainable business is the founding, in 2012, of the Sustainability Accounting Standards Board (SASB), an attempt to reflect TBL impacts in the world of corporate accounting.

SASB is a nonprofit organization that is creating accounting standards for publicly listed corporations to use when providing sustainability data to investors and the public.[13] This fledgling effort has already attracted support from a number of heavy hitters in the world of business, including financial backing from Bloomberg and participation by the highly influential California Public Employees' Retirement System (CalPERS) fund.

SASB is not merely a competitor with GRI for companies interested in reporting their TBL metrics. Jean Rogers, the founder and executive director of SASB, notes, "We're going after the 34,800 other potential issuers [of stock] that are not GRI reporters to get everyone reporting on a minimum set of things. That's our target market. For companies that are GRI reporters, SASB will be a piece of cake."[14]

SASB's ambitious program will undoubtedly take years to achieve. But if it succeeds, TBL metrics will routinely be considered alongside traditional financial measurements like revenues and profits, providing a uniform set of comparisons by which to judge the total performance of companies.

Finally, in the broadest sense of "value measurement," some economists are beginning to consider whether traditional measures of economic growth, such as gross domestic product (GDP), are an accurate reflection of the actual well-being of societies. Increasing numbers of scholars and analysts have started to question the assumption (built into statistics like GDP) that all economic activity is a net plus. For example, recovery efforts after the Deepwater Horizon oil spill, Hurricane Sandy, or even the terrorist attacks of 9/11 have all been measured as economic output, serving to increase the GDP and thereby boost the perception of "economic growth." But most people don't consider the work we do as a society to bounce back from horrific tragedies as a positive that belongs in the plus column of our national accounts.

So economists have been working to devise better measures for economic development on the national or even global level. For example, an international group called the Social Progress Imperative has developed a Social Progress Index that tracks the performance of fifty national economies in such areas as nutrition, medical care, shelter, environmental sustainability, and access to higher education. "We are measuring the things that really matter to people's lives," says economist Michael Green, who directs the project, "such as 'Do I have a roof over my head?' and 'Do I have enough to eat?'"[15] In the 2013 index, Sweden ranked highest, Ethiopia last; the United States came in sixth, just below Germany and above Australia. Comparable efforts to measure sustainable economic performance on the national level include the Better Life Index created by the Organization for Economic Cooperation and Development, and the UN's Human Development Index, which tracks national progress in health, education, and income.

These new macro-economic measures echo the same theme reflected in the proliferation and growing sophistication of multipurpose businesses: *The purpose and value of business cannot be measured by profit alone.* The confluence of all the trends described in this chapter suggests that millions of people around the world are coming to share this conviction.

Global Problems and Business Opportunities

Throughout this book, we've shown how the role of business is being redefined in an interdependent and interconnected world. In truth, the roles of all social institutions today are under scrutiny and facing redefinition. If it was once possible to draw bright lines separating the responsibilities of business, government, and the institutions of civil society, that day is past. In a world of rapid, unpredictable, and dangerous changes, pragmatism is the order of the day, and partnerships that shatter barriers, combine resources from many sectors, and (above all) get things done quickly and effectively are increasingly important.

You may have noticed that throughout this book, we have not relied on any altruistic or save-the-world justification for sustainability. That's deliberate. We do believe that most people, including most business managers, share at least some degree of what Adam Smith called "universal benevolence" (see Chapter Six)—that is, they care about their fellow human beings and would like to do their part in making the world a better place. But we also know that businesspeople are under intense pressure to produce growth and profits for their companies, and that any suggestion that a business should focus its efforts elsewhere than on profitability isn't likely to be warmly received in most boardrooms today. We've therefore tried to emphasize the sweet spot and the strong, growing evidence that it is possible, through creative management, to overcome most potential conflicts between being profitable and being responsible.

Still, we'd be remiss if we failed at least to suggest the tremendous and exciting opportunity for the corporate sustainability movement to make huge inroads in the major problems facing humankind in the twenty-first century. These problems include

- Global climate change and the need to adapt to melting ice, rising sea levels, and potential disruption to growing cycles and the food supply
- Worldwide or large-scale regional epidemics
- Millions of annual deaths from preventable diseases, crime, or environmental causes
- War, terrorism, and other forms of violence
- Global hunger and poverty
- Shortages of potable water and lack of sanitation

- Dwindling supplies of rare metals and other important natural resources
- Illiteracy and lack of educational resources for millions of children
- Aging and infirm populations in much of the developed world
- The growing economic gap between rich and poor
- Loss of personal privacy

Today some of these problems affect primarily the peoples of the developing world—Latin America, Asia, and sub-Saharan Africa. But others (such as climate change and dependence on fossil fuels) have implications for rich and poor alike. And all, unless they are solved, will increasingly trouble the nations of the developed northern hemisphere, as growing desperation in the south leads to increased migration, political and social upheaval, and regional wars with the potential to spark global conflict.

Governments and international institutions, from the United Nations to the World Bank, must work to solve these problems. But business will play a central role based not simply on altruism but also on enlightened self-interest. As Bjorn Stigson, former president of the World Business Council for Sustainable Development, likes to say, "Business cannot succeed in a society that fails."[16] And even if it could (for a time), do you really want to live in a world where 30 percent of the population lives in resplendent luxury while 70 percent live in ever-increasing squalor and misery and hopelessness . . . even if you happen to be among the fortunate few?

Self-interest in the most straightforward sense may yet play a major role in helping solve the problems of our century. As illustrated by the "base of the pyramid" movement, one aspect of the sustainability mind-set involves learning to see the opportunities hidden in problems—even problems as vast and daunting as those we listed above.

There's an old business parable that may be relevant here. According to the story, rival shoe companies sent consultants to visit a developing tropical nation newly opened for trade, asking that they report back on business prospects. After a week or so, the first consultant wired back to the home office, DON'T WASTE YOUR TIME HERE. EVERYONE IN THIS COUNTRY GOES BAREFOOT. The second consultant, however, had a different reaction. He sent a telegram exulting, FABULOUS BUSINESS OPPORTUNITY. MILLIONS OF PEOPLE AND THEY ALL NEED SHOES!

The seemingly intractable problems of our world are not simply invitations to philanthropy; they are also opportunities for corporate engagement, with the potential of producing benefits for all—provided we open our eyes to see them.

Appendix

Creating a Sustainability Management System

We believe that a systematic approach to sustainability requires at least the following elements:

Vision   How you see business, your industry, and your company in terms of the challenges associated with environmental, social, and economic issues. Example: "Our vision is to increase shareholder and societal value while decreasing our environmental footprint."

Strategy   A plan of action that puts your vision into effect (in other words, a plan that seeks the sweet spot). Example 1: Creating new products that will sell well and biodegrade. Example 2: Reducing the amount of energy and water used in manufacturing.

Goals   Specific aspirations or targets related to the strategy. Most useful when designated to be achieved by a certain date. Example 1: By the end of the year, develop a new biodegradable plastic with specific characteristics. Example 2: Conduct a global assessment of current water and energy use and identify opportunities for efficiencies, within eighteen months.

Procedures and protocols   Procedures that prescribe behavior designed to achieve the goals. Most useful when written down, well understood, and endorsed by affected employees. Example 1: Include the development of the new polymer in the annual performance objectives (that is, the incentive plan) of the head of R&D. Example 2: Establish procedures that require employees to shut off the lights before leaving work.

Key performance indicators (KPIs)   Measures or mileage markers that indicate whether procedures are actually working to help the company meet its goals. Example 1: Has the new polymer been designed and tested for biodegradability? Example 2: Have incentives been created to encourage waste reduction and energy savings at the plant level?

Measurement and reporting   Specific ways to account for or measure performance against the goals. Measurement, Example 1: Indicia of biodegradability: for example, new polymer biodegrades within eight months when exposed to air, but will not degrade when landfilled. Measurement, Example 2: Indicia of resource conservation: company is now using 6 percent less energy and 9 percent less water per employee. Internal reporting, Example 1: Provide monthly progress report on polymer creation to vice president for corporate strategy and sales. Internal reporting, Example 2: Plants provide monthly reports on water and energy usage and related costs, in standard format, to environmental department and office of the CFO. External reporting, Examples 1 and 2: Use GRI reporting indicators, including the following: 1.1, vision and strategy; 2.9, stakeholders; 2.14, significant changes in products; 3.9–3.12, stakeholder engagement; 3.16, initiatives to improve product design to minimize negative impacts associated with manufacturing, use, and final disposal; 3.19, programs related to environmental performance; EN14, significant environmental impacts of principal products; EN3 and EN4, energy use; EN5, total water use.

Stakeholder engagement   Interaction with stakeholders that influences the decisions and behavior of the company, from vision to measurement and reporting. Example 1: Meet with environmentalists, regulators, and end users to ensure that that new plastic will actually be discarded in such a way that it will biodegrade. Example 2: Work with community to understand the impact of plant water usage on surrounding community.

Culture   The pattern of actions, statements, and underlying beliefs that shape the behavior of an organization. In some cases, companies do and say the right things, but are stymied in their pursuit of TBL goals by underlying beliefs that are out of synch with sustainability. Example: The company that describes safety as its "highest priority" but that doesn't recognize, compensate, or promote employees based on their safety performance, due to an underlying belief that accidents are largely unavoidable and that safety rules tend to reduce productivity.

Key Action Steps

This list expands on the elements discussed in the glossary and serves as a framework for assessment, design, and implementation of a sustainability management system. It follows Part Two of the book, but there are many ways to start the process, and your approach need not follow the outline presented here.

I. Conduct a self-assessment.

Remember: When assessing where your company stands, make sure you look at sources outside the company and at what key stakeholders are saying.

A. Look at your company's sustainability or environmental reports.

- Are they balanced? (That is, do they contain positive and negative information?)
- Are they based on data and objective information?
- Are they comprehensive? (Do they "tell the whole story"?)
- Do they set forth specific goals for the future along with ways to measure progress?
- Do they include or incorporate feedback from stakeholders?

B. Look at how your company operates. Does your company

- Generally comply with laws and regulations and respect the role of regulators?
- Have positive relations with its employees and the communities in which it operates?
- Extend its analysis of TBL impacts to include its value chain (that is, impacts from cradle to grave)?
- Have minimization or optimization programs for environmental, social, or economic impacts?
- Have a good record of environmental protection?
- Consider social and environmental issues before taking major actions and work to minimize adverse impacts and maximize positive ones?

C. Understand the impacts of products and services your company provides.

- What are the primary environmental, social, and economic impacts of your company's products or services?

- What are their secondary impacts? (In other words, what are the company's side effects, e.g. in terms of product use or disposal?)
- Does the company serve or impact any protected or vulnerable people, operate in any environmentally sensitive areas, or confront any critical social issues?
- What specific industry issues is your company facing?

Consider: Organize the findings in a way that is most useful to you in terms of finding sweet spots. As you look at where the company stands, it might be useful to identify the organization's strengths, weaknesses, risks, and opportunities as a way of gaining further insight into the design and implementation of your programs.

II. Find your Sustainability Sweet Spot.

Remember: You can develop a sustainability strategy at any level of the organization, from corporate headquarters to departments to plants and offices. You can also develop strategies in collaboration with suppliers, customers, and others outside of the business itself.

A. Use the sustainability map to search for sweet spots.
- Plot different options in terms of their impacts on society and profitability.
- Look for overlaps between business objectives and sustainability considerations.
- Minimize adverse impacts ("be less bad"): identify and improve processes that create waste; look for areas of stakeholder conflict; compare your impacts with those of other companies or of the industry.
- Optimize positive impacts ("be more good"): push or build from minimization efforts; develop new products or service ideas to help; look for new markets "in plain sight."

B. Link environmental or social objectives to business strategy.
- Understand your organization's business objectives and how your part of the organization supports them.

- Find ways to support your business objectives through environmental, social, or economic programs (for example, conservation to support an objective of increased efficiency, sustainability education to support an objective of leadership development).

C. Leverage strengths and relationships.
  - Identify customer needs.
  - Differentiate from your competitors.
  - Leverage your skill sets and expertise (for example, if you're in the food business, focus on sustainability goals related to food or agriculture).
  - Anticipate future needs and trends.

Consider: Focus on the best three ideas you have and try to create projects by coordinating with other departments that would need to be involved. Make sure you emphasize the "wins" for that department in terms of its existing objectives.

III. Launch your program (goals, procedures, and KPIs).

Remember: Before establishing goals, procedures, and KPIs, look at the GRI guidelines and other reporting frameworks (for example, those of your competitors and in your industry). Also consider education and training on new goals, procedures, and KPIs.

A. Set goals.
  - Begin with existing business goals and with the TBL information you already have.
  - Identify possible environmental, social, and economic goals: Are they reasonable and achievable, clear and understandable, internally consistent and supportive of business goals?
  - Determine ways to advance toward business goals by addressing TBL issues.

B. Establish procedures.
  - What departments, business units, and facilities must participate to achieve the goals?

- Write simple paragraphs in plain language that describe what needs to happen in order to reach the goals. Describe the behaviors you seek to change and how these will differ with new procedures.
- Identify existing procedures into which new procedures can be embedded, or write new procedures that contain the required language.

C. Develop KPIs.

- Identify and clearly define all key terms used to describe goals.
- Identify ways to measure progress toward each goal (consider leading and lagging indicators).
- Strive to define all KPIs in terms of a number.
- For nonnumerical KPIs, look for objective descriptors.

Consider: Make sure that your goals, procedures, and KPIs tie together and form a cohesive framework: goals should suggest procedures, which should suggest KPIs, which measure progress toward achieving the goals. Each element should support both business objectives and sustainability strategies.

IV. Consider your resources and how to organize your efforts.

Remember: Organize your effort in a way that works best for your company or department. Benchmark your competitors or look at how other successful initiatives have been organized within your company.

A. Review your options. Should your company

- Assemble a task force to initiate and coordinate your efforts?
- Find or appoint one or more sustainability champions to drive your initiatives within their division?
- Establish a sustainability department?
- Create a virtual sustainability department?
- "Piggy-back" on existing department(s) (for example, environment or community relations)?

Consider: You will need two additional resources—funding and technical. Minimization programs (for example, water and energy conservation) can produce immediate savings, which can be used to support other programs with more long-term payback. Think about leveraging existing technical expertise when you choose what programs to develop.

V. Establish a process for stakeholder engagement.

Remember: Stakeholder engagement is the key to finding and staying on the sustainable path and can help you identify, move into, and expand the sweet spot. Even if you could do everything "right" without it, stakeholder engagement is an indispensable element of "doing business in an interdependent world." Try to get into a positive relationship with key stakeholders before you need them; it helps not to have a specific ulterior motive when launching new relationships.

A. Understand your current level of engagement with stakeholders and the means by which you engage with them (for example, Internet, phone calls, face-to-face meetings, memos). Does your company

- Engage in ongoing partnership?
- Engage in project-specific partnership?
- Engage in open multiparty or two-way dialogues?
- Listen actively?
- Listen passively?
- Refuse to listen (you talk, they listen)?
- React?
- Ignore?
- Antagonize?

B. Understand your current approach toward stakeholder engagement. Is it

- Systematic engagement or ad hoc?
- Proactive or reactive?
- Long-term or short-term in its perspective?
- Trusting or suspicious?

C. Map your stakeholders.

- Conduct a target analysis: Who are your stakeholders?

- Create an impact chart: What issues and activities affect your stakeholders?
- Create a priority table: How can your stakeholders affect you? Who is most important, and why?

D. Understand what you want from engagement.
- Use a simple map and engagement strategy if you want to develop a dialogue and a mutually beneficial relationship without trying to influence a specific outcome.
- Use advanced mapping and strategy if you have a specific objective and want to gain support or minimize opposition.

E. Choose the appropriate level of engagement.
- Do your homework and due diligence on stakeholders.
- Understand the likelihood of success, failure, and middle grounds.
- Develop a solid exit strategy.
- Be prepared for the unexpected.
- Be prepared for the long haul.
- Set expectations internally and externally—then lower them.

F. Develop radar.
- Establish networks: identify reliable sources of information on trends and issues that may affect your business in the future, and systematically work those networks.
- Follow as much relevant Web traffic as you can according to reasonable time constraints and priorities. Consider whether and how to participate in Web-based information forums.

Consider: Think about the three most recent unpleasant surprises that came from outside the company or department. Ask, How did we miss this? What can we do to make sure we are not surprised in that way again?

VI. Measure and report your results.

Remember: Reporting is the tail that wags the dog for many companies; they start with the need to report, then develop programs in order to have something to report, then try to justify what they are doing in terms of the business case. This is backwards.

A. Start with the business case.
- Make sure you have a strong business need or rationale for what you are measuring and how you are reporting or planning to report it.

B. Consider any need that might seem outside the business case for reporting.
- Look beyond your value chain to determine other important constituencies. The important point is to recognize why you are reporting, to whom, and for what purpose.

C. Consider the Global Reporting Initiative.
- Divide the indicators into three categories according to their relevance to your business: strong, moderate, weak business need.
- Look at all the indicators again and figure out whether you have the data, can easily obtain the data, or haven't a clue how to obtain them. Cross-reference data availability with the business case to determine how to proceed.

D. Take an incremental approach.
- Start with the indicators for which there are a strong business (or stakeholder) case and available data. Once those systems are complete, consider other indicators for which there is a strong business case but no available data. Add more information each year until you are reporting on the full range of indicators that pertain to your business.

E. Consider seeking stakeholder input.
- Following steps (A) through (D) will give you the makings of a reporting strategy. Next consider your stakeholders and what they might say about your overall reporting plans.

- Consider how and where you might be flexible in responding to stakeholder requests for additional or different information.
- Anticipate their specific requests and how you will respond.
- Work toward getting stakeholders involved in helping you determine the content and focus of your report.
- Make sure you have a workable reporting plan before you make a public commitment.
- As needed, continue internal reporting (for example, for management purposes) that is not reported publicly, provided this does not contradict your public report.

F. Engage in industry-specific planning.
- Make sure that you look for industry-specific reporting guidance and issues and for helpful technical protocols regarding ways to measure and report specific TBL issues.

G. Assess the costs and risks of reporting.
- Look carefully at the costs of reporting before you make a commitment: many companies underestimate the difficulty of obtaining and reporting information with sufficient precision for public reporting.
- Look at the hidden risks. Are you willing to publish bad news and unflattering information? If not, reconsider whether you want to report at all. Also consider whether you will verify the information in your report and how you will do so.

H. Be transparent.
- Although you do not need to make everything available, you do need to discuss the reasons for any omission.

Consider: Your ultimate goal should be integrated reporting—one unified report that doesn't distinguish financial and nonfinancial information but rather contains all information that would be relevant to a prudent investor.

VII. Consider whether your culture is supportive of your efforts.

Remember: Sustainability flourishes in companies with supportive cultures where actions, statements, and underlying beliefs are in alignment. If you are having trouble embedding sustainability throughout your organization, consider the possibility that opposing underlying beliefs may be thwarting your efforts. Understand your organization's culture or cultures (there may be more than one). What are employees doing, saying, and believing about sustainability? Does this vary from division to division or at the top, middle, or bottom of the organization?

   A. Identify opposition at a cultural or organizational level and find collaborative ways to change those opposing views.

   B. Role-model the behaviors and attitudes you want to have within your organization. If you don't believe in or act on sustainability, don't expect others to.

   C. Establish, promote, and glorify leaders who are making sustainability a reality. Many case studies we've cited depend on a strong executive or an inspired and determined midlevel manager. Companies that support and nurture their leaders and future leaders are far more likely to progress on sustainability than those who don't.

   D. Do leaders at the top express a clear sustainability message, in simple terms, that is repeated and disseminated throughout the organization? Are leaders putting resources behind their sustainability commitments? Is there accountability for goals and achievements?

   E. Engage in long-term thinking. Sustainable companies find ways to think and act in their long-term interests, despite enormous pressure to act only in the short-term interest of their investors.

And remember the words widely attributed to Mahatma Gandhi: "You must be the change you want to see in the world."

Notes

Introduction

1. The story of how the combination of overfishing, declining whale stocks, and the growing availability of alternative fuels (such as kerosene) gradually decimated the Atlantic whaling industry starting in the mid-nineteenth century is told in many sources, including such books as *Men and Whales*, by Richard Ellis (New York: Knopf, 1991).

2. Fiona Harvey, "Overfishing Causes Pacific Bluefin Tuna Numbers to Drop 96%," *Guardian*, January 9, 2013, http://www.guardian.co.uk/environment/2013/jan/09/overfishing-pacific-bluefin-tuna; "Overfishing Strips Tens of Millions from Southeast Economy," Environmental Initiatives Fact Sheet, Pew Charitable Trusts, September 4, 2012, http://www.pewenvironment.org/news-room/fact-sheets/overfishing-strips-tens-of-millions-from-southeast-economy-85899414509.

3. See John Elkington, *Cannibals with Forks: The Triple Bottom Line of 21st Century Business* (Philadelphia: New Society, 1998), especially ch. 4.

Chapter 1

1. Useful sources of background information on Milton S. Hershey and the history of the company he founded are *The Emperors of Chocolate: Inside the Secret World of Hershey and Mars*, by Joel Glenn Brenner (New York: Random House, 1999), and *Hershey: Milton S. Hershey's Extraordinary Life of Wealth, Empire, and Utopian Dreams*, by Michael D'Antonio (New York: Simon & Schuster, 2006).

2. "Company Profile," Hershey Company, October 1, 2012, http://www.thehershey company.com/investors/company-profile.aspx.

3. Jerry Kammer, "Hershey Leaves a Bitter Taste for Foreign Students," Center for Immigration Studies, August 23, 2011, http://www.cis.org/kammer/hershey-j1-students; Julia Preston, "Companies Point Fingers as Students Protest Conditions at Chocolate Plant," *New York Times*, August 15, 2011, http://www.nytimes.com/2011/08/19/us/19students.html?_r=0.

4. Jennifer Gordon, "America's Sweatshop Diplomacy," *New York Times*, August 24, 2011, http://www.nytimes.com/2011/08/25/opinion/americas-sweatshop-diplomacy.html.

5. Peter Jackson, "Student Workers at Hershey Facility Win Back Wages," Associated Press, November 14, 2012, http://bigstory.ap.org/article/student-workers -hershey-facility-win-back-wages.

6. *Corporate Social Responsibility Progress Report 2011*, Hershey Company, 2011, http://www.thehersheycompany.com/assets/pdfs/hersheycompany/Hershey2011 CSRReport.pdf.

7. Ibid., p. 2.

8. Ibid., pp. 21–22.

9. Gina-Marie Cheeseman, "Grocers Demand Hershey Ethically Source Cocoa," *TriplePundit*, August 24, 2012, www.triplepundit.com/2012/08/grocers-demand -hershey-ethically-source-cocoa/.

10. Jenara Nerenberg, "Hershey Gets a Not-So-Sweet Kiss for Fair Trade Month," *Fast Company*, October 5, 2010, http://www.fastcompany.com/1693089/hershey -gets-not-so-sweet-kiss-fair-trade-month.

11. Harry Stevens, "Child Labor Concerns Across Hershey's Supply Chain Prove It Pays to Be Proactive," *GreenBiz*, October 19, 2012, http://www.greenbiz .com/blog/2012/10/18/child-labor-concerns-hershey-supply-chain.

12. Global Exchange, Green America, the International Labor Rights Forum, and Oasis USA, *Time to Raise the Bar: The Real Corporate Social Responsibility Report for the Hershey Company*, September 2010, www.greenamerica.org/pdf /HersheyReport.pdf, pp. 4–5.

13. Our account of the attempted sale of Hershey Foods by the board of the Hershey Trust is based on numerous press accounts as well as interviews with many participants in the events described, including Joe Berning, Millie Landis Coyle, John Dunn, Michael Fisher, Ric Fouad, Bruce Hummel, John Long, Michael Macchioni, Bruce McKinney, Kathy Taylor, and Dick Zimmerman. A good contemporary account of the controversy can be found in "Hershey: Sweet Surrender," by John Helyar, *Fortune*, Oct. 1, 2002, www.fortune.com/fortune/subs /print/0,15935,366947,00.html. Specific quotations and details are cited in the notes that follow.

14. Shelley Branch, Sarah Ellison, and Gordon Fairclough, "Sweet Deal: Hershey Foods Is Considering a Plan to Put Itself Up for Sale," *Wall Street Journal*, July 25, 2002, p. A1.

15. Interview by Karl Weber, June 2005.

16. "How Hershey Made a Big Chocolate Mess," *BusinessWeek*, September 9, 2002, p. 54.

17. Dan Ackman, "Hershey Says No, Bankers Cry Foul," *Forbes*, September 18, 2002, www.forbes.com/2002/09/18/0918topnews.html.

18. Quoted in Robert Frank and Sarah Ellison, "Meltdown in Chocolate-town—Controlling Trust at Hershey Bows to Opposition to Sale; Company Faces Future Alone," *Wall Street Journal*, September 19, 2002, p. B1.

19. Quoted in Ackman, "Hershey Says No."

20. Frank and Ellison, "Meltdown in Chocolatetown."

21. "The Best and Worst Managers," *BusinessWeek*, January 13, 2003, p. 84.

22. Interview by Karl Weber, June 2005.

23. Rick Lenny, from an interview for J. Mack Robinson College of Business, Georgia State University, Oct. 1, 2004, http://robinson.gsu.edu/video/executive.

24. *Working Better Together: Our Corporate and Social Responsibility Report 2004*, Cadbury Schweppes, 2004, www.cadburyschweppes.com/NR/rdonlyres/8E1AF189 -9CC6-4CF8-8FEC-5CAF93CF10B6/0/00_2004CorporateSocialResponsibility Report.pdf.

Chapter 2

1. Quoted in Marc Gunther, "Money and Morals at GE," *Fortune*, November 15, 2004, p. 176.

2. Steve Bailey, "Forget the Elephant," *Boston Globe*, June 3, 2005, p. E1.

3. Interview with Beth Comstock, GE senior vice president and chief marketing officer, by Andrew W. Savitz and Karl Weber, May 9, 2011.

4. Quoted in "GE Hotline Gives Workers Some Clout," *Financial Times*, May 19, 2005, p. 19.

5. "No Kind of Hula Hoop: How GE Turned Wind Energy into Billion-Dollar Business," Arab Forum for Environment and Development, June 5, 2012, www.afedonline.org/en/inner.aspx?contentID=774.

6. "GE's Growth in Wind Reflects Changing Nature of World Markets," SustainableBusiness.com, November 20, 2012, www.sustainablebusiness.com/index.cfm /go/news.display/id/24296.

7. "GE's Ecomagination Reaches $105 Billion in Revenue," *Reuters*, June 28, 2012, www.reuters.com/article/2012/06/28/idUS208085+28-Jun-2012+ BW20120628.

8. Ian Davis, "The Biggest Contract," *Economist*, May 26, 2005, http://www .economist.com/node/4008642/.

9. Moran Zhang, "PepsiCo Inc. Betting on Emerging Markets for Continued Growth," *International Business Times*, April 2, 2012, http://www.ibtimes.com /pepsico-inc-betting-emerging-markets-continued-growth-432904.

10. Megha Bahree and Mike Esterl, "PepsiCo's Health Push: Global Nutrition Unit Sells 'Good for You' Products in India," *Wall Street Journal*, July 7, 2011. Available at http://online.wsj.com/article/SB100014240527023045631045763612501 40013250.html.

11. Stephanie Strom, "PepsiCo to Foster Chickpeas in Ethiopia," *New York Times*, September 10, 2011, http://www.nytimes.com/2011/09/21/business/pepsicos -chick-pea-plan-includes-taking-on-famine.html.

12. Amanda Little, "An Interview with Wal-Mart CEO H. Lee Scott," *Grist*, April 13, 2006, http://grist.org/article/griscom-little3/.

13. Stephanie Clifford, "Unexpected Ally Helps Wal-Mart Cut Waste," *New York Times*, April 13, 2012, http://www.nytimes.com/2012/04/14/business/wal-mart -and-environmental-fund-team-up-to-cut-waste.html.

14. David Barstow and Alejandra Xanic von Bertrab, "The Bribery Aisle: How Wal-Mart Got Its Way in Mexico," *New York Times*, December 17, 2012, http://www.nytimes.com/2012/12/18/business/walmart-bribes-teotihuacan.html?page wanted=all; Syed Zain Al-Mahmood, Tripti Lahiri, and Dana Mattiolo, "Bangladesh Fire: What Wal-Mart's Supplier Network Missed," *Wall Street Journal*, December 10, 2012, http://online.wsj.com/article/SB1000142412788732402 4004578169400995615618.html.

15. Data from *Sustainability Pays Off: An Analysis About the Stock Exchange Performance of Members of the World Business Council for Sustainable Development (WBCSD)* (Vienna: Kommunalkredit Dexia Asset Management, October 2004), http://issuu.com/hanac66/docs/sustainability-pays-off.

16. Charlie Kannel, "Socially Responsible Investments: How Do They Stack Up?" *Motley Fool*, September 14, 2012, http://www.dailyfinance.com/2012/09/14/socially-responsible-investments-how-do-they-stac/.

17. Robert G. Eccles, Ioannis Ioannou, and George Serafeim, "The Impact of a Corporate Culture of Sustainability on Corporate Behavior and Performance," Harvard Business School Working Paper no. 12-035, *Working Knowledge*, November 14, 2011.

18. The notion that sustainability can improve your business by helping you protect it, run it, and grow it was originally formulated by the World Business Council for Sustainable Development.

19. Steve Stecklow, "Virtual Battle: How a Global Web of Activists Gives Coke Problems in India," *Wall Street Journal*, June 7, 2005, p. A1.

20. Quoted in Andrew W. Singer, "The Perils of Doing the Right Thing," *Across the Board*, October 2000, p. 18.

21. "GM Food Banned at Monsanto Canteen," *Urban 75*, December 24, 1999, www.urban75.org/archive/news099.html.

22. Brian Hindo, "Monsanto: Winning the Ground War," *BusinessWeek*, December 5, 2007, www.businessweek.com/stories/2007-12-05/monsanto-winning-the-ground-war.

23. "140 Groups and Scientists Urge Senate to Oppose GM Clause in Global Food Security Act," Food Democracy Now! blog, April 16, 2010, http://food democracynow.org/blog/2010/apr/16/140-groups-scientists-urge-senate-oppose-gm-clause/.

24. "Eco-Efficiency Performance Overview," Unilever Global, 2012, http://www.unilever.com/sustainable-living/ourapproach/eco-efficiencyinmanufacturing/performance/.

25. Estimate for 2005 by U.S. Green Building Council, cited in Rebecca Smith, "Beyond Recycling: Manufacturers Embrace 'C2C' Design," *Wall Street Journal*, March 3, 2005, p. B1; estimate for 2011 from "Green and Sustainable Building Construction in the U.S.: Market Research Report," *IBISWorld*, December 2011, www.ibisworld.com/industry/green-sustainable-building-construction.html?partnerid=prweb.

26. C. K. Prahalad, *The Fortune at the Bottom of the Pyramid: Eradicating Poverty Through Profits* (Upper Saddle River, NJ: Wharton School Publishing, 2005).

27. "About Us," Wegman's, www.wegmans.com/webapp/wcs/stores/servlet /CategoryDisplay?storeId=10052&catalogId=10002&langId=-1&identifier= CATEGORY_507; Matthew Boyle, "The Wegman's Way," *Fortune*, January 24, 2005, p. 62; Adrian Slywotzky with Karl Weber, *Demand* (New York: Crown Business, 2011).

28. "Letter from William Clay Ford, Jr.," *Sustainability 2011/2012*, Ford Motor Company, 2012, http://corporate.ford.com/microsites/sustainability-report-2011 -12/review-letter-ford.

Chapter 3

1. "DuPont Corporate Profile," Pesticide Action Network, August 2010, www.panna.org/resources/corporate-accountability/profiles/dupont.

2. "Global Hazardous Waste," DuPont, www2.dupont.com/inclusive-innovations /en-us/gss/sustainability/commitments/global-hazardous-waste.html.

3. John Kenly Smith, "DuPont: The Enlightened Organization," http://www2 .dupont.com/Heritage/en_US/Enlightened/Enlightened.html.

4. "Core Values," DuPont, http://www2.dupont.com/Phoenix_Heritage/en_US /1805_detail.html.

5. Alex Taylor III, "The Greatest Business Decisions of All Time," *Fortune*, October 1, 2012, http://money.cnn.com/gallery/news/companies/2012/10/01/greatest -business-decisions.fortune/2.html.

6. Peter F. Drucker, *Management: Tasks, Responsibilities, Practices* (New York: HarperCollins, 1973), p. 314.

7. Economist Intelligence Unit, *Democracy Index 2011: Democracy Under Stress*, 2011, http://www.sida.se/Global/About%20Sida/Så%20arbetar%20vi /EIU_Democracy_Index_Dec2011.pdf.

8. "Social Responsibility," Procter & Gamble, http://www.pg.com/en_US /sustainability/social_responsibility/index.shtml.

9. "Chairman's Letter," *Procter & Gamble Annual Report*, 2012, http://annualreport .pg.com/annualreport2012/files/PG_2012_AnnualReport_letter.pdf.

10. "Apple Suppliers 2011," Apple, http://images.apple.com/supplierresponsibility /pdf/Apple_Supplier_List_2011.pdf.

11. "Global Manufacturing" [map], Nike, August 2012, www.nikeinc.com/pages /manufacturing-map.

12. "Detox Our Future," Greenpeace, http://www.greenpeace.org/international/en/ campaigns/toxics/water/detox/; Simon Birch, "How Activism Forced Nike to Change Its Ethical Game," *Guardian* GreenLiving blog, July 6, 2012, http://www .guardian.co.uk/environment/green-living-blog/2012/jul/06/activism-nike.

13. "Water Map Shows Billions at Risk of 'Water Insecurity,'" *BBC News*, www.bbc.co.uk/news/science-environment-11435522.

14. United Nations, Department of Economic and Social Affairs, "World Population Prospects: The 2010 Revision," December 6, 2012, http://esa.un.org/unpd/wpp/index.htm.
15. Sarah Murray, "Students Spread a Worthy Gospel," *Financial Times*, July 11, 2005, p. 10.
16. "Take Part Infographic: 2012—Social Activism," Take Part/TBWA, 2012, http://columnfivemedia.com/work-items/takepart-infographic-2012-social-activism/.
17. D. Steven White, "The Top 175 Global Economic Entities, 2011," August 11, 2012, http://dstevenwhite.com/2012/08/11/the-top-175-global-economic-entities-2011/.
18. Quoted in Andrew W. Savitz and Karl Weber, *Talent, Transformation, and the Triple Bottom Line: How Companies Can Leverage Human Resources to Achieve Sustainable Growth* (San Francisco: Jossey-Bass, 2013), p. 22.
19. "2013 Shareholder Resolutions," Interfaith Center on Corporate Responsibility, http://www.iccr.org/shareholder/trucost/index.php.
20. "Leading Corporate Sustainability Issues in the 2012 Proxy Season: Is Your Board Prepared?" Ernst & Young, 2012, www.ey.com/Publication/vwLUAssets/2012_proxy_season/$FILE/2012_proxy_season.pdf.
21. "SRI Basics," US SIF: The Forum for Sustainable and Responsible Investment, 2013, http://www.ussif.org/sribasics.
22. R. Edward Freeman, *Strategic Management: A Stakeholder Approach* (Boston: Pittman, 1984).
23. Edelman, "2012 Edelman Trust Barometer Executive Summary," retrieved from Scribd, www.scribd.com/doc/79026497/2012-Edelman-Trust-Barometer-Executive-Summary.

Chapter 4

1. Quoted in "The Debate over Doing Good," *Business Week*, August 15, 2005, p. 76.
2. Quoted in "Corporate Sustainability in the World Economy," UN Global Compact, 2011, http://www.unglobalcompact.org/docs/news_events/8.1/GC_brochure_FINAL.pdf.
3. *Insight Report: Global Risks 2012, Seventh Edition*, World Economic Forum, http://www3.weforum.org/docs/WEF_GlobalRisks_Report_2012.pdf.
4. "MBA in Corporate Social Responsibility (CSR) and Business Ethics," TopMBA, www.topmba.com/snippet/mba-corporate-social-responsibility-csr-and-business-ethics; "MBA Oath: Responsible Value Creation," MBA Oath, http://mbaoath.org/.
5. See, for example, Michael Robinson, Anne Kleffner, and Stephanie Bertels, "Signaling Sustainability Leadership: Empirical Evidence of the Value of DJSI Membership," *Journal of Business Ethics*, July 2011, available at http://link.springer.com/article/10.1007/s10551-011-0735-y?LI=true#page-1.

6. We are so convinced of the importance of HR to the sustainability movement that we've written an entire book on the subject: Andrew W. Savitz and Karl Weber, *Talent, Transformation, and the Triple Bottom Line: How Companies Can Leverage Human Resources to Achieve Sustainable Growth* (San Francisco: Jossey-Bass, 2013).

Chapter 5

1. Data available from the Responsible Care website, www.responsiblecare-us.com.
2. "Getting There: Ray's Story," Interface, http://www.interfaceinc.com/getting _there/Ray.html.
3. "Interview for *Women's Own* ('no such thing as society')," Margaret Thatcher Foundation, September 23, 1987, www.margaretthatcher.org/speeches/display document.asp?docid=106689.
4. Einer R. Elhauge, "Corporate Managers' Operational Discretion to Sacrifice Corporate Profits in the Public Interest," in Bruce L. Hay, Robert N. Stavins, and Richard H. K. Vietor (eds.), *Environmental Protection and the Social Responsibility of Firms: Perspectives from Law, Economics and Business* (Washington, DC: Resources for the Future Press, 2005).
5. See, for example, "Business Trusted More on Climate Change," *Environmental Leader*, January 17, 2013, http://www.environmentalleader.com/2013/01/17 /business-copes-better-with-climate-change/.
6. Jared Diamond, "What's Your Consumption Factor?" *New York Times*, January 2, 2008, http://www.nytimes.com/2008/01/02/opinion/02diamond.html ?pagewanted=all.
7. Adam Smith, "Of Universal Benevolence," in *The Theory of the Moral Sentiments* (1759, pt. 6, sect. 3, chap. 3).
8. Quoted from an interview in A. J. Vogl, "Managerial Correctness," *Across the Board*, July/Aug. 2004, www.conference-board.org/articles/atb_article.cfm?id =266.

Chapter 6

1. Quoted in Ian Urbina, "Dam Builder Becomes a Dam Breaker to Help Save a Species," *New York Times*, September 22, 2004, p. A20.
2. Our account of the Penobscot River restoration project developed by PPL and a consortium of Native American and environmental groups is based on extensive press coverage as well as interviews that Karl Weber conducted with several participants, including John Banks, Laura Rose Day, Scott D. Hall, and Gordon W. Russell, during August 2005. All quotations from these individuals are derived from those interviews. (Also see note 3.)
3. This passage and some other details about the history of the Penobscot River are drawn from the Penobscot Partners website, www.penobscotriver.org /histories.html.

4. James McCarthy, "More Energy, Fewer Dams: A New Approach to Hydro-power," *Mainebiz*, August 31, 2012, www.mainebiz.biz/apps/pbcs.dll/article
?AID=/20120903/CURRENTEDITION/308309997/1088&template=Mobile
Art.

5. "Fact Sheet," Penobscot River Restoration Trust, September 2012, www.penob
scotriver.org/assets/FactSheet-September2012Final.pdf.

6. McCarthy, "More Energy, Fewer Dams."

Chapter 7

1. Edward Lawler and Christopher Worley, *Management Reset* (San Francisco:
Jossey-Bass, 2011), pp. 21–22.

2. See the GRI website, http://database.globalreporting.org/.

3. *GreenBiz*, http://www.greenbiz.com; CSR Wire, www.csrwire.com; Business for
Social Responsibility, www.bsr.org; Interfaith Center on Corporate Responsibility, www.iccr.org.

4. *Connecting with Society*, Ford Motor Company, 1999, www.ford.com/en/company
/about/corporateCitizenship/connectingWithSociety/default.htm.

5. Michael Moss, "The Extraordinary Science of Addictive Junk Food," *New
York Times Magazine*, February 20, 2013, http://www.nytimes.com/2013/02/24
/magazine/the-extraordinary-science-of-junk-food.html?pagewanted=all.

Chapter 8

1. Ian Davis, "The Biggest Contract," *Economist*, May 26, 2005, http://www
.economist.com/node/4008642/.

2. Quoted in James Brooke, "At Tokyo Auto Show, a Focus on Fuel, Not Fenders,"
New York Times, November 4, 2005, p. C1.

3. Eric Louie, "3 Ways Walmart and Its Suppliers Are Reducing Packaging,"
GreenBiz, June 5, 2012, www.greenbiz.com/blog/2012/06/04/3-ways-walmart
-and-its-suppliers-are-reducing-packaging?page=full.

4. John Elkington, *Cannibals with Forks: The Triple Bottom Line of 21st Century
Business* (Philadelphia: New Society, 1998).

5. You can view this cartoon by entering the following URL into the Way-
back Machine (http://archive.org/web/web.php): www.geocities.com/Athens
/Acropolis/5232/comicmay97.htm.

6. "Newsmaker: Phil Knight," *NewsHour with Jim Lehrer*, May 13, 1998, www.pbs
.org/newshour/bb/business/jan-june98/nike_5–15a.html.

7. *Corporate Responsibility Report fy04*, Nike, 2004, http://nikeinc.com/system/assets
/1836/Nike_FY04_CR_report_original.pdf.

8. Amy Westervelt, "Target, Nike, Levi's Join Forces on Sustainable Clothing,"
Forbes, July 26, 2012, www.forbes.com/sites/amywestervelt/2012/07/26/target
-nike-levis-join-forces-on-sustainable-clothing/.

9. For a summary of the facts in the Kasky case, see "Kasky vs. Nike: Just the Facts," Reclaim Democracy! http://reclaimdemocracy.org/nike/kasky_nike_justfacts .html.

10. Sheila Shayon, "Nike Better World? Not for Converse Factory Workers in Indonesia," *BrandChannel*, July 13, 2011, www.brandchannel.com/home /post/2011/07/13/Nike-Just-Not-Doing-It-Right.aspx.

11. Mark Dice, "Wendy's New Obesity Burger," YouTube, www.youtube.com/watch ?v=YNB5LqkVCCg.

Chapter 9

1. "Our Vision," Unilever, www.unilever.com/aboutus/introductiontounilever /ourmission/.

2. "Fighting for the Next Billion Shoppers," *Economist*, June 30, 2012, www .economist.com/node/21557815.

3. *Unilever Sustainable Living Plan: Progress Report 2011*, Unilever, www.unilever .com/images/uslp-Unilever_Sustainable_Living_Plan_Progress_Report_2011 _tcm13-284779.pdf.

4. Sarah Murray, "Queen's Awards for Enterprise: Diversity of British Endeavour Wins the Greatest Accolade," *Financial Times*, April 21, 2005, p. 7.

5. Chester Dawson, "Proud Papa of the Prius," *BusinessWeek*, June 20, 2005, p. 20.

6. "Earth Day Voices: William McDonough," Worldchanging, April 16, 2007, http://www.worldchanging.com/archives/006492.html. Also see William McDonough and Michael Braungart, *Cradle to Cradle: Remaking the Way We Make Things* (New York: North Point Press, 2002).

7. Information on 3M's 3P program is available at "3P—Pollution Prevention Pays," 3M, http://solutions.3m.com/wps/portal/3M/en_US/3M-Sustainability /Global/Environment/3P/.

8. From interviews with internal human resources consultants at PwC conducted by Andrew W. Savitz.

9. Matthew Boyle, "Breakaway Brands—Subway," *Fortune*, October 31, 2005, p. 162; "Subway, the World's Biggest Restaurant Chain: by the Numbers," *Week*, March 11, 2011.

10. James Glanz, "Power, Pollution and the Internet," *New York Times*, September 22, 2012, www.nytimes.com/2012/09/23/technology/data-centers-waste-vast -amounts-of-energy-belying-industry-image.html?pagewanted=all&_r=0.

11. John Elkington, *Cannibals with Forks: The Triple Bottom Line of 21st Century Business* (Philadelphia: New Society, 1998), p. 203.

12. "Recycling Business Adds Global Value to Trash," *Asahi Shimbun*, June 9, 2005, p. 23.

13. "Brownfields and Land Revitalization: Basic Information," Environmental Protection Agency, http://www.epa.gov/brownfields/basic_info.htm#plan; Ray A. Smith, "Developers See Green in 'Brownfield' Sites," *Wall Street Journal*, June 1, 2005, p. B1.

14. Ibid.

15. Institute for Sustainable Development, "DuPont" [case study], *BSD Global*, www.bsdglobal.com/viewcasestudy.asp?id=123.

Chapter 10

1. Rob Bernard, "Earth Day 2012: A Progress Report," Microsoft Corporate Citizenship blog, April 16, 2012, http://blogs.technet.com/b/microsoftupblog/archive /2012/04/16/earth-day-2012-a-progress-report.aspx.

2. Charles O. Holliday Jr., Stephan Schmidheiny, and Philip Watts, *Walking the Talk: The Business Case for Sustainable Development* (Sheffield, England: Greenleaf, 2002), p. 147.

3. "Green Management 2015," Sony, www.sony.net/SonyInfo/csr_report/environ ment/management/gm2015/.

Chapter 11

1. Quoted in "The Perils of Doing the Right Thing," by Andrew W. Singer, *Across the Board*, Oct. 2000, p. 17.

2. "The Race to Save a Rainforest," *BusinessWeek*, November 24, 2003, p. 125.

3. Jared Diamond, *Collapse: How Societies Choose to Fail or Succeed* (New York: Viking, 2005).

4. Robert Lalasz, "Bringing Loggers and Villagers Together for Forest Conservation," Nature Conservancy, April 2009, www.nature.org/ourinitiatives/regions /asiaandthepacific/indonesia/explore/bringing-loggers-and-villagers-together -for-forest-conservation.xml.

5. Ibid.; Megan Sheehan, "Reduced Impact Logging," Nature Conservancy, April 2009, www.nature.org/ourinitiatives/urgentissues/global-warming-climate -change/explore/reduced-impact-logging.xml.

6. A useful and concise summary of the Brent Spar episode appears in "Lessons from Brent Spar," by Dirk Maxeiner, on the Maxeiner & Miersch website, www.maxeiner-miersch.de/lessons_from_brent_spar_e.htm.

7. Anthony K. Valley, "Southern Baptists End Disney Boycott," *In the Faith*, June 23, 2005, www.inthefaith.com/2005/06/23/southern-baptists-end-disney -boycott.

8. Interview by Karl Weber, June 2005.

Chapter 12

1. "Fact Sheet: Non-Governmental Organizations (NGOs) in the United States," HumanRights.gov, http://www.humanrights.gov/2012/01/12/fact-sheet-non -governmental-organizations-ngos-in-the-united-states/.

2. Quoted in John Elkington, *Cannibals with Forks: The Triple Bottom Line of 21st Century Business* (Philadelphia: New Society, 1998), pp. 134–135.

3. Quoted in Sarah Murray, "Campaigners Use Peace as a Weapon," *Financial Times*, May 5, 2005, p. 4.

4. *Corporate Responsibility Report fy04*, Nike, 2004, http://nikeinc.com/system/assets /1836/Nike_FY04_CR_report_original.pdf.

5. Disclosure: author Andy Savitz has worked with the leaders of AEP in his capacity as a corporate consultant.

6. "Letter to AEP from Ceres Stakeholder Team," in *2009 Corporate Responsibility Report*, American Electric Power, 2009, http://www.aepsustainability .com/fastfacts/reports/docs/CS_Report_2009_web.pdf, pp. 61–62.

7. Frances Beinecke, "How Many Lives Will the Utility Giant AEP Sacrifice to Get Weaker Clean Air Safeguards?" Switchboard (National Resources Defense Council staff blog), May 10, 2011, http://switchboard.nrdc.org/blogs/fbeinecke /how_many_lives_will_american_e.html.

8. *Corporate Responsibility Report fy04*, Nike, 2004, http://nikeinc.com/system/assets /1836/Nike_FY04_CR_report_original.pdf.

9. "Global Manufacturing" [map], Nike, http://manufacturingmap.nikeinc.com/.

10. *Linking Opportunity with Responsibility: Sustainability Report 2004*, Procter & Gamble, 2004, www.pg.com/content/pdf/01_about_pg/corporate_citizenship/sustain ability/reports/sustainability_report_2004.pdf.

11. Forbes Insights, "Procter & Gamble: Building a Community of Support," in *Global Diversity Rankings by Country, Sector and Occupation*, 2012, pp. 6–7, www.dpiap.org/resources/pdf/global_diversity_rankings_2012_12_03_20.pdf.

12. Syed Zain Al-Mahmood, Tripti Lahiri, and Dana Mattiolo, "Bangladesh Fire: What Wal-Mart's Supplier Network Missed," *Wall Street Journal*, December 10, 2012, http://online.wsj.com/article/SB1000142412788732402400457816940009 95615618.html.

13. Elkington, *Cannibals with Forks*, pp. 134–135.

14. "Walmart Launches the Sustainability Consortium in China, Sets Supplier Targets," *Environmental Leader*, October 25, 2012, www.environmentalleader .com/2012/10/25/walmart-launches-the-sustainability-consortium-in-china -sets-supplier-targets/.

15. Amy Westervelt, "Target, Nike, Levi's Join Forces on Sustainable Clothing," *Forbes*, July 26, 2012, www.forbes.com/sites/amywestervelt/2012/07/26/target -nike-levis-join-forces-on-sustainable-clothing/.

16. Quoted in Marc Gunther, "Who's Peddling Pulp Fiction in the SFI vs. FSC Forestry Wars?" *GreenBiz*, March 30, 2011, http://www.greenbiz.com /blog/2011/03/30/whos-peddling-pulp-fiction-sfi-vs-fsc-forestry-wars?page=full.

17. Stephanie Strom, "McDonalds Menu to Post Calorie Data," *New York Times*, September 12, 2012, www.nytimes.com/2012/09/13/business/mcdonalds-to -start-posting-calorie-counts.html.

18. Andrew W. Savitz and Karl Weber, *Talent, Transformation, and the Triple Bottom Line: How Companies Can Leverage Human Resources to Achieve Sustainable Growth* (San Francisco: Jossey-Bass, 2013), p. 331.

19. Quoted in Lauren K. Ohnesorge, "EMC Advice: Don't Regulate Social Media," *Triangle Business Journal*, March 28, 2013, http://www.bizjournals

.com/triangle/blog/socialmadness/2013/03/emc-advice-dont-regulate-social
-media.html?page=all.

20. Quoted in Charles O. Holliday Jr., Stephan Schmidheiny, and Philip Watts, *Walking the Talk: The Business Case for Sustainable Development* (Sheffield, England: Greenleaf, 2002), p. 128.

Chapter 13

1. "2003 Toxic Release Inventory Public Data Release eReport," Environmental Protection Agency, 2005, www.ep.gov/tri/tridata/tri03/2003eReport.pdf.

2. "Releases of Toxic Chemicals Increased by 8 Percent in 2011, EPA Data Show," *Bloomberg BNA*, January 18, 2013, available online at http://www.bna.com/releases-toxic-chemicals-n17179871917/.

3. Lynn Moore, "Wal-Mart Must Face the Music: Asked for 'Sustainability' Report," *Montreal Gazette*, June 3, 2005, p. B1.

4. "Current Corporate Social Responsibility Disclosure Efforts by National Governments and Stock Exchanges," Initiative for Responsible Investment and the Hauser Center for Nonprofit Organizations at Harvard University, http://www.stakeholderforum.org/fileadmin/files/Government%20disclosure%20efforts.pdf.

5. Statistic from "Sustainability Disclosure Database," GRI, http://database.globalreporting.org/.

6. Global Reporting Initiative, *Sustainability Reporting Guidelines*, Version 4, 2013, https://www.globalreporting.org/resourcelibrary/GRIG4-Part1-Reporting-Principles-and-Standard-Disclosures.pdf.

7. Raz Godelnik, "Why It's Time to Stop Accepting Unaudited CSR Reports," *TriplePundit*, December 21, 2011, http://www.triplepundit.com/2011/12/time-stop-accepting-unaudited-csr-reports/.

8. *Every Day, Around the Globe: The Coca-Cola Company 2004 Environmental Report*, Coca-Cola Company, 2004, www2.coca-cola.com/citizenship/environmental_report2004.pdf.

9. *2011/2012 GRI Report*, Coca-Cola Company, October 7, 2012, www.coca-colacompany.com/sustainabilityreport/downloads/2012-sustainability-report.pdf.

10. "Talisman Pulls out of Sudan," *BBC News*, March 10, 2003, http://news.bbc.co.uk/2/hi/business/2835713.stm.

11. "SEC to Require Rare Earth Purchase Accountability," *Energy Business Daily*, August 22, 2012, available online at http://www.energybusinessdaily.com/mobile-technology/sec-require-rare-earth-purchase-accountability/.

12. Aleksandra Dobkowski-Joy and Beth Brockland, "The State of Integrated Reporting: Innovation and Experimentation in the Merging of ESG and Financial Disclosure," Framework LLC, March 2013, http://framework-llc.com/wp-content/uploads/2013/03/FrameworkLLC_StateOfIR_Rev0313.pdf.

Chapter 14

1. Robert G. Eccles, Ioannis Ioannou, and George Serafeim, "The Impact of a Corporate Culture of Sustainability on Corporate Behavior and Performance," Harvard Business School Working Paper no. 12-035, *Working Knowledge*, November 14, 2011.

2. Edgar H. Schein, *The Corporate Culture Survival Guide*, New and Revised Edition (San Francisco: Jossey-Bass, 2009), p. 4.

3. Andrew W. Savitz and Karl Weber, *Talent, Transformation, and the Triple Bottom Line: How Companies Can Leverage Human Resources to Achieve Sustainable Growth* (San Francisco: Jossey-Bass, 2013).

4. For a more detailed discussion of capabilities that underlie sustainability, see *Talent, Transformation, and the Triple Bottom Line*, ch. 8, from which the discussion in this chapter is, in part, adapted.

5. Oxfam America, Coca-Cola Company, and SABMiller, *Exploring the Links Between International Business and Poverty Reduction: The Coca-Cola/ SABMiller Value Chain Impacts in Zambia and El Salvador*, December 2011, http://www.oxfamamerica.org/files/coca-cola-sab-miller-poverty-footprint-dec -2011.pdf. p. 68.

Chapter 15

1. Ian Davis, "The Biggest Contract," *Economist*, May 26, 2005, http://www .economist.com/node/4008642/.

2. Coauthor Karl Weber has collaborated on two books with Professor Yunus, *Creating a World Without Poverty* (2007) and *Building Social Business* (2010).

3. "Social Enterprise at Harvard," Harvard Social Enterprise Conference, http://socialenterpriseconference.org/about/social-enterprise-at-harvard/.

4. B Lab [B corporation website], http://www.bcorporation.net.

5. "Here's the Latest L3C Tally," interSector Partners, L3C, http://www .intersectorl3c.com/l3c_tally.html.

6. CIC Association, http://www.cicassociation.org.uk/about/what-is-a-cic.

7. Ironically, one of the first companies to participate in this trend—Ben & Jerry's—is now itself a B corp, perhaps presaging a new stage of business evolution.

8. For more information about these and other social businesses being launched with the help of Muhammad Yunus and his Grameen team, see the Grameen Creative Lab website, http://www.grameencreativelab.com/news.html. Also see Muhammad Yunus with Karl Weber, *Building Social Business: The New Kind of Capitalism That Serves Humanity's Most Pressing Needs* (New York: Public Affairs, 2010).

9. "What Is Patient Capital?" Acumen Fund, http://www.acumenfund.org/about -us/what-is-patient-capital.html.

10. "About Us," Echoing Green, http://www.echoinggreen.org/about.

11. "About New Profit," New Profit, http://newprofit.com/cgi-bin/iowa/about/index
    .html.
12. Paul Tullis, "Bloomberg's Push for Corporate Sustainability," *Fast Company*,
    May   30,   2011,   http://www.fastcompany.com/1739782/bloombergs-push
    -corporate-sustainability.
13. "Vision and Mission," SASB, http://www.sasb.org/sasb/about/.
14. Quoted in Joel Makower, "Why SASB Is a Game Changer for Sustainable Busi-
    ness," *GreenBiz*, October 1, 2012, http://www.greenbiz.com/blog/2012/10/01
    /why-sasb-game-changer-sustainable-business?page=0%2C2.
15. Quoted in Brenda Cronin, "Gauge Looks Beyond GDP," *Wall Street Journal*,
    April 11, 2013, p. A2.
16. From speeches attended by Andrew W. Savitz.

Acknowledgments

Every business book is a collaboration, and many friends and colleagues helped me along the way. I would like to thank them now.

First and foremost, Larry Tye, who, although under a deadline to deliver his own fourth book, gave me the confidence; the road map; and the monthly, weekly, daily, and at times the hourly encouragement I needed to start and finish my first. I am grateful for his support, for his friendship, and for the constant energy and inspiration that he provides.

Peter Barash, Mark Green, and the late, great congressman Benjamin S. Rosenthal started me thinking about corporations in terms of their impacts beyond the financial in my very first job. Later, John DeVillars gave me the opportunity to understand the relationship between public and private environmental interests, from the public side of the desk, where he has contributed so much.

Thereafter, PricewaterhouseCoopers let me take my knowledge and experience to the marketplace. I was fortunate to know and work with two of the firm's great chairmen, Gene Freedman and Samuel DiPiazza—who turned out to be a mentor and a friend, as well as a highly involved and committed leader in the service of accountability, business integrity, and meaningful corporate reporting. Chris Hughes, whose constant friendship, soaring intellect, and basic goodness have been a source of strength, read and commented on the final draft of this book, as he has on almost every important word I have written over the past fifteen years. Chris broadens and deepens the meaning of the word "partner" in everything he does, and what splendid good fortune for me that we met and stuck. Loraine Shuman cheerfully helped me wrestle with the manuscript, as she cheerfully helped me every day at PwC. Thanks also to Greg Bardnell, Dale Jensen, Eric

Howe, Karen Ethier, Jessica Shipps, Karen Burnette, and Holly Clack, my loyal teammates and colleagues, and especially to Mike Besly, an early reader, book supporter, and former captain of the Queen's Guard.

The World Business Council for Sustainable Development helped me and thousands of others think clearly and practically about sustainability. Bjorn Stigson, Margaret Flaherty, Travis Engen, Dan Gagnier, and Ron Nielsen (the latter three of whom are setting the standard for sustainability at Alcan), Matt Haddon (of Environmental Resources Management), Ian Goslin (of Caterpillar), Sunny Misser and Tess Mateo (both of PwC), Claude Fussler, Cheryl Hicks, and Laura Sanders, experts all, were generous with their time and thoughts. Bob Massie, Joan Bavaria, Mindy Lubber, and all the good people at CERES, and Allen L. White at Tellus have greatly enriched my thinking.

Speaking of ideas, Bill McDonough from McDonough, Braungart Design Chemistry and Anne Johnson from Green/Blue gave me many, and my collaboration with them continues to be a formative experience that is reflected on many pages herein.

I have had the pleasure to work with some outstanding clients over the years, but none more enjoyable than the fine people running with the sustainability ball, while juggling many others, at PepsiCo. I have learned much about how things actually get done in this world from Elaine Palmer, who is one of those heroic managers who make things happen in large companies through a combination of skill, smarts, and incredibly hard work—in this case moving PepsiCo in a sustainable direction. Tod McKenzie has inspired me (and many others) in every way, and Matt McKenna has impressed me with his personal and professional commitment to this issue. While they were at Northeast Utilities, Mike Morris was the first CEO I ever heard talk about managing based not so much on rules as on values; Dennis Welch was the first person I ever saw do it; and Greg Butler, Cheryl Grisé, and Barry Ilberman were each in their own way contributors to my understanding of that management philosophy. For two years, Stan Twardy, of Day, Berry, & Howard, gave me weekly tutorials on the science and art of environmental law enforcement. Keith Miller and Sara Ethier at 3M have been stalwarts. Roy Deitchman, Stan Bagley, and Bob Noonan at Amtrak helped me understand how responsibility works in the field. Thanks also to the environmental professionals at Sony and Shell, who are also among those in the book with whom we have worked.

I owe an enormous debt of gratitude to Morgan McVicar, a fine writer, who helped me with not one but twenty book proposals. Mark Katz introduced me to Evan Schwartz, who introduced me to Rafe Sagalyn, who has been far more than just a superb agent. Rafe gave me a world of good advice, and to the extent that this book rings true, he had a lot to do with it.

Many individuals were helpful to me and to my collaborator, Karl Weber, as we researched and reported the contents of this book. In particular, we want to thank those with past or present connections to the town of Hershey, Pennsylvania, and to the company after which the town is named, whose insights helped inform our chapter on Hershey. They include Joe Berning, Millie Landis Coyle, John Dunn, Michael Fisher, Ric Fouad, Bruce Hummel, John Long, Michael Macchioni, Bruce McKinney, Kathy Taylor, and Dick Zimmerman.

Thanks, too, to the people involved in the saga of PPL Corporation and the revitalization of the Penobscot River, who were generous with their time and advice. In particular, we want to thank John Banks, Laura Rose Day, Scott D. Hall, and Gordon W. Russell.

Naturally, our narratives concerning both Hershey and PPL reflect our own perspective, which shouldn't be identified with that of any individual we may have interviewed.

When we finished what I thought was a first readable draft, I looked around for actual readers and thought, "I'd better start with an immediate relative." Fortunately, my cousin Jeffrey Trachtenberg was more than willing. A lifelong pal and an accomplished author, journalist, and fisherman, he told me to "write it like a letter to your aunt." He gladly read the draft, gave me more helpful comments, and, most important, told my aunt that it was readable, knowing that his mother would pass that compliment along to my mother, who already knew the book was great, without having to read it.

My other reader-coaches, Mindy Lubber, Dawn Rittenhouse, Allen L. White, and Elizabeth Ames, provided shockingly targeted and diverse insights, all of which changed the book for the better, and did so over their holidays, for which I will be forever grateful. Penny McGee Savitz, my wife, provided me with uncountable mornings, evenings, and weekends of quietude (no mean feat with six-year-old Noah and four-year-old Zuzzie), and offered some excellent editorial suggestions. Brother Peter gave me the Wall Street perspective, which led to some late-night discussions and positive changes.

Max Bazerman spent many of his precious hours reading and commenting, chapter by chapter, concept by concept, case by case, with the thoughtfulness, balance, and rigor of a world-class thinker, scholar, and business consultant, and with the fierce integrity that he brings to every aspect of his life and, by a happy osmosis, to many around him.

Our editor at Jossey-Bass, Susan Williams, has been a staunch supporter from beginning to end and an astute guide through the writing, editing, and publication process. She has supported this first-time author with all the help he needed, providing it in a firm, low-key, and generous way, with incredible dexterity and insight. Thanks for her insights and advice on the book itself, which have added significantly to the quality of the work.

Thanks also to Mark Linton, who helped with the research; Scott Cohen, the publisher of Compliance Week, who provided some last-minute assistance and encouragement; Rabbi William Hamilton; Kert Davies; Dutch Leonard; Jane Nelson; Ralph Earle; and Rob Stavins, who got me thinking about fishing.

Finally, my collaborator and now friend, Karl Weber, was magnificent in every way. A clear thinker and writer, a gentle editor, and a fellow follower of baseball and politics, he took my ideas and my words, added some of both (and cut some too, thank goodness), and helped arranged them into what we both hope is a compelling, informative, and entertaining book.

To all of you—my friends, my family, my collaborators—go my heartfelt thanks.

A.W.S.

Additional Thanks and Acknowledgments for the Revised Edition

I'm honored to thank some old and new friends and colleagues who have contributed to this revision of *The Triple Bottom Line* (*TBL*).

Thanks go first to Genoveva Llhosa at Wiley for thinking that this book might be worthy of an update, and for being such a total pleasure to work with. Genoveva passed the editorial baton to John Maas, who raced forward in the same collaborative spirit. Susan Williams, our editor on the first edition, has continued to support *TBL*, as has Jessie Wiley and our incomparable copyeditor, Michele Jones.

Ed Lawler and Sue Mohrman from the Center for Effective Organizations at USC helped with the culture, employee engagement, and strategic human resources aspects of this revision, as did Gregg Ribatt and John Berger. Friends and colleagues Ken Frazier, Sandy Nessing, and Dennis Welch provided the guidance and information we needed about culture change inside AEP.

Oxfam America continues to do cutting-edge work based in large measure on the efforts of Chris Jochnik and Minor Sinclair, for whom Andy provided consulting assistance. Allen White, from Tellus, and Mindy Lubber, the CEO of Ceres, also continue to be helpful in many ways.

After *TBL* came out the first time, I continued to work with PepsiCo, and I owe a strong debt of thanks to Paul Boykas, Rob Schasel, Dan Bena, and Derek Yach. Liz Maw, the indefatigable CEO of Net Impact, has expanded my thinking, and Margaret Flaherty, formerly of the World Business Council for Sustainable Development, continues to do so. The Society for Human Resource Management is working for a more sustainable future, and my thanks go to Frank Scanlan, Sue Meissinger, and Jennifer Schramm, who have been unwavering in their support.

My friend Chris Hughes helped me with this book as he has with everything else. "Thanks, Chris" doesn't quite do, but it will have to suffice under the circumstances.

I didn't know Devon Long-Lytle when *TBL* was first published, but without her this revision would not have been nearly as strong.

Devon is remarkable in every way. She and Karl Weber have made the past few years an exciting period of intellectual, professional, and personal growth for me. I am grateful for what they have done and excited about what remains to do.

To those whom I have not mentioned by name, I hope to have another chance in next revision.

Andrew W. Savitz

August 2013

About the Authors

Andrew W. Savitz is an author, consultant, and speaker on how companies can create goods, services, and processes that meet business needs and serve the interests of society and the planet at the same time. His organization, Sustainable Business Strategies, helps companies find such sweet spots and improve their Triple Bottom Lines (TBL).

Andy was a lead partner in the sustainability services practice at the global auditing firm PricewaterhouseCoopers LLP (PwC), where he developed and helped implement TBL programs for global clients in many industries.

Andy wrote the first edition of *The Triple Bottom Line*, with Karl Weber, in 2006. He also wrote *Talent, Transformation, and the Triple Bottom Line* (Jossey-Bass, 2013) with Karl, which shows how employees and HR professionals can advance sustainability within their organizations through employee engagement, change management, capacity building, and corporate culture change programs.

As a staff member of a U.S. House subcommittee, Andy helped draft the 1980 Corporate Democracy Act, requiring public companies to nominate directors with specific expertise on environmental, employee, housing, and community-related issues. He also worked on other corporate governance issues, including consumer protection, fair trade, and environmental justice. While working in the Executive Office of Management and Budget, he was responsible for drafting guidelines related to the disclosure of personal information held by the federal government under the Right to Privacy Act.

Andy later served as general counsel of Environmental Affairs for Massachusetts, conceived of and helped create the Massachusetts Environmental Crimes Strike Force, founded the

Massachusetts League of Environmental Voters, and served on the steering committee of the Environmental and Natural Resources Department of Harvard's Kennedy School of Government and on the advisory board of the Boston Zoos.

Andy graduated from the Johns Hopkins University; New College, Oxford (where he was a Rhodes Scholar); and the Georgetown University Law Center. He has given up all hope of playing any major league sport, but he is a Life Master at bridge and, in a stroke of unimaginable luck, made the final table at a World Series of Poker event in 2011. Now that this book is revised, he is learning to cook. He resides and recycles in Brookline, Massachusetts.

For more information, please visit www.getsustainable.net.

• • •

Karl Weber is a writer and editor who specializes in topics from business, politics, current affairs, history, and social issues. He is particularly interested in exploring the area where business, politics, and innovative forms of activism, such as social entrepreneurship, overlap.

Karl's publishing projects include the *New York Times* best seller *Creating a World Without Poverty* (2008), coauthored with Muhammad Yunus, founder of Grameen Bank and winner of the 2006 Nobel Peace Prize, and its sequel, *Building Social Business* (2010); Scott McClellan's *New York Times* number-one best seller *What Happened: Inside the Bush White House and Washington's Culture of Deception* (2008), which Weber edited; and three best-selling companion books to acclaimed films, *Food Inc.* (2009), *Waiting for "Superman"* (2010), and Steven Spielberg's *Lincoln* (2012), all of which Karl edited. He lives in Irvington, New York, with his wife, Mary-Jo Weber.

Index